ANIMAL RIGHTS

**OPPOSING
VIEWPOINTS®**

Other Books of Related Interest

ANIMAL RIGHTS

OPPOSING VIEWPOINTS®

David Bender & Bruno Leone, *Series Editors*

Andrew Harnack, Professor of English, Eastern
Kentucky University, *Book Editor*

OPPOSING
VIEWPOINTS®
SERIES

Greenhaven Press, Inc., San Diego, CA

Cover photo: Dover Books

Greenhaven Press, Inc.
PO Box 289009
San Diego, CA 92198-9009

Library of Congress Cataloging-in-Publication Data

Animal rights : opposing viewpoints / Andrew Harnack, book
    editor.
        p.   cm. — (Opposing viewpoints series)
    Includes bibliographical references and index.
    ISBN 1-56510-399-8 (lib. : alk. paper). — ISBN 1-56510-398-X
(pbk. : alk. paper)
    1. Animal rights. 2. Animal welfare. 3. Animal rights move-
ment. I. Harnack, Andrew, 1937–   . II. Series: Opposing
viewpoints series (Unnumbered)
HV4711.A58   1996
179'.3—dc20   95-52147
                                                              CIP

"Congress shall make no law . . .
abridging the freedom of speech,
or of the press."

First Amendment to the U.S. Constitution

The basic foundation of our democracy is the First Amendment guarantee of freedom of expression. The Opposing Viewpoints Series is dedicated to the concept of this basic freedom and the idea that it is more important to practice it than to enshrine it.

Contents

Why Consider Opposing Viewpoints?

"The only way in which a human being can make some approach to knowing the whole of a subject is by hearing what can be said about it by persons of every variety of opinion and studying all modes in which it can be looked at by every character of mind. No wise man ever acquired his wisdom in any mode but this."

John Stuart Mill

In our media-intensive culture it is not difficult to find differing opinions. Thousands of newspapers and magazines and dozens of radio and television talk shows resound with differing points of view. The difficulty lies in deciding which opinion to agree with and which "experts" seem the most credible. The more inundated we become with differing opinions and claims, the more essential it is to hone critical reading and thinking skills to evaluate these ideas. Opposing Viewpoints books address this problem directly by presenting stimulating debates that can be used to enhance and teach these skills. The varied opinions contained in each book examine many different aspects of a single issue. While examining these conveniently edited opposing views, readers can develop critical thinking skills such as the ability to compare and contrast authors' credibility, facts, argumentation styles, use of persuasive techniques, and other stylistic tools. In short, the Opposing Viewpoints Series is an ideal way to attain the higher-level thinking and reading skills so essential in a culture of diverse and contradictory opinions.

In addition to providing a tool for critical thinking, Opposing Viewpoints books challenge readers to question their own strongly held opinions and assumptions. Most people form their opinions on the basis of upbringing, peer pressure, and personal, cultural, or professional bias. By reading carefully balanced opposing views, readers must directly confront new ideas as well as the opinions of those with whom they disagree. This is not to simplistically argue that everyone who reads opposing views will—or should—change his or her opinion. Instead, the series enhances readers' depth of understanding of their own views by encouraging confrontation with opposing ideas. Careful examination of others' views can lead to the readers' understanding of the logical inconsistencies in their own opinions, perspective on why they hold an opinion, and the consideration of the possibility that their opinion requires further evaluation.

Evaluating Other Opinions

To ensure that this type of examination occurs, Opposing Viewpoints books present all types of opinions. Prominent spokespeople on different sides of each issue as well as well-known professionals from many disciplines challenge the reader. An additional goal of the series is to provide a forum for other, less known, or even unpopular viewpoints. The opinion of an ordinary person who has had to make the decision to cut off life support from a terminally ill relative, for example, may be just as valuable and provide just as much insight as a medical ethicist's professional opinion. The editors have two additional purposes in including these less known views. One, the editors encourage readers to respect others' opinions—even when not enhanced by professional credibility. It is only by reading or listening to and objectively evaluating others' ideas that one can determine whether they are worthy of consideration. Two, the inclusion of such viewpoints encourages the important critical thinking skill of objectively evaluating an author's credentials and bias. This evaluation will illuminate an author's reasons for taking a particular stance on an issue and will aid in readers' evaluation of the author's ideas.

As series editors of the Opposing Viewpoints Series, it is our hope that these books will give readers a deeper understanding of the issues debated and an appreciation of the complexity of even seemingly simple issues when good and honest people disagree. This awareness is particularly important in a democratic society such as ours in which people enter into public debate to determine the common good. Those with whom one disagrees should not be regarded as enemies but rather as people whose views deserve careful examination and may shed light on one's own.

Thomas Jefferson once said that "difference of opinion leads to inquiry, and inquiry to truth." Jefferson, a broadly educated man, argued that "if a nation expects to be ignorant and free . . . it expects what never was and never will be." As individuals and as a nation, it is imperative that we consider the opinions of others and examine them with skill and discernment. The Opposing Viewpoints Series is intended to help readers achieve this goal.

David L. Bender & Bruno Leone,
Series Editors

Introduction

Discussion of animal rights issues is often highly emotional and dramatic. In an attempt to evoke sympathy and outrage, animal rights activists frequently publish shockingly graphic images and descriptions of animals being used in laboratories and on farms. On the other hand, critics of the movement often portray animal rights activists as fanatics who commit terrorist acts against medical laboratories and other facilities in which animals are thought to be mistreated. Beneath this extreme rhetoric and imagery, however, lie complex philosophical questions about humankind's relationship with, and responsibilities toward, the animal kingdom.

The animal rights movement is founded on the belief that a moral order exists in the universe and that within that moral order animals and human beings are equal. One prominent supporter of this view is Peter Singer, a professor of philosophy and the director of the Centre for Human Bioethics at Monash University in Melbourne, Australia, and the author of *Animal Liberation*, which is considered by many to be the "bible" of the animal rights movement. Philosophically, Singer is a utilitarian. In *The Animals Rights Crusade: The Growth of a Moral Protest*, James Jasper and Dorothy Nelkin summarize his position:

> For utilitarians, ethical decisions should be made by adding up all pleasures and pains that would result from different choices, and choosing the option yielding the greatest aggregate pleasure (or happiness). . . Singer believes that all

pleasures and pains, even of nonhumans, must be tallied for a proper moral calculus. . . . Singer argues that humans must take into account the fact that animals are capable of suffering and enjoyment. It is just as arbitrary to disregard the suffering of animals as that of women or people with dark skin. To assume that humans are inevitably superior to other species is "speciesism"—an injustice parallel to racism and sexism.

In short, Singer holds that because animals share with humans the capacity to experience pain and suffering, they are worthy of the same degree of moral consideration as is granted to humans. Consequently, Singer urges people to become vegetarians and otherwise adopt a lifestyle that avoids causing cruelty to animals.

Another who argues that animals and humans should be subjected to identical moral yardsticks is Tom Regan, the University Alumni Distinguished Professor of Philosophy at North Carolina State University and the author of numerous books, including *The Struggle for Animal Rights* and *Animal Sacrifices: Religious Perspectives on the Use of Animals in Science*. Like Singer, Regan advocates a cruelty-free, vegetarian lifestyle. Unlike Singer, however, Regan rejects utilitarianism. Regan contends that the utilitarian approach—taking the action that results in the greatest aggregate pleasure and the least aggregate pain—could be used to justify causing animals to suffer in order to bring humans greater pleasure. In *The Case for Animal Rights*, Regan argues that rather than a utilitarian value, animals possess an inherent value that is equal to that of humans. Therefore, he contends, animals have the right to be treated with the same respect as that afforded to people.

Other philosophers believe that animals are not morally equal to humans. One such critic is Mary Anne Warren, who teaches philosophy at San Francisco State University. Warren argues that while all sentient animals have moral rights, the rights of nonhuman animals are weaker than those of humans. Warren maintains that humans have stronger rights than animals because people, unlike animals, are capable of rational thought. According to Warren, this capacity makes humans more dangerous than animals and therefore requires humans to establish a "system of morality" that recognizes "the equal moral status of all persons." Because animals cannot be reasoned with, according to Warren, they cannot be included in this system of morality and therefore cannot be viewed as people's moral equals.

Another philosopher who believes animals are not the moral equals of humans is R.G. Frey, a professor of philosophy at Bowling Green State University in Ohio and the author of *Interests and Rights: The Case Against Animals* and *Rights, Killing, and Suffering*. Frey agrees with advocates who contend that animals possess moral standing and that their suffering should be taken into account by humans. However, Frey differs from many in that he explicitly states that "animal life is less valuable than human life." Human life is more valuable than animal life, according to Frey, because it is richer:

> Part of the richness of our lives involves activities that we have in common with animals but there are as well whole dimensions to our lives—love, marriage, educating children, jobs, hobbies, sporting events, cultural pursuits, intellectual development and striving, etc.—that greatly expand our range of absorbing behaviors and so significantly deepen the texture of our lives.

Frey contends that the richness of human life is made possible by autonomy. Unlike animals, he argues, humans are able to choose among various conceptions of how they want to live, and exercising this freedom creates the potential for "further, important dimensions of value to their lives."

Whether human life is richer or more valuable than animal life is one of the issues debated in *Animal Rights: Opposing Viewpoints*, which contains the following chapters: Do Animals Have Rights? Is Animal Experimentation Justified? Should Animals Be Used for Food and Other Commodities? Does Wildlife Need to Be Protected? What Issues Need to Be Resolved Within the Animal Rights Movement? Underlying all of these issues is the fundamental philosophical question of whether or not animals and humans are moral equals.

Do Animals
Have Rights?

Chapter Preface

The birth of the present-day animal rights movement took place in the mid-1970s. In 1975, Peter Singer published *Animal Liberation: A New Ethics for Our Treatment of Animals*, often called the "bible" of the animal rights movement. Two years later, in December 1977, a group of activists led by Henry Spira forced the American Museum of Natural History in New York to terminate a twenty-year series of experiments in which researchers mutilated cats in order to investigate their sexual behavior. Shortly thereafter, in the early 1980s, People for the Ethical Treatment of Animals (PETA) successfully closed down Edward Taub's independent Institute of Behavioral Research at Silver Spring, Maryland, where experiments involved severing nerves in the limbs of seventeen monkeys. In 1984 Tom Regan, one of the movement's most prolific writers, published *The Case for Animal Rights*. In 1989, members of the underground Animal Liberation Front (ALF) broke into a laboratory at the University of Arizona in Tucson and set free more than 1,200 frogs, mice, rabbits, and pigs. By the end of the decade, scientific communities, medical schools, and federal health officials found it necessary to defend themselves against charges of unethical and inhumane treatment of animals. As a result of these publications and actions, philosophers, theologians, ethicists, scientists, physicians, veterinarians, attorneys, and thousands of other thoughtful people are reexamining what, if any, moral responsibilities humans have toward animals.

Whether or not animals do in fact possess rights as individuals and/or as species continues to be a question of serious debate. Animal rights advocates believe that because animals are capable of experiencing pain and suffering in a way similar to people, they have rights equal to those of humans. Opponents contend that animals do not possess rights and that it is ethical to use them in research and for food and other commodities (although most agree that animals should always be treated humanely). This chapter presents six viewpoints that argue for and against the possibility of rights for animals.

"If a being suffers, there can be no moral justification for refusing to take that suffering into consideration."

All Animals Are Equal

Peter Singer

Peter Singer, professor of philosophy and director at Monash University, Melbourne, Australia, is best known for his book *Animal Liberation*, in which he argues that humans must recognize that animals are capable of experiencing pain and pleasure. This ability, Singer asserts, brings animals into humanity's moral calculus. When humans fail to measure the capacity of animals to suffer, he contends, they become guilty of "speciesism," an injustice parallel to racism and sexism.

As you read, consider the following questions:

1. What, in Singer's view, do racism, sexism, and speciesism have in common?
2. According to Singer, how did Jeremy Bentham help people understand their moral relationship with animals?
3. Although the author believes it is best not to claim that animals have "rights," why is he willing to let the media use the word *rights* when discussing animal liberation?

Reprinted from *Animal Liberation* by Peter Singer, 2nd ed. (New York: New York Review of Books, 1990), by permission of the author.

"Animal Liberation" may sound more like a parody of other liberation movements than a serious objective. The idea of "The Rights of Animals" actually was once used to parody the case for women's rights. When Mary Wollstonecraft, a forerunner of today's feminists, published her *Vindication of the Rights of Woman* in 1792, her views were widely regarded as absurd, and before long an anonymous publication appeared entitled *A Vindication of the Rights of Brutes*. The author of this satirical work (now known to have been Thomas Taylor, a distinguished Cambridge philosopher) tried to refute Mary Wollstonecraft's arguments by showing that they could be carried one stage further. If the argument for equality was sound when applied to women, why should it not be applied to dogs, cats, and horses? The reasoning seemed to hold for these "brutes" too; yet to hold that brutes had rights was manifestly absurd. Therefore the reasoning by which this conclusion had been reached must be unsound, and if unsound when applied to brutes, it must also be unsound when applied to women, since the very same arguments had been used in each case.

Clarifying the General Principle of Equality

In order to explain the basis of the case for the equality of animals, it will be helpful to start with an examination of the case for the equality of women. Let us assume that we wish to defend the case for women's rights against the attack by Thomas Taylor. How should we reply?

One way in which we might reply is by saying that the case for equality between men and women cannot validly be extended to nonhuman animals. Women have a right to vote, for instance, because they are just as capable of making rational decisions about the future as men are; dogs, on the other hand, are incapable of understanding the significance of voting, so they cannot have the right to vote. There are many other obvious ways in which men and women resemble each other closely, while humans and animals differ greatly. So, it might be said, men and women are similar beings and should have similar rights, while humans and nonhumans are different and should not have equal rights.

The reasoning behind this reply to Taylor's analogy is correct up to a point, but it does not go far enough. There are obviously important differences between humans and other animals, and these differences must give rise to some differences in the rights that each have. Recognizing this evident fact, however, is no barrier to the case for extending the basic principle of equality to nonhuman animals. The differences that exist between men and women are equally undeniable, and the supporters of Women's Liberation are aware that these differences may give rise to different rights. Many feminists hold that women have the right to an abortion on request. It does not follow that since these same feminists are campaigning for equality between men and women they must support the right of men to have abortions too. Since a man cannot have an abortion, it is meaningless to talk of his right to have one. Since dogs can't vote, it is meaningless to talk of their right to vote. There is no reason why either Women's Liberation or Animal Liberation should get involved in such nonsense. The extension of the basic principle of equality from one group to another does not imply that we must treat both groups in exactly the same way, or grant exactly the same rights to both groups. Whether we should do so will depend on the nature of the members of the two groups. The basic principle of equality does not require equal or identical *treatment*; it requires equal consideration. Equal consideration for different beings may lead to different treatment and different rights.

So there is a different way of replying to Taylor's attempt to parody the case for women's rights, a way that does not deny the obvious differences between human beings and nonhumans but goes more deeply into the question of equality and concludes by finding nothing absurd in the idea that the basic principle of equality applies to so-called brutes. At this point such a conclusion may appear odd; but if we examine more deeply the basis on which our opposition to discrimination on grounds of race or sex ultimately rests, we will see that we would be on shaky ground if we were to demand equality for blacks, women, and other groups of oppressed humans while denying equal consideration to nonhumans. To make this clear we need to see, first, exactly why racism and sexism are wrong. When we say that all human beings, whatever their race, creed, or sex, are equal, what is it that we are asserting? Those who wish to defend hierarchical, inegalitarian societies have often pointed out that by whatever test we choose it simply is not true that all humans are equal. Like it or not we must face the fact that humans come in different shapes and sizes; they come with different moral capacities, different intellectual abilities, different amounts of benevolent feeling and sensitivity to the needs of others, different abilities to communicate effectively, and different capacities to experience pleasure and pain. In short, if the demand for equality were based on the actual equality of all human beings, we would have to stop demanding equality.

Considering Differences

Still, one might cling to the view that the demand for equality among human beings is based on the actual equality of the different races and sexes. Although, it may be said, humans differ as individuals, there are no differences between the races and sexes as such. From the mere fact that a person is black or a woman we cannot infer anything about that person's intellectual or moral capacities. This, it may be said, is why racism and sexism are wrong. The white racist claims that whites are superior to blacks, but this is false; although there are differences among individuals, some blacks are superior to some whites in all of the capacities and abilities that could conceivably be relevant. The opponent of sexism would say the same: a person's sex is no guide to his or her abilities, and this is why it is unjustifiable to discriminate on the basis of sex.

The Rights of Animals

1. All animals are born with an equal claim on life and the same rights to existence.

2. All animals are entitled to respect. Man as an animal species shall not arrogate to himself the right to exterminate or inhumanely exploit other species. It is his duty to use his knowledge for the welfare of animals. All animals have the right to the attention, care, and protection of man.

3. No animals shall be ill-treated or be subject to cruel acts. If an animal has to be killed, this must be instantaneous and without distress.

4. All wild animals have the right to liberty in their natural environment, whether land, air, or water, and should be allowed to procreate. Deprivation of freedom, even for educational purposes, is an infringement of this right.

International League of the Rights of Animals, "Universal Declaration of the Rights of Animals," September 1977.

The existence of individual variations that cut across the lines of race or sex, however, provides us with no defense at all against a more sophisticated opponent of equality, one who proposes that, say, the interests of all those with IQ scores below 100 be given less consideration than the interests of those with ratings over 100. Perhaps those scoring below the mark would, in this society, be made the slaves of those scoring higher. Would a hierarchical society of this sort really be so much better than one based on race or sex? I think not. But if we tie the moral principle of equality to the factual equality of the different races or sexes, taken as a whole, our opposition to racism and sexism does not provide us with any basis for objecting to this kind of inegalitarianism.

There is a second important reason why we ought not to base

our opposition to racism and sexism on any kind of factual equality, even the limited kind that asserts that variations in capacities and abilities are spread evenly among the different races and between the sexes: we can have no absolute guarantee that these capacities and abilities really are distributed evenly, without regard to race or sex, among human beings. So far as actual abilities are concerned there do seem to be certain measurable differences both among races and between sexes. These differences do not, of course, appear in every case, but only when averages are taken. More important still, we do not yet know how many of these differences are really due to the different genetic endowments of the different races and sexes, and how many are due to poor schools, poor housing, and other factors that are the result of past and continuing discrimination. Perhaps all of the important differences will eventually prove to be environmental rather than genetic. Anyone opposed to racism and sexism will certainly hope that this will be so, for it will make the task of ending discrimination a lot easier; nevertheless, it would be dangerous to rest the case against racism and sexism on the belief that all significant differences are environmental in origin. The opponent of, say, racism who takes this line will be unable to avoid conceding that if differences in ability did after all prove to have some genetic connection with race, racism would in some way be defensible.

Equality as a Moral Idea

Fortunately there is no need to pin the case for equality to one particular outcome of a scientific investigation. The appropriate response to those who claim to have found evidence of genetically based differences in ability among the races or between the sexes is not to stick to the belief that the genetic explanation must be wrong, whatever evidence to the contrary may turn up; instead we should make it quite clear that the claim to equality does not depend on intelligence, moral capacity, physical strength, or similar matters of fact. Equality is a moral idea, not an assertion of fact. There is no logically compelling reason for assuming that a factual difference in ability between two people justifies any difference in the amount of consideration we give to their needs and interests. *The principle of the equality of human beings is not a description of an alleged actual equality among humans: it is a prescription of how we should treat human beings.*

Jeremy Bentham, the founder of the reforming utilitarian school of moral philosophy, incorporated the essential basis of moral equality into his system of ethics by means of the formula: "Each to count for one and none for more than one." In other words, the interests of every being affected by an action are to be taken into account and given the same weight as the like interests of any other being. A later utilitarian, Henry Sidgwick, put the point in this way: "The good of any one individual is of no more importance, from the point of view (if I may say so) of the Universe, than the good of any other." More recently the leading figures in contemporary moral philosophy have shown a great deal of agreement in specifying as a fundamental presupposition of their moral theories some similar requirement that works to give everyone's interests equal consideration—although these writers generally cannot agree on how this requirement is best formulated.

It is an implication of this principle of equality that our concern for others and our readiness to consider their interests ought not to depend on what they are like or on what abilities they may possess. Precisely what our concern or consideration requires us to do may vary according to the characteristics of those affected by what we do: concern for the well-being of children growing up in America would require that we teach them to read; concern for the well-being of pigs may require no more than that we leave them with other pigs in a place where there is adequate food and room to run freely. But the basic element—the taking into account of the interests of the being, whatever those interests may be—must, according to the principle of equality, be extended to all beings, black or white, masculine or feminine, human or nonhuman. . . .

Speciesism

It is on this basis that the case against racism and the case against sexism must both ultimately rest; and it is in accordance with this principle that the attitude that we may call "speciesism," by analogy with racism, must also be condemned. Speciesism—the word is not an attractive one, but I can think of no better term—is a prejudice or attitude of bias in favor of the interests of members of one's own species and against those of members of other species. It should be obvious that the fundamental objections to racism and sexism . . . apply equally to speciesism. If possessing a higher degree of intelligence does not entitle one human to use another for his or her own ends, how can it entitle humans to exploit nonhumans for the same purpose?

Considering an Animal's Capacity to Suffer

Many philosophers and other writers have proposed the principle of equal consideration of interests, in some form or other, as a basic moral principle; but not many of them have recognized that this principle applies to members of other species as well as to our own. Jeremy Bentham was one of the few who did realize this. In a forward-looking passage written at a time when black slaves had been freed by the French but in the

British dominions were still being treated in the way we now treat animals, Bentham wrote:

> The day *may* come when the rest of the animal creation may acquire those rights which never could have been withholden from them but by the hand of tyranny. The French have already discovered that the blackness of the skin is no reason why a human being should be abandoned without redress to the caprice of a tormentor. It may one day come to be recognized that the number of the legs, the villosity of the skin, or the termination of the *os sacrum* are reasons equally insufficient for abandoning a sensitive being to the same fate. What else is it that should trace the insuperable line? Is it the faculty of reason, or perhaps the faculty of discourse? But a full-grown horse or dog is beyond comparison a more rational, as well as a more conversable animal, than an infant of a day or a week or even a month, old. But suppose they were otherwise, what would it avail? The question is not, Can they *reason*? nor Can they *talk*? but, Can they *suffer*?

In this passage Bentham points to the capacity for suffering as the vital characteristic that gives a being the right to equal consideration. The capacity for suffering—or more strictly, for suffering and/or enjoyment or happiness—is not just another characteristic like the capacity for language or higher mathematics. Bentham is not saying that those who try to mark "the insuperable line" that determines whether the interests of a being should be considered happen to have chosen the wrong characteristic. By saying that we must consider the interests of all beings with the capacity for suffering or enjoyment Bentham does not arbitrarily exclude from consideration any interests at all—as those who draw the line with reference to the possession of reason or language do. The capacity for suffering and enjoyment is *a prerequisite for having interests at all*, a condition that must be satisfied before we can speak of interests in a meaningful way. It would be nonsense to say that it was not in the interests of a stone to be kicked along the road by a schoolboy. A stone does not have interests because it cannot suffer. Nothing that we can do to it could possibly make any difference to its welfare. The capacity for suffering and enjoyment is, however, not only necessary, but also sufficient for us to say that a being has interests—at an absolute minimum, an interest in not suffering. A mouse, for example, does have an interest in not being kicked along the road, because it will suffer if it is.

Although Bentham speaks of "rights" in the passage I have quoted, the argument is really about equality rather than about rights. Indeed, in a different passage, Bentham famously described "natural rights" as "nonsense" and "natural and imprescriptable rights" as "nonsense upon stilts." He talked of moral rights as a shorthand way of referring to protections that people and animals morally ought to have; but the real weight of the moral argument does not rest on the assertion of the existence of the right, for this in turn has to be justified on the basis of the possibilities for suffering and happiness. In this way we can argue for equality for animals without getting embroiled in philosophical controversies about the ultimate nature of rights.

In misguided attempts to refute the arguments of this [viewpoint] some philosophers have gone to much trouble developing arguments to show that animals do not have rights. They have claimed that to have rights a being must be autonomous, or must be a member of a community, or must have the ability to respect the rights of others, or must possess a sense of justice. These claims are irrelevant to the case for Animal Liberation. The language of rights is a convenient political shorthand. It is even more valuable in the era of thirty-second TV news clips than it was in Bentham's day; but in the argument for a radical change in our attitude to animals, it is in no way necessary.

If a being suffers, there can be no moral justification for refusing to take that suffering into consideration. No matter what the nature of the being, the principle of equality requires that its suffering be counted equally with the like suffering—insofar as rough comparisons can be made—of any other being. If a being is not capable of suffering, or of experiencing enjoyment or happiness, there is nothing to be taken into account. So the limit of sentience (using the term as a convenient if not strictly accurate shorthand for the capacity to suffer and/or experience enjoyment) is the only defensible boundary of concern for the interests of others. To mark this boundary by some other characteristic like intelligence or rationality would be to mark it in an arbitrary manner. Why not choose some other characteristic, like skin color?

Racists violate the principle of equality by giving greater weight to the interests of members of their own race when there is a clash between their interests and the interests of those of another race. Sexists violate the principle of equality by favoring the interests of their own sex. Similarly, speciesists allow the interests of their own species to override the greater interests of members of other species. The pattern is identical in each case.

> "Normal (adult) human life is of a much higher
> quality than animal life, not because of species,
> but because of richness; the value of a life is a
> function of its quality."

All Animals
Are Not Equal

R.G. Frey

R.G. Frey is professor of philosophy at Bowling Green State University in Ohio. As the author of *Interests and Rights: The Case Against Animals* and *Rights, Killing, and Suffering*, Frey has written extensively against the arguments of those who advocate the rights and liberation of animals. In the following viewpoint, Frey contends that whenever one species of life is demonstrably more rich and developed than another species, the former is always of more value than the latter. For this reason, Frey maintains, humans may legitimately use animals in medical and scientific research in order to maintain and promote the higher value of human life.

As you read, consider the following questions:

1. What three propositions capture Frey's views of the differing value of human and animal life?
2. Why, in the author's estimate, is human life usually more valuable than animal life?
3. As Frey describes the process, how does autonomy make human life more valuable than animal life?

From "Moral Standing, the Value of Lives, and Speciesism," by R.G. Frey, *Between the Species*, Summer 1988. Reprinted by permission of the publisher.

The question of who or what has moral standing, of who or what is a member of the moral community, has received wide exposure in recent years. Various answers have been extensively canvassed; and though controversy still envelops claims for the inclusion of the inanimate environment within the moral community, such claims on behalf of animals (or, at least, the "higher" animals) are now widely accepted. Morally, then, animals count. I do not myself think that we have needed a great deal of argument to establish this point; but numerous writers, obviously, have thought otherwise. In any event, no work of mine has ever denied that animals count. In order to suffer, animals do not have to be self-conscious, to have interests or beliefs or language, to have desires and desires related to their own future, to exercise self-critical control of their behaviour, or to possess rights; and I, a utilitarian, take their sufferings into account, morally. Thus, the scope of the moral community, at least so far as ("higher") animals are concerned, is not something I contest. I may disagree with some particular way of trying to show that animals possess moral standing, e.g., by ascribing them some variant of moral rights, but I have no quarrel with the general claim that they possess such standing. Indeed, my reformist position with respect to vegetarianism, vivisection, and our general use of animals in part turns upon this very fact.

As I have indicated in my two books [*Interests and Rights: The Case Against Animals* (1980) and *Rights, Killing, and Suffering* (1983)] and numerous articles on animal issues, my reservations come elsewhere. . . . There, I have focussed upon the comparative value of human and animal life; I have taken the notion of autonomy to be central to this issue, since the exercise of autonomy by normal adult humans is the source of an immense part of the value of their lives. Here, I want to sketch one way this concern with the comparative value of human and animal life comes to have importance and to interact with the charge of speciesism.

Animal Life Is Less Valuable Than Human Life

Those who concern themselves with the moral considerability of animals may well be tempted to suppose that their work is finished, once they successfully envelop animals within the moral community. Yet, to stop there is never *per se* to address the issue of the value of animal life and so never to engage the position that I, and others, hold on certain issues. Thus, I am a restricted vivisectionist, not because I think animals are outside the moral community but because of views I hold about the value of their lives. Again, I think it is permissible to use animal parts in human transplants, not because I think animals lack moral standing but because I think animal life is less valuable than human life.

(As some readers may know, I argue that experiments upon animals and the use of animal parts in human transplants are only permissible if one is prepared to sanction such experiments upon and the use of certain humans. I think the benefits to be derived from these practices are *sometimes* substantial enough to compel me to endorse the practices in the human case, unless the side-effects of any such decision offset these benefits. . . .

I have written of views that I hold; the fact is, I think, that the vast majority of people share my view of the differing value of human and animal life. This view we might capture in the form of three propositions:

1. Animal life has some value;
2. Not all animal life has the same value;
3. Human life is more valuable than animal life.

Very few people today would seem to believe that animal life is without value and that, therefore, we need not trouble ourselves morally about taking it. Equally few people, however, would seem to believe that all animal life has the same value. Certainly, the lives of dogs, cats, and chimps are very widely held to be more valuable than the lives of mice, rats, and worms, and the legal protections we accord these different creatures, for example, reflect this fact. Finally, whatever value we take the lives of dogs and cats to have, most of us believe human life to be more valuable than animal life. We believe this, moreover, even as we oppose cruelty to animals and acknowledge value—in the case of some animals, considerable value—to their lives. I shall call this claim about the comparative value of human and animal life the unequal value thesis. A crucial question, obviously, is whether we who hold this thesis can defend it.

Defending the Unequal Value Thesis

Many "animal rightists" themselves seem inclined to accept something like the unequal value thesis. With respect on the oft-cited raft example, in which one can save a man or a dog but not both, animal rightists often concede that, other things being equal, one ought to save the man. To be sure, this result only says something about our intuitions and about those *in extremis*; yet, what it is ordinarily taken to say about them—that we take human life to be more valuable than animal life—is not something we think in extreme circumstances only. Our intuitions about the greater value of human life seem apparent in and affect all our relations with animals, from the differences in the ways we regard, treat, and even bury humans and animals to the differences in the safeguards for their protection that we construct and the differences in penalties we exact for violation of those safeguards.

In a word, the unequal value thesis seems very much a part of the approach that most of us adopt towards animal issues. We oppose cruelty to animals as well as humans, but this does not lead us to suppose that the lives of humans and animals have the same value. Nor is there any entailment in the matter: one can perfectly consistently oppose cruelty to all sentient creatures without having to suppose that the lives of all such creatures are equally valuable.

We might note in passing that if this is right about our intuitions, then it is far from clear that it is the defender of the unequal value thesis who must assume the burden of proof in the present discussion. Our intuitions about pain and suffering are such that if a theorist today suggested that animal suffering did not count morally, then he would quickly find himself on the defensive. If I am right about our intuitions over the comparative value of human and animal life, why is the same not true in the case of the theorist who urges or assumes that these lives are of equal value? If, over suffering, our intuitions force the exclusion of the pains of animals to be defended, why, over the value of life, do they not force an *equal* value thesis to be defended? In any event, I have not left this matter of the burden of proof to chance in any other work, where I have *argued* for the unequal value thesis. Here, I want only to stress that our intuitions *do not obviously endorse*, as it were, a starting-point of equality of value in the lives of humans and animals. On the strength of this consideration alone, we seem justified in at least treating sceptically arguments and claims that proceed from or implicitly rely upon some initial presumption of equal value, in order to undermine the unequal value thesis from the outset.

When the Value of Life Is the Central Issue

Where pain and suffering are the central issue, most of us tend to think of the human and animal cases in the same way; thus, cruelty to a child and cruelty to a dog are wrong and wrong for the same reason. Pain is pain; it is an evil, and the evidence suggests that it is as much an evil for dogs as for humans. Furthermore, autonomy or agency (or the lack thereof) does not seem a relevant factor here, since the pains of nonautonomous creatures count as well as the pains of autonomous ones. Neither the child nor the dog is autonomous, at least in any sense that captures why autonomy is such an immensely important value; but the pains of both child and dog count and affect our judgments of rightness and wrongness with respect to what is done to them.

Where the value of life is the central issue, however, we do not tend to think of the human and animal cases alike. Here, we come down in favor of humans, as when we regularly experiment upon and kill animals in our laboratories for (typically) human benefit; and a main justification reflective people give for according humans such advantage invokes directly a difference in value between human and animal life. Autonomy or agency is now, moreover, of the utmost significance, since the exercise of autonomy by normal adult humans is one of the central ways they make possible further, important dimensions of value to their lives.

Arguably, even the extended justification of animal suffering in, say, medical research may make indirect appeal to the unequal value thesis. Though pain remains an evil, the nature and size of some benefit determine whether its infliction is justified in the particular cases. Nothing precludes this benefit from accruing to human beings, and when it does, we need an independent defence of the appeal to benefit in this kind of case. For the appeal is typically invoked in cases where those who suffer are those who benefit, as when we go to the dentist, and in the present instance human beings are the beneficiaries of animal suffering. Possibly the unequal value thesis can provide the requisite defence; what justifies the infliction of pain, if anything does, is the appeal to benefit; but what justifies use of the appeal in those cases where humans are the beneficiaries of animal suffering is, arguably, that human life is more valuable than animal life. Thus, while the unequal value thesis cannot alter the character of pain, which remains an evil, and cannot directly, independently of benefit, justify the infliction of pain, it can, the suggestion is, anchor a particular use of the appeal to benefit.

Animals Have No Rights

Animals (that is, nonhuman animals, the ordinary sense of that word) lack [the] capacity for free moral judgment. They are not beings of a kind capable of exercising or responding to moral claims. Animals therefore have no rights, and they can have none.

Carl Cohen, *New England Journal of Medicine*, October 2, 1986.

I do not have space to discuss what constitutes a benefit, the magnitude of benefit required in order to justify the infliction of pain, and some principle of proportionality that rejects even a significant benefit at a cost of immense and excruciating suffering. In general, my views on these matters favor animals, especially when further commercial products are in question but also even when much medical/scientific research is under consideration. More broadly, I think a presumption, not in favor of, but against the use of animals in medical/scientific research would be desirable. Its intended effect would be to force researchers as a matter of routine to argue in depth a case for animal use. Such a presumption coheres with my earlier remarks. The unequal value thesis in no way compels its adherents to deny that animal lives have value; the destruction or impairment of such lives, therefore, needs to be argued for, which a presumption against use of animals would force researchers to do.

Clearly, a presumption against use is not the same thing as a bar; I allow, therefore, that researchers can make a case. That they must do so, that they must seek to justify the destruction or impairment of lives that have value, is the point.

Evaluating the Quality of Various Lives

How might we defend the unequal value thesis? At least the beginnings of what I take to be the most promising option in this regard can be briefly sketched.

Pain is one thing, killing is another, and what makes killing wrong—a killing could be free of pain and suffering—seems to be the fact that it consists in the destruction of something of value. That is, killing and the value of life seem straightforwardly connected, since it is difficult to understand why taking a particular life would be wrong if it had no value. If few people consider animal life to be without value, equally few, I think, consider it to have the same value as normal (adult) human life. They need not be speciesist as a result: in my view, normal (adult) human life is of a much higher quality than animal life, not because of species, but because of richness; and the value of a life is a function of its quality.

Part of the richness of our lives involves activities that we have in common with animals but there are as well whole dimensions to our lives—love, marriage, educating children, jobs, hobbies, sporting events, cultural pursuits, intellectual development and striving, etc.—that greatly expand our range of absorbing endeavors and so significantly deepen the texture of our lives. An impoverished life for *us* need not be one in which food or sex or liberty is absent; it can equally well be a life in which these other dimensions have not taken root or have done so only minimally. When we look back over our lives and regret that we did not make more of them, we rarely have in mind only the kinds of activities that we share with animals; rather, we think much more in terms of precisely these other dimensions of our lives that equally go to make up a rich, full life.

The lives of normal (adult) humans betray a variety and richness that the lives of rabbits do not; certainly, we do not think of ourselves as constrained to live out our lives according to some (conception of a) life deemed appropriate to our species. Other conceptions of a life for ourselves are within our reach, and we can try to understand and appreciate them and to choose among them. Some of us are artists, others educators, still others mechanics; the richness of our lives is easily enhanced through developing and molding our talents so as to enable us to live out these conceptions of the good life. Importantly, also, we are not condemned to embrace in our lifetimes only a single conception of such a life; in the sense intended, the artist can choose to become an educator and the educator a mechanic. We can embrace at different times different conceptions of how we want to live.

No Direct Duties

But so far as animals are concerned, we have no direct duties. Animals are not self-conscious and are there merely as a means to an end. That end is man. We can ask, "Why do animals exist?" But to ask, "Why does man exist?" is a meaningless question. Our duties towards animals are merely indirect duties towards humanity. Animal nature has analogies to human nature, and by doing our duties to animals in respect of manifestations of human nature, we indirectly do our duty towards humanity.

Immanuel Kant, "Duties to Animals and Spirits," in *Lectures on Ethics*.

Choosing among conceptions of the good life and trying to live out such a conception are not so intellectualized a set of tasks that only an elite few can manage them. Some reflection upon the life one wants to live is necessary, and some reflection is required in order to organize one's life to live out such a conception; but virtually all of us manage to engage in this degree of reflection. (One of the tragic aspects of Alzheimer's disease is how it undoes a person in just this regard, once it has reached advanced stages.) Even an uneducated man can see the choice between the army and professional boxing as one that requires him to sit down and ponder what he wants to do, whether he has the talents to do it, and what his other, perhaps conflicting desires come to in strength. Even an habitual street person, if free long enough from the influence of drink or drugs to be capable of addressing himself to the choice, can see the life the Salvation Army holds out before him as different in certain respects, some appealing, others perhaps not, from his present life. Choosing how one will live one's life can often be a matter of simply focussing upon these particulars and trying to gauge one's desires with respect to them.

Now, in the case of the rabbit the point is not that the activities which enrich an adult human's life are different from those which enrich its life; it is that the scope or potentiality for enrichment is truncated or severely diminished in the rabbit's case. The quality of a life is a function of its richness, which is a function of its scope or potentiality for enrichment; the scope or potentiality for enrichment in the rabbit's case never approaches that of the human. Nothing we have ever observed about rabbits, nothing we know of them, leads us to make judgments about the variety and richness of their life in anything even remotely comparable to the judgments we make in the human case. To assume as present in the rabbit's life dimensions that supply the full variety and richness of ours, only that these dimensions are hidden from us, provides no real answer, especially when the evidence we have about their lives runs in the other direction.

The Importance of Autonomy

Autonomy is an important part of the human case. By exercising our autonomy we can mold our lives to fit a conception of the good life that we have decided upon for ourselves; we can then try to live out this conception, with all the sense of achievement, self-fulfillment, and satisfaction that this can bring. Some of us pursue athletic or cultural or intellectual endeavors; some of us are good with our hands and enjoy mechanical tasks and manual labor; and all of us see a job—be it the one we have or the one we should like to have—as an important part of a full life. (This is why unemployment affects more than just our incomes.) The emphasis is upon agency: we can *make* ourselves into repairmen, pianists, and accountants; by exercising our autonomy, we can *impose* upon our lives a conception of the good life that we have for the moment embraced. We can then try to live out this conception, with the consequent sense of fulfillment and achievement that this makes possible. Even failure can be part of the picture: a woman can try to make herself into an Olympic athlete and fail; but her efforts to develop and shape her talents and to take control of and to mold her life in the appropriate ways can enrich her life. Thus, by exercising our autonomy and trying to live out some conception of how we want to live, we make possible further, important dimensions of value to our lives.

We still share certain activities with rabbits, but no mere record of those activities would come anywhere near accounting for the richness of our lives. What is missing in the rabbit's case is the same scope or potentiality for enrichment; and lives of less richness have less value.

The kind of story that would have to be told to make us think that the rabbit's life *was* as rich as the life of a normal (adult) human is one that either postulates in the rabbit potentialities and abilities vastly beyond what we observe and take it to have, or lapses into a rigorous scepticism. By the latter, I mean that we should have to say either that we know nothing of the rabbit's life (and so can know nothing of that life's richness and quality) or that what we know can never be construed as adequate for grounding judgments about the rabbit's quality of life. Such sceptical claims, particularly after Ryle and Wittgenstein on the one hand and much scientific work on the other, may strike many as misplaced, and those who have recourse to them, at least in my experience, have little difficulty in pronouncing pain and suffering, stress, loss of liberty, monotony, and a host of other things to be detrimental to an animal's quality of life. But the real puzzle is how this recourse to scepticism is supposed to make us think that a rabbit's life is as varied and rich as a human's life. If I can know nothing of the rabbit's life, presumably because I do not live that life and so cannot experience it from the inside (this whole way of putting the matter sets ill with a post-Ryle, post-Wittgenstein understanding of psychological concepts and inner processes), then how do I know that the rabbit's life is as rich as a human's life? Plainly, if I cannot know this, I must for the argument's sake assume it. But why should I do this? Nothing I observe and experience leads me to assume it; all the evidence I have about rabbits and humans seems to run entirely in the opposite direction. So, why make this assumption? Most especially, why assume animal lives are as rich as human lives, when we do not even assume, or so I suggest, that all *human* lives have the same richness?

"The rights view, I believe, is rationally the most satisfactory moral theory."

The Case for Strong Animal Rights

Tom Regan

Tom Regan is University Alumni Distinguished Professor at North Carolina State University and general editor of *The Heritage Project*, a fourteen volume series on the foundations of philosophy. In the following viewpoint, he presents a condensed version of his argument in *The Case for Animal Rights*. Regan contends that all sentient animals are "subjects of a life"; that is, they all have inherent worth as living creatures. Humans, therefore, ought to recognize the moral rights of animals and never use them as commodities or resources for exploitation.

As you read, consider the following questions:

1. According to Regan, what is fundamentally wrong with the way people usually describe their relationship with animals?
2. What does Regan mean when he asserts that animals have inherent value?
3. What are the implications of "the rights view" for farming and science, according to the author?

From "The Case for Animal Rights" by Tom Regan, in *In Defense of Animals*, edited by Peter Singer; ©1985 by Peter Singer. Reprinted by permission of the publisher, Basil Blackwell Inc.

I regard myself as an advocate of animal rights—as a part of the animal rights movement. That movement, as I conceive it, is committed to a number of goals, including:

- the total abolition of the use of animals in science;
- the total dissolution of commercial animal agriculture;
- the total elimination of commercial and sport hunting and trapping.

Why the System Is Fundamentally Wrong

There are, I know, people who profess to believe in animal rights but do not avow these goals. Factory farming, they say, is wrong—it violates animals' rights—but traditional animal agriculture is all right. Toxicity tests of cosmetics on animals violates their rights, but important medical research—cancer research, for example—does not. The clubbing of baby seals is abhorrent, but not the harvesting of adult seals. I used to think I understood this reasoning. Not any more. You don't change unjust institutions by tidying them up.

What's wrong—fundamentally wrong—with the way animals are treated isn't the details that vary from case to case. It's the whole system. The forlornness of the veal calf is pathetic, heart wrenching; the pulsing pain of the chimp with electrodes planted deep in her brain is repulsive; the slow, torturous death of the raccoon caught in the leg-hold trap is agonizing. But what is wrong isn't the pain, isn't the suffering, isn't the deprivation. These compound what's wrong. Sometimes—often—they make it much, much worse. But they are not the fundamental wrong.

The fundamental wrong is the system that allows us to view animals as *our resources*, here for *us*—to be eaten, or surgically manipulated, or exploited for sport or money. Once we accept this view of animals—as our resources—the rest is as predictable as it is regrettable. Why worry about their loneliness, their pain, their death? Since animals exist for us, to benefit us in one way or another, what harms them really doesn't matter—or matters only if it starts to bother us, makes us feel a trifle uneasy when we eat our veal escalop, for example. So, yes, let us get veal calves out of solitary confinement, give them more space, a little straw, a few companions. But let us keep our veal escalop.

But a little straw, more space and a few companions won't eliminate—won't even touch—the basic wrong that attaches to our viewing and treating these animals as our resources. A veal calf killed to be eaten after living in close confinement is viewed and treated in this way: but so, too, is another who is raised (as they say) 'more humanely'. To right the wrong of our treatment of farm animals requires more than making rearing methods 'more humane'; it requires the total dissolution of commercial animal agriculture.

How we do this, whether we do it or, as in the case of animals in science, whether and how we abolish their use—these are to a large extent political questions. People must change their beliefs before they change their habits. Enough people, especially those elected to public office, must believe in change—must want it—before we will have laws that protect the rights of animals. This process of change is very complicated, very demanding, very exhausting, calling for the efforts of many hands in education, publicity, political organization and activity, down to the licking of envelopes and stamps. As a trained and practising philosopher, the sort of contribution I can make is limited but, I like to think, important. The currency of philosophy is ideas—their meaning and rational foundation—not the nuts and bolts of the legislative process, say, or the mechanics of community organization. That's what I have been exploring over the past ten years or so in my essays and talks and, most recently, in my book, *The Case for Animal Rights*. I believe the major conclusions I reach in the book are true because they are supported by the weight of the best arguments. I believe the idea of animal rights has reason, not just emotion, on its side. . . .

The Importance of Recognizing Inherent Value

What to do? Where to begin anew? The place to begin, I think, is with the utilitarian's view of the value of the individual—or, rather, lack of value. In its place, suppose we consider that you and I, for example, do have value as individuals—what we'll call *inherent value*. To say we have such value is to say that we are something more than, something different from, mere receptacles. Moreover, to ensure that we do not pave the way for such injustices as slavery or sexual discrimination, we must believe that all who have inherent value have it equally, regardless of their sex, race, religion, birthplace and so on. Similarly to be discarded as irrelevant are one's talents or skills, intelligence and wealth, personality or pathology, whether one is loved and admired or despised and loathed. The genius and the retarded child, the prince and the pauper, the brain surgeon and the fruit vendor, Mother Teresa and the most unscrupulous used-car salesman—all have inherent value, all possess it equally, and have an equal right to be treated with respect, to be treated in ways that do not reduce them to the status of things, as if they existed as resources for others. My value as an individual is independent of my usefulness to you. Yours is not dependent on your usefulness to me. For either of us to treat the other in ways that fail to show respect for the other's independent value is to act immorally, to violate the individual's rights. . . .

The rights view, I believe, is rationally the most satisfactory moral theory. It surpasses all other theories in the degree to which it illuminates and explains the foundations of our duties to one another—the domain of human morality. On this score it has the best reasons, the best arguments, on its side. Of course, if it were possible to show that only human beings are included within its scope, then a person like myself, who believes in animal rights, would be obliged to look elsewhere.

Peanuts by Charles Schulz is reprinted by special permission of United Feature Syndicate, Inc.

But attempts to limit its scope to humans only can be shown to be rationally defective. Animals, it is true, lack many of the abilities humans possess. They can't read, do higher mathematics, build a bookcase or make *baba ghanoush*. Neither can many human beings, however, and yet we don't (and shouldn't) say that they (these humans) therefore have less inherent value, less of a right to be treated with respect, than do others. It is the *similarities* between those human beings who most clearly, most non-controversially have such value (the people reading this, for example), not our differences, that matter most. And the really crucial, the basic similarity is simply this: we are each of us the experiencing subject of a life, a conscious creature having an individual welfare that has importance to us whatever our usefulness to others. We want and prefer things, believe and feel things, recall and expect things. And all these dimensions of our life, including our pleasure and pain, our enjoyment and suffering, our satisfaction and frustration, our continued existence or our untimely death—all make a difference to the quality of our life as lived, as experienced, by us as individuals. As the same is true of those animals that concern us (the ones that are eaten and trapped, for example), they too must be viewed as the experiencing subjects of a life, with inherent value of their own.

Some there are who resist the idea that animals have inherent value. 'Only humans have such value,' they profess. How might this narrow view be defended? Shall we say that only humans have the requisite intelligence, or autonomy, or reason? But there are many, many humans who fail to meet these standards and yet are reasonably viewed as having value above and beyond their usefulness to others. Shall we claim that only humans belong to the right species, the species *Homo sapiens*? But this is blatant speciesism. Will it be said, then, that all—and only—humans have immortal souls? Then our opponents have their work cut out for them. I am myself not ill-disposed to the proposition that there are immortal souls. Personally, I profoundly hope I have one. But I would not want to rest my position on a controversial ethical issue on the even more controversial question about who or what has an immortal soul. That is to dig one's hole deeper, not to climb out. Rationally, it is better to resolve moral issues without making more controversial assumptions than are needed. The question of who has inherent value is such a question, one that is resolved more rationally without the introduction of the idea of immortal souls than by its use.

Well, perhaps some will say that animals have some inherent value, only less than we have. Once again, however, attempts to defend this view can be shown to lack rational justification. What could be the basis of our having more inherent value than animals? Their lack of reason, or autonomy, or intellect? Only if we are willing to make the same judgement in the case of humans who are similarly deficient. But it is not true that such humans—the retarded child, for example, or the mentally deranged—have less inherent value than you or I. Neither, then, can we rationally sustain the view that animals like them in being the experiencing subjects of a life have less inherent value. *All* who have inherent value have it *equally*, whether they be human animals or not.

Animals Are Subjects of a Life

Inherent value, then, belongs equally to those who are the experiencing subjects of a life. Whether it belongs to others—to rocks and rivers, trees and glaciers, for example—we do not know and may never know. But neither do we need to know, if we are to make the case for animal rights. We do not need to know, for example, how many people are eligible to vote in the next presidential election before we can know whether I am. Similarly, we do not need to know how many individuals have inherent value before we can know that some do. When it comes to the case for animal rights, then, what we need to know is whether the animals that, in our culture, are routinely eaten, hunted and used in our laboratories, for example, are like us in being subjects of a life. And we do know this. We do know that many—literally, billions and billions—of these animals are the subjects of a life in the sense explained and so have inherent value if we do. And since, in order to arrive at the best theory of our duties to one another, we must recognize our equal inherent value as individuals, reason—not sentiment, not emotion—reason compels us to recognize the equal inherent value of these animals and, with this, their equal right to be treated with respect.

Two Points

That, *very* roughly, is the shape and feel of the case for animal rights. Most of the details of the supporting argument are missing. They are to be found in the book to which I alluded earlier. Here, the details go begging, and I must, in closing, limit myself to [two] points.

The first is how the theory that underlies the case for animal rights shows that the animal rights movement is a part of, not antagonistic to, the human rights movement. The theory that rationally grounds the rights of animals also grounds the rights of humans. Thus those involved in the animal rights movement are partners in the struggle to secure respect for human rights—the rights of women, for example, or minorities, or workers. The animal rights movement is cut from the same moral cloth as these.

Second, having set out the broad outlines of the rights view, I can now say why its implications for farming and science, among other fields, are both clear and uncompromising. In the case of the use of animals in science, the rights view is categorically abolitionist. Lab animals are not our tasters; we are not their kings. Because these animals are treated routinely, systematically as if their value were reducible to their usefulness to others, they are routinely, systematically treated with a lack of respect, and thus are their rights routinely, systematically violated. This is just as true when they are used in trivial, duplicative, unnecessary or unwise research as it is when they are used in studies that hold out real promise of human benefits. We can't justify harming or killing a human being (my Aunt Bea, for example) just for these sorts of reason. Neither can we do so even in the case of so lowly a creature as a laboratory rat. It is not just refinement or reduction that is called for, not just larger, cleaner cages, not just more generous use of anesthetic or the elimination of multiple surgery, not just tidying up the system. It is complete replacement. The best we can do when it comes to using animals in science is—not to use them. That is where our duty lies, according to the rights view.

As for commercial animal agriculture, the rights view takes a similar abolitionist position. The fundamental moral wrong here is not that animals are kept in stressful close confinement or in isolation, or that their pain and suffering, their needs and preferences are ignored or discounted. All these *are* wrong, of course, but they are not the fundamental wrong. They are symptoms and effects of the deeper, systematic wrong that allows these animals to be viewed and treated as lacking independent value, as resources for us—as, indeed, a renewable resource. Giving farm animals more space, more natural environments, more companions does not right the fundamental wrong, any more than giving lab animals more anesthesia or bigger, cleaner cages would right the fundamental wrong in their case. Nothing less than the total dissolution of commercial animal agriculture will do this, just as, for similar reasons I won't develop at length here, morality requires nothing less than the total elimination of hunting and trapping for commercial and sporting ends. The rights view's implications, then, as I have said, are clear and uncompromising.

"*The rights of most non-human animals may be overridden in circumstances which would not justify overriding the rights of persons.*"

The Case for Weak Animal Rights

Mary Anne Warren

In the following viewpoint, Mary Anne Warren argues against the contention that nonhuman animals have the same basic moral rights as humans, an argument she labels as the strong animal rights position. In contrast to such a position (advocated by Tom Regan, for example), Warren prefers a weak animal rights position, one that bases animal rights on a rationality that, she contends, nonhuman animals do not possess. Warren teaches philosophy at San Francisco State University.

As you read, consider the following questions:

1. Why is the notion of inherent rights unclear and obscure, according to the author?
2. Why is rationality morally relevant, according to Warren?
3. In what ways does Warren, in fact, argue for the rights of animals, even though those rights are weak?

From "Difficulties with the Strong Animal Rights Position" by Mary Anne Warren, *Between the Species*, Fall 1987. Reprinted by permission of the publisher.

Tom Regan has produced what is perhaps the definitive defense of the view that the basic moral rights of at least some non-human animals are in no way inferior to our own. In *The Case for Animal Rights*, he argues that all normal mammals over a year of age have the same basic moral rights. Non-human mammals have essentially the same right not to be harmed or killed as we do. I shall call this "the strong animal rights position," although it is weaker than the claims made by some animal liberationists in that it ascribes rights to only some sentient animals.

I will argue that Regan's case for the strong animal rights position is unpersuasive and that this position entails consequences which a reasonable person cannot accept. I do not deny that some non-human animals have moral rights; indeed, I would extend the scope of the rights claim to include all sentient animals, that is, all those capable of having experiences, including experiences of pleasure or satisfaction and pain, suffering, or frustration. However, I do not think that the moral rights of most non-human animals are identical in strength to those of persons. The rights of most non-human animals may be overridden in circumstances which would not justify overriding the rights of persons. There are, for instance, compelling realities which sometimes require that we kill animals for reasons which could not justify the killing of persons. I will call this view "the weak animal rights" position, even though it ascribes rights to a wider range of animals than does the strong animal rights position. . . .

The Obscurity of Inherent Value

Inherent value is a key concept in Regan's theory. It is the bridge between the plausible claim that all normal, mature mammals—human or otherwise—are subjects-of-a-life and the more debatable claim that they all have basic moral rights of the same strength. But it is a highly obscure concept, and its obscurity makes it ill-suited to play this crucial role.

Inherent value is defined almost entirely in negative terms. It is not dependent upon the value which either the inherently valuable individual or anyone else may place upon that individual's life or experiences. It is not (necessarily) a function of sentience or any other mental capacity, because, Regan says, some entities which are not sentient (e.g., trees, rivers, or rocks) may, nevertheless, have inherent value. It cannot attach to anything other than an individual; species, eco-systems, and the like cannot have inherent value.

These are some of the things which inherent value is not. But what is it? Unfortunately, we are not told. Inherent value appears as a mysterious non-natural property which we must take on faith. Regan says that it is a *postulate* that subjects-of-a-life have inherent value, a postulate justified by the fact that it avoids certain absurdities which he thinks follow from a purely utilitarian theory. But why is the postulate that *subjects-of-a-life* have inherent value? If the inherent value of a being is completely independent of the value that it or anyone else places upon its experiences, then why does the fact that it has certain sorts of experiences constitute evidence that it has inherent value? If the reason is that subjects-of-a-life have an existence which can go better or worse for them, then why isn't the appropriate conclusion that all sentient beings have inherent value, since they would all seem to meet that condition? Sentient but mentally unsophisticated beings may have a less extensive range of possible satisfactions and frustrations, but why should it follow that they have—or may have—no inherent value at all?

In the absence of a positive account of inherent value, it is also difficult to grasp the connection between being inherently valuable and having moral rights. Intuitively, it seems that value is one thing, and rights are another. It does not seem incoherent to say that some things (e.g., mountains, rivers, redwood trees) are inherently valuable and yet are not the sorts of things which can have moral rights. Nor does it seem incoherent to ascribe inherent value to some things which are not individuals, e.g., plant or animal species, though it may well be incoherent to ascribe moral rights to such things.

In short, the concept of inherent value seems to create at least as many problems as it solves. If inherent value is based on some natural property, then why not try to identify that property and explain its moral significance, without appealing to inherent value? And if it is not based on any natural property, then why should we believe in it? That it may enable us to avoid some of the problems faced by the utilitarian is not a sufficient reason, if it creates other problems which are just as serious.

Is There a Sharp Line?

Perhaps the most serious problems are those that arise when we try to apply the strong animal rights position to animals other than normal, mature mammals. Regan's theory requires us to divide all living things into two categories: those which have the same inherent value and the same basic moral rights that we do, and those which have no inherent value and presumably no moral rights. But wherever we try to draw the line, such a sharp division is implausible.

It would surely be arbitrary to draw such a sharp line between normal, mature mammals and all other living things. Some birds (e.g., crows, magpies, parrots, mynahs) appear to be just as mentally sophisticated as most mammals and thus are equally strong candidates for inclusion under the subject-of-a-life criterion. Regan is not in fact advocating that we draw the line here. His claim is only that normal, mature mammals are clear cases, while other cases are less clear. Yet, on his theory, there must be such a sharp line *somewhere*, since there are no degrees of inherent value. But why should we believe that there is a sharp line between creatures that are subjects-of-a-life and creatures that are not? Isn't it more likely that "subjecthood" comes in degrees, that some creatures have only a little self-awareness, and only a little capacity to anticipate the future, while some have a little more, and some a good deal more?

Reprinted by permission of Chuck Asay and Creators Syndicate.

Should we, for instance, regard fish, amphibians, and reptiles as subjects-of-a-life? A simple yes-or-no answer seems inadequate. On the one hand, some of their behavior is difficult to explain without the assumption that they have sensations, beliefs, desires, emotions, and memories; on the other hand, they do not seem to exhibit very much self-awareness or very much conscious anticipation of future events. Do they have enough mental sophistication to count as subjects-of-a-life? Exactly how much is enough?

It is still more unclear what we should say about insects, spiders, octopi, and other invertebrate animals which have brains and sensory organs but whose minds (if they have minds) are even more alien to us than those of fish or reptiles. Such creatures are probably sentient. Some people doubt that they can feel pain, since they lack certain neurological structures which are crucial to the processing of pain impulses in vertebrate animals. But this argument is inconclusive, since their nervous systems might process pain in ways different from ours. When injured, they sometimes act as if they are in pain. On evolutionary grounds, it seems unlikely that highly mobile creatures with complex sensory systems would not have developed a capacity for pain (and pleasure), since such a capacity has obvious survival value. It must, however, be admitted that we do not *know* whether spiders can feel pain (or something very like it), let alone whether they have emotions, memories, beliefs, desires, self-awareness, or a sense of the future.

The Unclear Cases

Even more mysterious are the mental capacities (if any) of mobile microfauna. The brisk and efficient way that paramecia move about in their incessant search for food *might* indicate some kind of sentience, in spite of their lack of eyes, ears, brains, and other organs associated with sentience in more complex organisms. It is conceivable—though not very probable—that they, too, are subjects-of-a-life.

The existence of a few unclear cases need not pose a serious problem for a moral theory, but in this case, the unclear cases constitute most of those with which an adequate theory of animal rights would need to deal. The subject-of-a-life criterion can provide us with little or no moral guidance in our interactions with the vast majority of animals. That might be acceptable if it could be supplemented with additional principles which would provide such guidance. However, the radical dualism of the theory precludes supplementing it in this way. We are forced to say that either a spider has the same right to life as you and I do, or it has no right to life whatever—and that only the gods know which of these alternatives is true.

Regan's suggestion for dealing with such unclear cases is to apply the "benefit of the doubt" principle. That is, when dealing with beings that may or may not be subjects-of-a-life, we should act as if they are. But if we try to apply this principle to the entire range of doubtful cases, we will find ourselves with moral obligations which we cannot possibly fulfill. In many climates, it is virtually impossible to live without swatting mosquitoes and exterminating cockroaches, and not all of us can afford to hire someone to sweep the path before we walk, in order to make sure that we do not step on ants. Thus, we are still faced with the daunting task of drawing a sharp line somewhere on the continuum of life forms—this time, a line demarcating the limits of the benefit of the doubt principle.

The weak animal rights theory provides a more plausible way of dealing with this range of cases, in that it allows the rights of animals of different kinds to vary in strength. . . .

Why Are Animal Rights Weaker Than Human Rights?

How can we justify regarding the rights of persons as generally stronger than those of sentient beings which are not persons? There are a plethora of bad justifications, based on religious premises or false or unprovable claims about the differences between human and non-human nature. But there is one difference which has a clear moral relevance: people are at least sometimes capable of being moved to action or inaction by the force of reasoned argument. Rationality rests upon other mental capacities, notably those which Regan cites as criteria for being a subject-of-a-life. We share these capacities with many other animals. But it is not just because we are subjects-of-a-life that we are both able and morally compelled to recognize one another as beings with equal basic moral rights. It is also because we are able to "listen to reason" in order to settle our conflicts and cooperate in shared projects. This capacity, unlike the others, may require something like a human language.

Why is rationality morally relevant? It does not make us "better" than other animals or more "perfect." It does not even automatically make us more intelligent. (Bad reasoning reduces our effective intelligence rather than increasing it.) But it is morally relevant insofar as it provides greater possibilities for cooperation and for the nonviolent resolution of problems. It also makes us more dangerous than non-rational beings can ever be. Because we are potentially more dangerous and less predictable than wolves, we need an articulated system of morality to regulate our conduct. Any human morality, to be workable in the long run, must recognize the equal moral status of all persons, whether through the postulate of equal basic moral rights or in some other way. The recognition of the moral equality of other persons is the price we must each pay for their recognition of our moral equality. Without this mutual recognition of moral equality, human society can exist only in a state of chronic and bitter conflict. The war between the sexes will persist so long as there is sexism and male domination; racial conflict will never be eliminated so long as there are racist laws and practices. But, to the extent that we achieve a mutual recognition of equality, we can hope to live together, perhaps as peacefully as wolves, achieving (in part) through explicit moral principles what they do not seem to need explicit moral principles to achieve.

Why not extend this recognition of moral equality to other

creatures, even though they cannot do the same for us? The answer is that we cannot. Because we cannot reason with most non-human animals, we cannot always solve the problems which they may cause without harming them—although we are always obligated to try. We cannot negotiate a treaty with the feral cats and foxes, requiring them to stop preying on endangered native species in return for suitable concessions on our part.

> If rats invade our houses . . . we cannot reason with them, hoping to persuade them of the injustice they do us. We can only attempt to get rid of them. [Bonnie Steinbock]

Reasoning with Animals

Aristotle was not wrong in claiming that the capacity to alter one's behavior on the basis of reasoned argument is relevant to the full moral status which he accorded to free men. Of course, he was wrong in his other premise, that women and slaves by their nature cannot reason well enough to function as autonomous moral agents. Had that premise been true, so would his conclusion that women and slaves are not quite the moral equals of free men. In the case of most non-human animals, the corresponding premise is true. If, on the other hand, there are animals with whom we can (learn to) reason, then we are obligated to do this and to regard them as our moral equals.

Thus, to distinguish between the rights of persons and those of most other animals on the grounds that only people can alter their behavior on the basis of reasoned argument does not commit us to a perfectionist theory of the sort Aristotle endorsed. There is no excuse for refusing to recognize the moral equality of some people on the grounds that we don't regard them as quite as rational as we are, since it is perfectly clear that most people can reason well enough to determine how to act so as to respect the basic rights of others (if they choose to), and that is enough for moral equality.

But what about people who are clearly not rational? It is often argued that sophisticated mental capacities such as rationality cannot be essential for the possession of equal basic moral rights, since nearly everyone agrees that human infants and mentally incompetent persons have such rights, even though they may lack those sophisticated mental capacities. But this argument is inconclusive, because there are powerful practical and emotional reasons for protecting non-rational human beings, reasons which are absent in the case of most non-human animals. Infancy and mental incompetence are human conditions which all of us either have experienced or are likely to experience at some time. We also protect babies and mentally incompetent people because we care for them. We don't normally care for animals in the same way, and when we do—e.g., in the case of much-loved pets—we may regard them as having special rights by virtue of their relationship to us. We protect them not only for their sake but also for our own, lest we be hurt by harm done to them. Regan holds that such "side-effects" are irrelevant to moral rights, and perhaps they are. But in ordinary usage, there is no sharp line between moral rights and those moral protections which are not rights. The extension of strong moral protections to infants and the mentally impaired in no way proves that non-human animals have the same basic moral rights as people.

Why Speak of "Animal Rights" at All?

If, as I have argued, reality precludes our treating all animals as our moral equals, then why should we still ascribe rights to them? Everyone agrees that animals are entitled to some protection against human abuse, but why speak of animal *rights* if we are not prepared to accept most animals as our moral equals? The weak animal rights position may seem an unstable compromise between the bold claim that animals have the same basic moral rights that we do and the more common view that animals have no rights at all.

It is probably impossible to either prove or disprove the thesis that animals have moral rights by producing an analysis of the concept of a moral right and checking to see if some or all animals satisfy the conditions for having rights. The concept of a moral right is complex, and it is not clear which of its strands are essential. Paradigm rights holders, i.e., mature and mentally competent persons, are *both* rational and morally autonomous beings and sentient subjects-of-a-life. Opponents of animal rights claim that rationality and moral autonomy are essential for the possession of rights, while defenders of animal rights claim that they are not. The ordinary concept of a moral right is probably not precise enough to enable us to determine who is right on purely definitional grounds.

If logical analysis will not answer the question of whether animals have moral rights, practical considerations may, nevertheless, incline us to say that they do. The most plausible alternative to the view that animals have moral rights is that, while they do not have *rights*, we are, nevertheless, obligated not to be cruel to them. Regan argues persuasively that the injunction to avoid being cruel to animals is inadequate to express our obligations towards animals, because it focuses on the mental states of those who cause animal suffering, rather than on the harm done to the animals themselves. Cruelty is inflicting pain or suffering and either taking pleasure in that pain or suffering or being more or less indifferent to it. Thus, to express the demand for the decent treatment of animals in terms of the rejection of cruelty is to invite the too easy response that those who subject animals to suffering are not being cruel because they regret the suffering they cause but sincerely believe that what they do is justified. The injunction to avoid cruelty is also inadequate in that it does not preclude the killing of animals—for any reason, however trivial—so long as it is done relatively painlessly.

The Only Way

The inadequacy of the anti-cruelty view provides one practical reason for speaking of animal rights. Another practical reason is that this is an age in which nearly all significant moral claims tend to be expressed in terms of rights. Thus, the denial that animals have rights, however carefully qualified, is likely to be taken to mean that we may do whatever we like to them, provided that we do not violate any human rights. In such a context, speaking of the rights of animals may be the only way to persuade many people to take seriously protests against the abuse of animals.

Why not extend this line of argument and speak of the rights of trees, mountains, oceans, or anything else which we may wish to see protected from destruction? Some environmentalists have not hesitated to speak in this way, and, given the importance of protecting such elements of the natural world, they cannot be blamed for using this rhetorical device. But, I would argue that moral rights can meaningfully be ascribed only to entities which have some capacity for sentience. This is because moral rights are protections designed to protect rights holders from harms or to provide them with benefits which matter *to them*. Only beings capable of sentience can be harmed or benefitted in ways which matter to them, for only such beings can like or dislike what happens to them or prefer some conditions to others. Thus, sentient animals, unlike mountains, rivers, or species, are at least logically possible candidates for moral rights. This fact, together with the need to end current abuses of animals—e.g., in scientific research and intensive farming—provides a plausible case for speaking of animal rights.

Conclusion

I have argued that Regan's case for ascribing strong moral rights to all normal, mature mammals is unpersuasive because (1) it rests upon the obscure concept of inherent value, which is defined only in negative terms, and (2) it seems to preclude any plausible answer to questions about the moral status of the vast majority of sentient animals. Moreover, (3) the strong animal rights position leads to unacceptable conclusions: e.g., that we may not kill rodents when they invade our houses or protect endangered species by killing introduced predators. The weak animal rights position allows for the necessary flexibility in dealing with animals when they pose a threat to our well-being, or that of other animals, or ecological systems. On the other hand, it also ascribes moral rights to a much wider range of animals: not just normal, mature mammals but all sentient beings, whether warm- or cold-blooded, vertebrate or invertebrate.

The weak animal rights theory asserts that (1) any creature whose natural mode of life includes the pursuit of certain satisfactions has the right not to be forced to exist without the opportunity to pursue those satisfactions; (2) any creature which is capable of pain, suffering, or frustration has the right that such experiences not be deliberately inflicted upon it without some compelling reason; and (3) no sentient being should be killed without good reason. However, moral rights are not an all-or-nothing affair. The strength of the reasons required to override the rights of a non-human organism varies, depending upon— among other things—the probability that it is sentient and (if it is clearly sentient) its probable degree of mental sophistication.

"In all our dealings with animals, whether direct or indirect, the ethic for the liberation of life requires that we render unto animals what they are due, as creatures with an independent integrity and value."

Christianity Supports Animal Rights

Annecy Report to the World Council of Churches

In 1988 fourteen theologians from different traditions and different parts of the world gathered in Annecy, France, under the aegis of the World Council of Churches, to deliberate upon the integrity of creation. The following viewpoint is excerpted from "Liberating Life," their report to the WCC. It contends that Christians have a responsibility to God to maintain ecological systems and biodiversity, and to pay special respect to individual animals. Because of God's love for all life forms, the report urges, Christians should work to alleviate the suffering of animals, especially in commercial research, in fashion and entertainment industries, in processing animals as food, and in educational settings.

As you read, consider the following questions:

1. According to the authors, how do the stories of the creation and Noah urge Christians to value the integrity of animals?
2. What practical suggestions does this viewpoint make as to how Christians may liberate all forms of life from suffering?

Excerpted from "Liberating Life: A Report to the World Council of Churches," in *Liberating Life: Contemporary Approaches to Ecological Theology*, edited by Charles Birch, William Eakin, and Jay B. McDaniel (Maryknoll, NY: Orbis Books, 1991). Copyright 1991. Reprinted with permission of the publisher.

Christian visions of the world and of salvation are profoundly shaped by the biblical story of creation. For many generations in the West, this story was read primarily in human-centered terms; human beings were created in the image of God, commanded to be fruitful and multiply, given dominion over the rest of creation, only to disobey God and fall. This one-sided interpretation led to reading the remainder of the Bible as the story of human salvation alone. It also supported exploitative attitudes and practices in relation to the remainder of creation and the destruction of the habitat of many species.

Rereading the Creation Story

As the disastrous consequences of this exploitation, both for the rest of creation and for humanity as a whole, have become manifest, Christians have reread the creation story. We have found that it locates the story of humanity in a much wider context, as a cosmic one. Before and apart from the creation of human beings, God sees that the animals are good. When humanity is added creation as a whole is very good. The command to human beings to be fruitful and to multiply does not nullify the identical command to animals. The image of God with its associated dominion is not for exploitation of animals but for responsible care. The plants that are good in themselves are given to both animals and human beings for their food. This is the integrity of creation in its ideal form.

According to the biblical stories, human sin disrupts this integral creation. As a consequence, there emerges competition and war between farmers and pastoralists. Injustice and strife proceed so far that God repents having created the world. Nevertheless, God saves the Noah family from the deluge, and at God's command this human family exercises its rightful dominion in saving all animal species from a watery death. When the waters recede God makes a covenant with the animals. From this vision of creation and human sin there follows a longing for inclusive salvation. The whole creation praises God, but this whole creation also groans in travail. As human sin has caused the subjection of all creation to futility, so the liberation of all life can come about only through the liberation of humanity from its bondage to Mammon.

The ideas expressed in the creation and Noah stories and the consequent vision of universal salvation have profound relevance today. All creatures have value in themselves as well as for one another and for God. Each, therefore, claims respect from human beings. The whole creation in all its rich complexity has a special value that is diminished when forests are turned into grasslands and grasslands are turned into deserts. The Noah story highlights God's concern for the preservation of species.

From these stories we acquire a distinctive understanding of "the integrity of creation." *The value of all creatures in and for themselves, for one another, and for God, and their interconnectedness in a diverse whole that has unique value for God, together constitute the integrity of creation.*

Restoring Peace and Justice

As human beings who participate in this creation we have a unique responsibility to respect its integrity, but in fact we have violated it in many ways. Indeed, our violence against one another and against the rest of creation threatens the continuation of life on the planet. It is now our opportunity and our duty, by God's grace, to be restored to peace and justice both in our relations to one another and in our relations with the rest of creation. As long as human beings order their lives to short-sighted economic gain or increased wealth, there will be no end to violence, oppression, or to the exploitation of the other creatures. Only a society ordered to the regeneration of the earth will attain peace and justice. Only in such a world is the integrity of creation respected and achieved.

Within the message of Jesus we find a profound deepening of the importance of our treatment of one another and especially of the weak and oppressed. "Truly, I say to you as you did it to one of the least of these my brothers and sisters, you did it to me" (Mt 25:40). Primarily this refers to our treatment of human beings, but on the lips of the Jesus who speaks of God's care for the grass of the field and the fallen sparrow, these too are included among "the least of these." In the hunger of millions of children, in the loneliness and humiliation of the homeless, in the wretchedness of the raped, in the suffering of the tortured, and also in the pain of myriads of animals used for human gain without regard to their own worth, Christ is crucified anew (Eph 1:10). . . .

Imaging the New Sensibility

A contemporary reading of scripture suggests an interrelatedness of all creatures within the earth and with God. Likewise, the story of the universe emerging from the sciences indicates that all that exists is part of everything else. How should Christians image this sensibility when speaking of God and of world? Whenever human beings attempt to speak about God, we do so in the language of our own time, our various cultures, and from familiar and important relationships. In biblical times, this language was of God as king and lord, but also of God as creator, father, mother, healer, and liberator. As we think about the way to express the relationship of God to the world in our time, we realize that metaphors such as king and lord limit God's activity to the human sphere; moreover, these metaphors suggest that God is external to the world and distant from it.

The creation narrative of our time, the awesome story of the beginning of the universe some ten billion years ago, evolving into our incredibly complex and intricate cosmos in which "everything that is" is interrelated, suggests the need for different symbolic language. Instead of a king relating to his realm, we picture God as the creator who "bodies forth" all that is, who creates not as a potter or an artist does, but more as a mother. That is to say, the universe, including our earth and all its creatures and plants, "lives and moves and has its being" in God (cf. Acts 17:28), though God is beyond and more than the universe. Organic images seem most appropriate for expressing both the immanence of God in and to the entire creation as well as God's transcendence of it. In the light of the incarnation, the whole universe appears to us as God's "body." Just as we transcend our bodies, so also the divine spirit transcends the body of the universe. And, just as we are affected by what happens to our body, so also God is affected by what happens in the world. The sufferings and joys of people and other creatures are shared by God.

The Body

When we express the relationship between God and the world (or universe) in organic images, several things become clearer. First, all of us, humans and other living creatures, live together within this body—we are part of each other and can in no way exist separately. Second, unlike the king-realm image which is hierarchical and dualistic and encourages human beings to adopt similar postures toward other members of their own species as well as toward other species, the organic symbolism underscores the inherent worth of all the different parts of the body, different species as well as individuals within those species. Third, while the body metaphor has been used since the time of Paul to express Christ, the Church (1 Corinthians 12:12–26), extending it to the cosmos (we are all members of the body of God, the universe) places us in intimate relations with all our fellow human beings as well as with all other forms of life. We not only empathize with all who are oppressed and suffer—victims of war and injustice, both humans and other living creatures—but we also feel responsibility for helping to bring about peace and justice to the suffering members of God's "body." God's glory and God's closeness are expressed in this image. We stand in awe of the One upon whom this universe depends, whether we view it through a telescope in which its vastness enthralls and terrifies us or through a microscope in which the intricate patterns of the veins of a leaf amaze us. And at a molecular level of life, the complex and beautiful structure of the DNA molecule that can exist in an indefinite variety of forms gives us a sense of awe and wonder. We also, each of us, are part of this universe, this body, in which God is present to us. We feel God's presence here in our world as we touch one another, love and serve one another, that is, all the others that make up the fabric of existence.

Our scripture speaks of the cosmic Christ (Colossians 1), the presence of God in the cosmos, God's embodiment, God's "incarnation." In this image of divine embodiment, we have a helpful way of talking about creation that is biblical, consonant with contemporary science, and experientially illuminating. The universe, everything that is, each and every living thing and the ecosystem that supports all things, is bound together, intrinsically and inextricably, with its creator. Within this bond, the oppression of life is common history, the liberation of life is our common responsibility and our common hope.

An Ethic for the Liberation of Life

An ethic for the liberation of life calls for seeing the whole of creation in its integrity and therefore demands respect of every creature. Human respect for fellow creatures properly emphasizes individual members of the human community itself. Peace among nations and justice both within and between them are crucial. But this human community is part of a larger community of creatures whose health is essential for the well-being of human beings. An ethic for the liberation of life involves concern for this larger community not only because of its importance to human beings but also for the sake of its other members. . . .

Respect for Individual Animals

The biblical and theological messages about the value of animals speak with one voice: Animals do not exist for the sake of the unbridled pursuit of human avarice and greed. And yet the increasingly powerful transnational corporations prefer that people not know, or not care, about the pain and death literally billions of animals are made to suffer every year in the name of corporate mass-production and consumer over-consumption. Some examples follow.

Cosmetics and Household Products. Many areas of the world have an abundance of toothpastes, colognes, after-shaves, deodorants, perfumes, powders, blushes, detergents, oven and window cleaners, furniture and floor polishes, and other cosmetics and household products. This is well-known. What is not well-known is that these items routinely are tested on animals in a variety of painful ways, including acute eye-irritance tests as well as so-called "lethal dose" tests, in which animals are force-fed a deodorant or floor polish, for example, until a specific number die. When we purchase the products of the major cosmetic and household products' corporations, we support massive animal pain and death—all of which is unnecessary. For there are alternatives. Attractive cosmetics and effective household products that are both safe and economical, that have not been tested on animals, already exist and are available, and others would be if enough consumers demanded them.

Fashion. Mass-production and over-consumption encourage ignorance and indifference in the name of fashion. Nowhere is this more evident than in the case of fur products (coats, capes, gloves, and the like). Fur-bearing animals trapped in the wild inevitably suffer slow, agonizing deaths, while those raised on "modern" fur-farms live in unnatural conditions that severely limit their ability to move, groom, form social units, and engage in other patterns of behavior that are natural to their kind. When we purchase the products of commercial furriers, we support massive animal pain and death—all of which is unnecessary. For there are alternatives. Many attractive coats, capes, gloves, and the like, which are not directly linked to the commercial exploitation of animals, already exist and are available, and others would be if enough consumers demanded them.

Animals Are Family

Of course Christians affirm that God is Redeemer as well as Creator. The redemption is progressive and involves the interdependence of family working together to restore broken relationships. We are thus enabled to see animals as our brothers and sisters rather than as commodities. That involves our own being liberated from seeing ourselves as consumers and machines. We cannot respect ourselves in fullness without respect for animals; we cannot know our full physical selves without animals. Indeed, completed redemption will involve a great community of creatures who participate together in God's household. The recognition that we are family carries us one step in that direction.

L. Shannon Jung, *Good News for Animals? Christian Approaches to Animal Well-Being,* eds. Charles Pinches and Jay B. McDaniel, 1993.

Food. Increasingly, the family farm is being replaced by national and often multi-national interests, business ventures void of any roots in the land or bonds to the animals they raise. The goal of mass-production is to raise the largest number of animals in the shortest time with the least investment. The "good shepherd" has given way to the corporate factory.

Corporate animal agriculture relies on what are called "close-confinement" or "intensive rearing" methods. The animals are taken off the land and raised permanently indoors. There is no sunlight, no fresh air, often not even room enough to turn around. In many cases six to eight laying hens are packed in a wire-mesh metal cage three-quarters of the size of a page of daily newspaper. For up to five years, many breeding sows are confined to stalls barely larger than their bodies. Veal calves (typically male calves born to dairy herds) routinely are taken from their mothers at birth and raised in permanent isolation. Increasingly even dairy cattle are being taken off the land and raised indoors.

Because of the massive numbers of farm animals raised for slaughter (upwards of 4 billion annually, just in the United States), huge amounts of grains are used as feed. More than 90 percent of the oats, corn, rye, barley, and sorghum crops grown in the United States, for example, are fed to animals, and this use of food is enormously wasteful. Every pound of complete protein produced by beef cattle requires eight to nine pounds of complete vegetable protein, while every pound of complete protein supplied by hogs requires four to five pounds of complete vegetable protein. When more protein is being used to produce less, it is no exaggeration to say that we have a protein production system running in reverse.

On the corporate factory that is today's animal farm, virtually every natural form of behavior is thwarted, from preening and dust bathing in chickens to nursing and gamboling in veal calves. When we purchase the products of corporate factory farming, we support massive animal deprivation and death—all of which is unnecessary. For alternatives exist. People can choose to purchase the products of the remaining small-scale family farms or explore a dietary life-style free from all direct commercial connections with the suffering death of animals.

Means to Human Ends

Entertainment. Many different animals are used for commercial purposes in entertainment. The forms of entertainment include circuses, stage and aquatic shows, rodeos, bullfights, and organized cock and dog fights. In whatever form, the animals are treated as mere means to human ends. Sometimes (as in the case of bull and bronco busting in rodeos) the animals are caused more than incidental pain. Sometimes (in the case of the housing and transportation of circus and other "performing" animals) the animals are subjected to severe and often protracted deprivation. Sometimes (as in the case of animals who perform "tricks" in stage and aquatic shows) the animals are rewarded for their ability to mimic human behavior (for example, by balancing themselves on balls or jumping through hoops). And sometimes (as in the case of bull, cock, and dog fights) some of the animals are killed and all are made to endure acute suffering.

When we patronize these forms of entertainment, we support those commercial interests that reduce the value of animals to the status of the purely instrumental, often at the cost of great pain (and sometimes even death) for the animals themselves—and all of this is unnecessary. For alternatives exist. We do not have to train, exploit, outwit, or outmuscle animals, or to support those who make a profit from doing so, in order to take pleasure in their presence or their beauty. Benign forms of recreation involving animals exist. For some people this may involve photography, scuba, and other forms of ocean diving, or the viewing of any one of the thousands of films about wildlife. For all people this can involve becoming attentive to and appreciative of many forms of animal life that live in community with us, wherever we live.

Education. A traditional rite-of-passage for children and adolescents in the affluent world is compulsory dissection of animals. Those students who resist or refuse for reasons of conscience routinely are ridiculed or punished for their moral sensitivity. Often they stand alone, abandoned even by their parents, ostracized by their peers. And yet this exercise in scholastic coercion is totally unnecessary. For alternatives exist. These include detailed drawings of animal anatomy and physiology, state-of-the art videos of relevant dissections, and even computer programs that enable students to "dissect" a frog, for example, on a screen rather than dissect a once living organism. When we support an educational system that callously punishes young people for being concerned about the integrity and value of animals, we tacitly support not only the unnecessary pain and death of countless numbers of animals but also the moral damage done to our children.

The examples given above are only that: examples. There are many other ways in which people fail to show minimal respect for animals as creatures of God. These include instances of wasteful, needlessly duplicative, and poorly executed scientific use of animals, the "sport" of hunting, and the killing of members of rare and endangered species, such as the African elephant and the black rhino. Like the previous examples, these further ones have a common denominator: A creature having intrinsic value is reduced to one having only instrumental value—as an object of mere scientific curiosity, a trophy, or a source of illegal profit.

A Call to Christian Action

The ethic of the liberation of life is a call to Christian action. In particular, how animals are treated is not "someone else's worry," it is a matter of our individual and collective responsibility. Christians are called to act respectfully towards "these, the least of our brothers and sisters." This is not a simple question of kindness, however laudable that virtue is. *It is an issue of strict justice.* In all our dealings with animals, whether direct or indirect, the ethic for the liberation of life requires that *we render unto animals what they are due, as creatures with an independent integrity and value.* Precisely because they cannot speak for themselves or act purposively to free themselves from the shackles of their enslavement, the Christian duty to speak and act for them is the greater, not the lesser. . . .

Much else remains to be considered. Laws and institutions that permit or encourage the oppression of animals need to be identified and changed. The truth about the ways animals are oppressed needs to be made known, beginning in the church itself. Our children need to be sustained in their natural empathy with and compassion for animals, and this means that certain traditional practices in their education, including in particular compulsory dissection, will have to be altered. Clearly, the struggle to liberate life is not for the faint of heart.

Yet just as clearly it is a struggle no thoughtful Christian can avoid. When St. Paul says that "the whole creation has been groaning in travail together until now," he speaks to our time and our circumstances. For the animals have been groaning, though we have heard them not. We hear them now. They cry for justice. We cannot fail to answer.

"Despite everything the Bible says about kindness to animals, it says nothing explicitly about their rights."

Christianity Does Not Support Animal Rights

James Parker

James Parker is the information officer for Oregon Regional Primate Research Center, Beaverton, Oregon. In the following viewpoint, Parker reviews the theological contributions of three theologians who support, to varying degrees, the rights of animals. After reviewing their theological presentations, along with the 1991 Annecy report to the World Council of Churches, he concludes that animal rights theologians have failed to convince Christians because their arguments, while interesting and new, are unworkable and ineffective.

As you read, consider the following questions:

1. In Parker's estimation, why is Lewis Regenstein's precritical approach to the rights of animals ineffective?
2. Why does the author consider Andrew Linzey's theology of creation unpersuasive?
3. Why, according to Parker, have Christian theologians not been more successful in promoting the rights of animals?

Excerpted from "With New Eyes: The Animal Rights Movement and Religion" by James Parker, *Perspectives in Biology and Medicine*, vol. 36, no. 3, Spring 1993; ©1993 by The University of Chicago. All rights reserved. Reprinted by permission of the author and the publisher, the University of Chicago Press.

The contemporary animal rights movement has taken a religious turn. One of its most vocal leaders, Ingrid Newkirk, president of People for the Ethical Treatment of Animals (PETA), has expressed her goal by evoking the biblical image of a world where the lamb will lie down with the lion. Another, philosopher Tom Regan, has distributed a videotape called *Noah's Ark* that makes the connection between animal rights and belief and attempts to recruit religious groups to the cause. Two-hundred-fifty pastors and a handful of theologians have declared in the *Glauberg Confession* that they now ". . . read the statements in the Bible about Creation and regard for our fellow-creatures with new eyes and new interest. . . ." The editors of a 1992 issue of *Animals' Voice* magazine have published what amounts to a handbook explaining how readers can make their voice heard in the churches. "Progress with the churches," it declares, "should now become one of the major concerns of the [animal rights] movement.". . .

The approaches of contemporary theologians interested in the animal issue fall into three categories. The first, staying well within traditional orthodoxy, calls attention to the biblical and Judeo-Christian doctrine of kindness toward animals. The second operates with traditional notions of God, but argues for a theology of creation in which animals have rights. The third and most radical type takes up the questions about God raised by the animal rights movement and answers them with notions taken from contemporary "process" theologians. All three approaches call into question the use of animals in biomedical research.

An Evaluation of Regenstein's Precritical Approach

The most comprehensive and coherent spokesman for the first approach is Lewis Regenstein. He has addressed church audiences with *Replenish the Earth*, "a history of organized religion's treatment of animals and nature." Regenstein strings together all the texts from the Bible and from church and synagogue leaders through the centuries that inculcate kindness toward animals. This approach, used also by pamphleteers for animal welfare organizations, provides a useful resource, a beginning point for the person who has never noticed the Bible's references to animals. In addition it highlights prescriptions that are central to the tradition of animal welfare. Even if that tradition hasn't always been honored, it has prevailed in Jewish and Christian history.

Standing by themselves, however, the texts on kindness give no answer to someone asking if the Bible has anything to say about animal rights. If we want to apply those texts to present-day concerns without the mistake of reading our own interests into them, we must determine what they meant to the people who first spoke and heard them. Only if we investigate their historical settings and their changes over time can we safely establish a future trajectory that could point beyond the doctrine of kindness. Texts, whether they are love letters or laws or poems or any of the many diverse literary forms in the Bible, beg critical interpretation.

Animals Have No "Rights"

If that term be used correctly, animals have no "rights," for these can belong only to persons, endowed with reason and responsibility. Cruelty to animals is certainly wrong: not because it outrages animal "rights" which are non-existent, but because cruelty in a human being is an unworthy and wicked disposition and, objectively, because ill-treatment of animals is an abuse and perversion of God's design. Man has been given dominion over the animal kingdom, and it is to be exercised in conformity with human reason and God's will.

Catholic Hierarchy of England and Wales, *A Catholic Dictionary*, 1962.

Regenstein's precritical approach opens the door to arbitrary interpretations of the texts. One example of such is Newkirk's already mentioned citation, in which she declares herself for a world where lamb and lion will lie down together, where "man will live in harmony with nature, (and) where when two animals fight, human beings will intervene." Her image of the lamb and the lion comes from the Hebrew prophet Isaiah, and the dream of a perfect world derives from the Bible's expectation of God's final age of peace. However, overlooking the fact that lamb and lion lying down together constitutes a powerful symbol of what God will accomplish in the end-time, she assumes that such harmony is a real possibility in this world and proposes the preposterous mission of intervening in natural predation—as if animals were children squabbling on a schoolyard.

Another example of arbitrary interpretation is Regenstein's own reflection on animal sacrifice. He interprets the prophetic denunciation of animal sacrifice and the eventual ending of the practice by both Jews and Christians as milestones in the long march toward animal liberation. People have conducted ritual slaughter as a symbol of the gift of themselves to God. When Hebrew prophets thundered against the practice, it was not primarily because the slaughter was going on, but because the bending of human will to the just and compassionate will of God wasn't happening; the symbol was empty. They called people away from the distractions of sacrifice back to the religion of the commandments. Nevertheless, sacrifice continued down to the days when the site of sacrifice, the temple, was destroyed by the Romans. Christians never began the practice of animal sacrifice because they consider the death of Jesus as an offering to God so perfect that none other is required. Neither group faced the issue directly from the perspective of the animals concerned; the liberation of animals was not an issue for them.

A second problem with Regenstein's approach is that it doesn't allow him to ask further questions of the texts. He has nothing to offer writers whom he quotes approvingly—Colman McCarthy, who asks for a theology of animal rights, or L. Charles Birch, who wants the churches to support the rights movement. Cutting and pasting texts together can't answer the question of whether the Scriptures provide a foundation for recognizing the rights of animals. Despite everything the Bible says about kindness to animals, it says nothing explicitly about their rights.

Since he does no more than advance the traditional doctrine of kindness to animals, Regenstein can fault only those practices such as hunting or bullfighting that appear cruel. He studiously avoids the question of the use of animals in biomedical research. He does, however, make a case for vegetarianism. Again, it is a case marred by arbitrary and curious interpretation. He declares that certain Mosaic precepts, if strictly obeyed, preclude the eating of meat, even though the rabbinic tradition of interpretation hasn't discovered this. Jesus, he suggests, might have been a vegetarian. After all, through the preachings of Isaiah, God promised a child who would have curds and honey for his diet. Regenstein neglects the fact that the child's diet is symbolic of his dwelling in the promised land.

An Assessment of Linzey's Theology of Creation

Representative of what the Glauberg signatories identify as a theology of creation are the writings of Andrew Linzey. Linzey knows that the meaning of scriptural texts emerges through critical reading. He has embarked on an interpretation from the viewpoint of concern for animals and creation. Because Jewish and Christian theologians have traditionally been concerned more with human salvation than with creation, Linzey's effort amounts to a rereading of the Bible. He is convinced that his rereading results not in a reversal of doctrine, but in a fresh start. Christian history is still in its infancy, so a theology of creation that includes the doctrine of animal rights is still on the ground floor of tradition. "It is not that Christian tradition has faced the question (of animal rights) and given unsatisfactory answers," he says, "[but] rather [that] the question has never really been put . . . [and] the thinking . . . has yet to be done."

Before constructing his creation theology, Linzey clears away some of the rubble of old debates. Proponents of animal use, for example, have often dismissed animal rights advocates with the words of God on the sixth day of creation: "You shall have dominion over the fish of the sea, the birds of heaven, and all the creatures that move on the earth" (Gen. 1:28). Linzey rightly points out that the word "dominion" translates a Hebrew word for a type of lordship that was supposed to characterize Israel's kings. Far from being absolute monarchs, they were only vice-regents of God. As stand-ins for God, humans are to exercise responsible and compassionate stewardship. It is not for us to dispose of creation in any way we see fit.

In his own effort to move the central concern of theology from the human family to creation, Linzey retrieves the biblical theme of God's glory: nature and all living beings exist for the purpose of reflecting the glory of God. Their usefulness to humans is strictly secondary. More basic than their instrumental value is their intrinsic meaning and worth to God.

The Right of God

God has a right that his creation be honored and respected. This objective *right of God* sustains subjective individuals as bearers of what Linzey calls *theos rights*. All individuals? Not quite all. Amoebae and bacteria, for instance, do not possess theos rights. Piecing together texts in which the notions of spirit, flesh, and blood appear, Linzey concludes that God's rights accrue only to spirit-filled (i.e., breathing) creatures of "flesh and blood."

Linzey's invention of theos rights keeps him from getting bogged down or even lost in the paths of philosophers who have attempted to extend the eighteenth-century notion of rights to animals. It doesn't, however, avoid the problem that in the world of nature there is no recognition of rights, either theos rights or natural rights. The lion, "seeking whom he may devour," is exercising a "right" to survive that violates the similar rights of the hyenas or gazelles that are his prey.

The painful question about creation is theological: what kind of God does it glorify? Linzey wants to overcome the popular notion that God is responsible for a creation that is "red in tooth and claw." The world of nature, he reminds us, is a world fallen and at fundamental variance from the Creator and his purpose. The world intended by God is the world of the biblical creation story, an Eden in which there is eternal life and perfect harmony. Only Eden can serve as a basis for ethical thinking. "The world of nature," he asserts, "*cannot* simply be read as a moral textbook."

Linzey's assertion is true as far as it goes: what *is* is not necessarily what *ought* to be. Yet, for moral guidelines to mean anything, the world to which they lead, the world that *ought* to be, must be humanly achievable. The world in which lambs lie down with lions is a work of God alone. Isaiah, who envisioned this world, was describing the end-time that will be ushered in by the long awaited Messiah, the anointed agent of God. Isaiah's image was transferred by later theologians who composed Genesis 1–11, back to an original, prehistorical, and mythological time when universal vegetarianism was imagined to prevail. The point of the transfer was to suggest that God's messianic, end-time world will arrive not as an afterthought but the realization at last of his intention from the beginning.

In the present and historical world, however, the joy of motherhood comes with the pain of childbirth, the satisfaction of creativity with the sweat of the brow, the delightful variety of plant and animal life from the cycle of growth and decay, life and death. We can't remove ourselves from the web of life and death any more than we can separate the admixed joy and labor in childbirth and creativity. Lamb and lion are powerful symbols of God's end-time that point us to the beyond, but they hardly comprise a workable ethic in this real world in which we continually ask what is right and wrong.

The ethical conclusion coming from Linzey's creation theology is that animals may not be used as raw material for human designs, no matter how laudable the designs. There are ills that humans should be prepared to bear rather than inflict them on animals. We may wonder if Linzey is not naive about the scope and magnitude of those ills, but he is consistent. If animals have rights, then with them as with humans, the end never justifies the means.

A Summary of McDaniel's Process Theology

Theologian Jay B. McDaniel also is convinced of the urgent need for a Christian theology of creation. In *Of God and Pelicans: A Theology of Reverence for Life*, he proposes a "life-centered ethic" to correct "that human centeredness that sees humans as the measure of all things and that believes humans, and humans alone, are worthy of moral regard." Like Linzey he develops his life-centered ethic from the intrinsic value of living beings.

The title of McDaniel's book comes from a bit of ethological lore that raises the question dramatically. Females of a species of white pelicans lay two eggs. The earlier hatched chick is first in line for food and protects his interests against the younger chick. The younger chick has to go out and forage on its own. If it fails and returns to the nest, the parents, unable to raise two offspring, will turn it out again to die. The second chick is a back-up creature, nurtured only if the elder dies.

Such behavior is a successful strategy for survival of the pelican species. This strategy poses no problem to Aldo Leopold, who attempted to reverse the anthropocentrism of ethical thinking but was concerned about biotic communities rather than individual animals. For Leopold, the ethical imperative is to help preserve species, all of which have their ecological niche and function.

McDaniel, however, is concerned about individual animals. In his view, each individual has an intrinsic value that is more fundamental than its instrumental value to its biotic community or to other species. This intrinsic value, which comes from the animal having interests and experiences of its own, is sufficient to ground rights.

Traditionally, of course, rights have been recognized in moral *agents*—humans beings, who discover that they have to constitute themselves through a lifetime of decisions, and on whom, consequently, it is wrong to impose another will. McDaniel joins the philosopher Tom Regan (*The Case for Animal Rights*) in claiming rights for moral *patients*—animals who are not possessed of conscience, who are not responsible even to themselves, and who, in traditional thought, may serve others' ends as long as they are treated with humane care. For McDaniel, subjective experiences and interests are basis enough for rights.

Having claimed rights for individual animals, McDaniel must ask what kind of God would create a world in which these rights are violated wholesale, in which pelicans survive by turning on their own offspring. Archibald MacLeish once put the problem into a jingle: "If God is God he is not good; if God is good he is not God; choose the even, choose the odd." Traditional theologians have chosen "the even": God is God, the all-powerful creator, and how he is good and loving in view of the evil in his creation is hidden in the mystery of his God-ness. McDaniel follows process theologians such as Charles Hartshorne and John Cobb in choosing "the odd." The God who notices every sparrow that falls (Luke 12:6) is all-loving but not all-powerful. His is the powerlessness of love. God cannot prevent the emergence of behaviors, such as those of pelicans, that are necessary to the process of evolution. In that sense, the natural world's creativity is independent of God's. All God can do is coax and lure the world to his loving purposes. He is not powerful enough to end its suffering, and he is in everything as the one who suffers. Having chosen "the odd," McDaniel can undercut the argument that an all-powerful God approves, or at least permits, the carnage that is nature. God is on the side of animal rights activists against the present order of the universe. The only problem is that he is powerless.

Humans Are Powerless

Powerless, too, are humans. McDaniel cautions against intervening à la Newkirk in nature's war. To animals in the wild, he would apply Leopold's ethic: preserve species and bracket your concern for the intrinsic value of each individual. To animals that have been subjugated or domesticated, he would apply the ethic of animal rights. A resulting paradox is not lost on McDaniel: domestication is a violation of an animal's intrinsic value, but, at the same time, even in the researcher's laboratory, it means salvation from the world of predation and gruesome death.

Because McDaniel acknowledges the problem of competing rights in nature, he allows that the rights of animals must be weighed against those of humans. He thus winds up being softer on biomedical researchers than Linzey. Animals may be used for research purposes if their use can be proved "absolutely necessary" and without pain. McDaniel's argument with researchers ultimately falls back, then, from ethics to questions of medical science and history. How many animals are "absolutely necessary" for basic research? for experimental verification? for testing? What constitutes pain, stress, suffering? What are the benefits of biomedical research?

Limited Success

Despite its problems, the theological quest outlined in the approaches of creation and process theology manages to be something new. Several Victorian antivivisectionists—Cardinal Manning and Frances Power Cobbe being the most prominent—were religious, but their use of the biblical and church traditions was, like that of Regenstein, precritical. Their attempts to persuade the churches were largely ineffective.

Will Linzey and McDaniel and others in their wake succeed where the Victorian antivivisectionists failed? Linzey, an Anglican priest who has served on various ethics study committees of the Church of England, has seen some of his concerns, if not his theology, reflected in his church's documents. McDaniel has been effective in moving the cause of animals into the discussions and debates of committees of the World Council of Churches.

Until now, however, the animal rights' theologians haven't moved churches from their traditional animal welfare position. Animal rights groups have sprung up within churches—The Society for Animal Rights (originally the National Catholic Society for Animal Welfare), the Unitarian Universalist Federation for the Ethical Treatment of Animals, Jews for Animal Rights—but, in response, official denominational statements have done no more than touch up the doctrine of humane care and kindness with cautions about the use of animals for what some deem frivolous purposes—for the testing of cosmetic and household products. A report by a group of theologians including McDaniel to a committee of the World Council of Churches (not yet a report of the committee) adds concerns about the fur, entertainment (circuses and rodeos), sports (hunting), and "factory" farming industries. It also contains one sentence condemning unspecified "instances of wasteful, needlessly duplicative and poorly executed scientific use of animals."

The reason for their limited success may be that animal rights theologians of the creation and process schools are struggling against a down-to-earth tradition that takes as the starting point for ethical thinking the real world of human/animal interdependence. The absolutist ethic of creation theology collapses because it can't be achieved. The more moderate conclusion of process theology leaves its partisans arguing the nature and merits of science, an argument even harder for them to win than it was for their Victorian ancestors.

Just before the turn of the last century, the English Jesuit George Tyrell responded to an attack by the religious leader of the antivivisectionists, Frances Power Cobbe. After arguing that humans have obligations not to animals but to God concerning animals, Tyrell concluded:

> Whatever one may think of the old fashioned psychology (that distinguishes humans from animals) on which this system (of concern for animal welfare) rests, no one can deny that it is at least coherent and in keeping with the common sense of the best part of mankind, and that it offers a full and firm basis for a humane and reasonable treatment of animals without entailing any of those hopeless problems which Miss Cobbe has to encounter in the application of her system.

Tyrell's judgment about the hopeless problems encountered in the application of the antivivisectionist system may well stand for the attempts of creation and process theology to view the human/animal relationship with new eyes and interest as this century draws to its close.

Periodical Bibliography

The following articles have been selected to supplement the diverse views presented in this chapter. Addresses are provided for periodicals not indexed in the *Readers' Guide to Periodical Literature*, the *Alternative Press Index*, or the *Social Sciences Index*.

John Balzar
: "Creatures Great and—Equal?" *Los Angeles Times*, December 25, 1993. Available from Reprints, Times Mirror Square, Los Angeles, CA 90053.

Tom Beauchamp
: "Why Treat the Human Animal Differently?" *World & I*, April 1995. Available from 3600 New York Ave. NE, Washington, DC 20002.

Joan Biskupic
: "Supreme Court Weighs Rights of Churches, Animals," *Washington Post*, November 5, 1992. Available from Reprints, 1150 15th St. NW, Washington, DC 20071.

Charles Fink
: "The Moderate View on Animal Rights," *Between the Species*, Fall 1991. Available from PO Box 8496, Landscape Station, Berkeley, CA 94707.

Donald Gould
: "An Emotional Appeal for Animals," *New Scientist*, July 25, 1992. Available from IPC Specialist Group, King's Reach Tower, Stamford St., London SE1 9LS, U.K.

Vicki Hearne
: "Philosophy Goes to the Polls," *Yale Review*, July 1994. Available from Yale University Press, 302 Temple St., New Haven, CT 06520.

Harold Herzog Jr.
: "The Movement Is My Life: The Psychology of Animal Rights Activism," *Journal of Social Issues*, Spring 1993.

Morton Kaplan
: "A Different Position on Animal Rights," *World & I*, April 1995.

Colman McCarthy
: "Two Kinds of Kindness to Animals," *Washington Post*, January 18, 1992.

Daniel McShea
: "On the Rights of an Ape," *Discover*, February 1994.

Susan Opotow
: "Animals and the Scope of Justice," *Journal of Social Issues*, Spring 1993.

S. Plous
: "The Role of Animals in Human Society," *Journal of Social Issues*, Spring 1993.

Matthew Scully	"Creature Teachers," *National Review*, May 10, 1993.
Janine Stanley-Dunham	"Extending Our Circle of Compassion," *Wilson Library Bulletin*, June 1994.
Gary Varner	"The Prospects for Consensus and Convergence in the Animal Rights Debate," *Hastings Center Report*, January/February 1994.
Nicholas Wade	"Our Cousins' Keepers," *New York Times Magazine*, May 1, 1994.
Junda Woo	"Lawyers Choose Animal Rights as Pet Projects," *Wall Street Journal*, December 2, 1993.

CHAPTER 2

Is Animal
Experimentation
Justified?

ANIMAL
RIGHTS

Chapter Preface

The use of animals for medical research is a source of contentious debate. Animal rights activists believe that confining animals in laboratories and subjecting them to painful and sometimes life-threatening procedures is unjustifiably inhumane. Others insist that the suffering these animals experience is easily justified by the medical benefits humans reap from such research. This debate becomes particularly divisive when the animals in question are primates.

Animal rights activists contend that apes and monkeys are physically and psychologically similar to humans and that such creatures experience pain and suffering the way people do. Therefore, activists insist, using primates for medical research is no more ethically acceptable than using humans for such purposes. One proponent of this view is Geza Teleki, a conservationist who has worked with chimpanzees. Teleki writes that chimpanzees are "the closest living relatives we humans have on this planet" and that "every chimpanzee has rights to the freedom and the self-determination we so highly value for ourselves."

Proponents of animal research maintain that it is precisely because primates are similar to humans that they are valuable—even indispensable—for medical research. For example, the American Medical Association (AMA) argues that because primates are susceptible to many of the same diseases as humans, they can be used to discover the causes of, and to develop treatments and vaccines for, diseases that afflict people. According to the AMA, primates were essential in the development of the vaccine for polio and may in the future prove pivotal in the discovery of treatments for Parkinson's disease and AIDS.

Whether the use of primates as research subjects is justified by the medical breakthroughs such experiments make possible is among the issues discussed in the following chapter on animal experimentation.

"Biomedical advances depend on research with animals, and not using them would be unethical because it would deprive humans and animals of the benefits of research."

Animal Experimentation Is Justified

American Medical Association

The American Medical Association (AMA) is one of the largest organizations supporting the use of animals in biomedical research, education, and drug and product testing. In the following viewpoint, which is excerpted from an AMA white paper, the organization argues that experimenting on animals in biological research "increases understanding of how biological systems function and advances medical knowledge." With the advancement of such knowledge, the AMA contends, scientists, researchers, and medical providers are able to reduce human and animal suffering and disease.

As you read, consider the following questions:

1. According to the AMA, why is it often preferable to experiment on animals rather than on humans?
2. What evidence does the AMA provide to support its argument that animal experimentation has been scientifically beneficial?
3. What alternatives would remain if animal research were banned, according to the authors?

Excerpted from "Use of Animals in Biomedical Research: The Challenge and Response," American Medical Association white paper, Chicago, 1989; ©1989, American Medical Association. Reprinted with permission.

Animals have been used in experiments for at least 2,000 years, with the first reference made in the third century B.C. in Alexandria, Egypt, when the philosopher and scientist Erisistratus used animals to study body functions.

Five centuries later, the Roman physician Galen used apes and pigs to prove his theory that veins carry blood rather than air. In succeeding centuries, animals were employed to discover how the body functions or to confirm or disprove theories developed through observation. Advances in knowledge made through these experiments included Harvey's demonstration of the circulation of blood in 1622, the effect of anesthesia on the body in 1846, and the relationship between bacteria and disease in 1878.

Types of Experiments That Require the Use of Animals

Today, animals are used in experiments for three general purposes: (1) biomedical and behavioral research, (2) education, (3) drug and product testing.

Biomedical research increases understanding of how biological systems function and advances medical knowledge. Biomedical experiments are conducted in accordance with the principles of the scientific method developed by the French physiologist Claude Bernard in 1865. This method established two requirements for the conduct of a valid experiment: (1) control of all variables so that only one factor or set of factors is changed at a time, and (2) the replication of results by other laboratories. Unless these requirements are met, an experiment is not considered scientifically valid. Behavioral research is a type of biomedical research that is directed toward determining the factors that affect behavior and how various organisms and organs respond to different stimuli. Much behavioral research is environmental in nature but some involves the study of responses to physical stimuli or manipulation of biological systems or organs, such as the brain.

Educational experiments are conducted to educate and train students in medicine, veterinary medicine, physiology, and general science. In many instances, these experiments are conducted with dead animals.

Animals also are employed to determine the safety and efficacy of new drugs or the toxicity of chemicals to which humans or animals may be exposed. Most of these experiments are conducted by commercial firms to fulfill government requirements.

As with all scientific research, biomedical research may be subdivided into two types: basic and applied. Basic biomedical research is conducted to increase the base knowledge and understanding of the physical, chemical, and functional mechanisms of life processes and disease. The aim of applied research is to attain specific, targeted objectives, such as the development of a new drug, therapy, or surgical procedure, and usually involves the application of existing knowledge, much of which is obtained by basic research. Applied research can be either experimental—that is, conducted with animals or some non-animal alternative method—or clinical—that is, conducted with human beings. Clinical trials are the last step in the biomedical research process and are performed only after the procedure, drug, or device being investigated has been thoroughly tested in experimental research conducted under guidelines designed to protect both patients and volunteers.

Use of Animals Rather than Humans

A basic assumption of all types of research is that man should relieve human and animal suffering. One objection to the use of animals in biomedical research is that the animals are used as surrogates for human beings. This objection presumes the equality of all forms of life; animal rights advocates argue that if the tests are for the benefit of man, then man should serve as the subject of the experiments. There are limitations, however, to the use of human subjects both ethically, such as in the testing of a potentially toxic drug or chemical, and in terms of what can be learned. The process of aging, for instance, can best be observed through experiments with rats, which live an average of two to three years, or with some types of monkeys, which live 15 to 20 years. Some experiments require numerous subjects of the same weight or genetic makeup or require special diets or physical environments; these conditions make the use of human subjects difficult or impossible. By using animals in such tests, researchers can observe subjects of uniform age and background in sufficient numbers to determine if findings are consistent and applicable to a large population.

Animals are important in research precisely because they have complex body systems that react and interact with stimuli much as humans do. The more true this is with a particular animal, the more valuable that animal is for a particular type of research. One important property to a researcher is discrimination—the extent to which an animal exhibits the particular quality to be investigated. The greater the degree of discrimination, the greater the reliability and predictability of the information gathered from the experiment.

For example, dogs have been invaluable in biomedical research because of the relative size of their organs compared to humans. The first successful kidney transplant was performed in a dog and the techniques used to save the lives of "blue babies," babies with structural defects in their hearts, were developed with dogs. Open-heart surgical techniques, coronary bypass surgery and heart transplantation all were developed using dogs.

Another important factor is the amount of information available about a particular animal. Mice and rats play an extensive role in research and testing, in part because repeated experiments and controlled breeding have created a pool of data to which the findings from a new experiment can be related and given meaning. Their rapid rate of reproduction also has made them important in studies of genetics and other experiments that require observation over a number of generations. Moreover, humans cannot be bred to produce "inbred strains" as can be done with animals; therefore, humans cannot be substituted for animals in studies where an inbred strain is essential.

Scientists argue repeatedly that research is necessary to reduce human and animal suffering and disease. Biomedical advances depend on research with animals, and not using them would be unethical because it would deprive humans and animals of the benefits of research. . . .

Missing the Point

The arguments advanced by animal rights activists in opposing the use of animals in biomedical research . . . are scientific, emotional, and philosophic. . . .

The scientific challenge raised by animal rights activists goes to the heart of the issue by asking whether animal experiments are necessary for scientific and medical progress and whether all the experiments being performed and all the animals being used are justified and required. Scientists insist that they are; animal rights activists insist that they are not.

Scientists justify use of animals in biomedical research on two grounds: the contribution that the information makes to human and animal health and welfare, and the lack of any alternative way to gain the information and knowledge. Animal rights activists contest experiments that utilize animals on both these grounds and assert that this practice no longer is necessary because alternative methods of experimentation exist for obtaining the same information.

In an appearance on the Today show in 1985, Ingrid Newkirk, representing People for the Ethical Treatment of Animals (PETA) stated: "If it were such a valuable way to gain knowledge, we should have eternal life by now." This statement is similar in spirit to one made in 1900 by an antivivisectionist who stated that, given the number of experiments on the brain done up to then, the insane asylums of Washington, D.C., should be empty.

Scientists believe that such assertions miss the point. The issue is not what *has not* been accomplished by animal use in biomedical research, but what *has* been accomplished. A longer life span has been achieved, decreased infant mortality has occurred, effective treatments have been developed for many diseases, and the quality of life has been enhanced for mankind in general.

Animals Play a Critical Role

One demonstration of the critical role that animals play in medical and scientific advances is that 54 of 76 Nobel Prizes awarded in physiology or medicine since 1901 have been for discoveries and advances made through the use of experimental animals. Among these have been the Prize awarded in 1985 for the studies (using dogs) that documented the relationship between cholesterol and heart disease; the 1966 Prize for the studies (using chickens) that linked viruses and cancer; and the 1960 Prize for studies (using cattle, mice, and chicken embryos) that established that a body can be taught to accept tissue from different donors if it is inoculated with different types of tissue prior to birth or during the first year of life, a finding expected to help simplify and advance organ transplants in the future. Studies using animals also resulted in successful culture of the poliomyelitis virus; a Nobel Prize was awarded for this work in 1954. The discovery of insulin and treatment of diabetes, achieved through experiments using dogs, also earned the Prize in 1923.

In fact, virtually every advance in medical science in the 20th century, from antibiotics and vaccines to antidepressant drugs and organ transplants, has been achieved either directly or indirectly through the use of animals in laboratory experiments. The result of these experiments has been the elimination or control of many infectious diseases—smallpox, poliomyelitis, measles— and the development of numerous life-saving techniques—blood transfusions, burn therapy, open-heart and brain surgery. This has meant a longer, healthier, better life with much less pain and suffering. For many, it has meant life itself. Often forgotten in the rhetoric is the fact that humans *do* participate in biomedical research in the form of clinical trials. They experience pain and are injured and, in fact, some of them die from this participation. Hence, scientists are not asking animals to be "guinea pigs" alone for the glory of science. Some medical breakthroughs accomplished through research with animals are described in Table 1.

Scientists feel that it is essential for the public to understand that had scientific research been restrained in the first decade of the 20th century as antivivisectionists and activists were then and are today urging, many millions of Americans alive and healthy today would never have been born or would have suffered a premature death. Their parents or grandparents would have died from diphtheria, scarlet fever, tuberculosis, diabetes, appendicitis, and countless other diseases and disorders.

Animal rights activists attribute advances in longevity and

Table 1. Some Medical Advances Made Using Animals

Pre-1900	• Treatment of rabies, anthrax, beriberi (thiamine deficiency) and smallpox • Principles of infection control and pain relief • Management of heart failure
Early 1900s	• Treatment of histamine shock, pellagra, (niacin deficiency) and rickets (Vitamin D deficiency) • Electrocardiography and cardiac catheterization
1920s	• Discovery of thyroxin • Intravenous feeding • Discovery of insulin—diabetes control
1930s	• Therapeutic use of sulfa drugs • Prevention of tetanus • Development of anticoagulants, modern anesthesia and neuromuscular blocking agents
1940s	• Treatment of rheumatoid arthritis and whooping cough • Therapeutic use of antibiotics, such as penicillin, aureomycin and streptomycin • Discovery of Rh factor • Treatment of leprosy • Prevention of diphtheria
1950s	• Prevention of poliomyelitis • Development of cancer chemotherapy • Open-heart surgery and cardiac pacemaker
1960s	• Prevention of rubella • Corneal transplant and coronary bypass surgery • Therapeutic use of cortisone • Development of radioimmunoassay for the measurement of minute quantities of antibodies, hormones and other substances in the body
1970s	• Prevention of measles • Modern treatment of coronary insufficiency • Heart transplant • Development of non-addictive painkillers
1980s	• Use of cyclosporin and other anti-rejection drugs • Artificial heart transplantation • Identification of psychophysiological factors in depression, anxiety and phobias • Development of monoclonal antibodies for treating disease

American Medical Association, *Use of Animals in Biomedical Research*, 1989.

health to public health measures and better nutrition. Scientists agree that for a number of infectious diseases such as typhoid fever, influenza and tuberculosis, such measures were important; however, for most infectious diseases, improved public health and nutrition have played only a minor role. This is clear when one considers the marked reduction in the incidence of infectious diseases such as whooping cough, rubella, measles and poliomyelitis. Despite advances in public health and nutrition, eradication or control of these and most other infectious diseases was not achieved until the development of vaccines and drugs through research using animals. . . . Many physicians have become concerned recently over pertussis immunization resulting in some cases of brain damage. Only through additional studies of pertussis vaccines will scientists be able to eliminate these unpredictable events, and animals are imperative for these studies. Similarly, the development of a vaccine against AIDS is dependent upon continued studies conducted in animals. . . .

A Ban Would Be Dangerous

The activities and arguments of animal rights and animal welfare activists and organizations present the American people with some fundamental decisions that must be made regarding the use of animals in biomedical research.

The fundamental issue raised by the philosophy of the animal rights movement is whether man has the right to use animals in a way that causes them to suffer and die. To accept the philosophical and moral viewpoint of the animal rights movement would require a total ban on the use of animals in any scientific research and testing. The consequences of such a step were set forth by the Office of Technology Assessment (OTA) in its report to Congress: "Implementation of this option would effectively arrest most basic biomedical and behavioral research and toxicological testing in the United States." The economic and public health consequences of that, the OTA warned Congress, "are so unpredictable and speculative that this course of action should be considered dangerous."

No nation and no jurisdiction within the United States has yet adopted such a ban. Although, as noted earlier, laws to ban the use of animals in biomedical research have been introduced into a number of state legislatures, neither a majority of the American people nor their elected representatives have ever supported these bills.

Another aspect of the use of animals in biomedical research that has received little consideration is the economic consequences of regulatory change. Clearly, other nations are not curtailing the use of animals to any significant degree. Some of these, like Japan, are major competitors of the United States in biomedical research. Given the economic climate in the United States, our massive trade imbalance and our loss of leadership

in many areas, can the United States afford not to keep a leading industry, i.e., biomedical science, developing as rapidly as
possible? Many nations are in positions to assume leadership
roles, and the long-term economic impact on our citizens could
be profound. This economic impact would be expressed in
many ways, not the least of which would certainly be a reduction in the quality and number of health services available for
people who need them.

Research Using Animals Is Essential

Through polls and by other means, the American people have
indicated that they support the use of animals in research and
testing. At the same time they have expressed a strong wish that
the animals be protected against any unnecessary pain and suffering. The true question, therefore, is how to achieve this without interfering with the performance of necessary research.
Scientists already comply with a host of federal, state, munici-
pal, and institutional guidelines and laws. However, in this era
of cost containment, they fear that overregulation will become
so costly that research progress will suffer. Scientists emphasize
that a reasonable balance must be achieved between increased
restrictions and increased cost.

What must be recognized, say scientists, is that it is not possible to protect all animals against all pain and still conduct meaningful research. No legislation and no standard of humane care
can eliminate this necessity. The only alternative is either to
eliminate the research, as animal rights adherents urge, and
forego the knowledge and the benefits of health-related research
that would result, or to inflict the pain and suffering on human
beings by using them as research subjects.

The desire by animal welfare proponents to ensure maximum
comfort and minimal pain to research animals is understandable
and appeals to scientists, the public, and to legislators. But what
also must be recognized and weighed in the balance is the price
paid in terms of human pain and suffering if overly protective
measures are adopted that impede or prevent the use of animals
in biomedical research.

In short, the American people should not be misled by emotional appeals and philosophic rhetoric on this issue. Biomedical
research using animals is essential to continued progress in clinical medicine. Animal research holds the key for solutions to
AIDS, cancer, heart disease, aging and congenital defects. In discussing legislation concerning animal experimentation, the
prominent physician and physiologist Dr. Walter B. Cannon
stated in 1896 that ". . . the antivivisectionists are the second of
the two types Theodore Roosevelt described when he said,
'Common sense without conscience may lead to crime, but con-

science without common sense may lead to folly, which is the handmaiden of crime.'"

The American Medical Association has been an outspoken proponent of biomedical research for over 100 years, and that tradition continues today. The Association believes that research involving animals is absolutely essential to maintaining and improving the health of the American people. The Association is opposed to any legislation or regulation that would inappropriately limit such research, and actively supports all legislative efforts to ensure the continued use of animals in research, while providing for their humane treatment.

"*On any theory of morality, a basic principle is that we have an obligation to avoid causing harm to others.*"

Animal Experimentation Is Not Justified

Michael Allen Fox

Michael Allen Fox is professor of philosophy at Queen's University, Kingston, Ontario. In 1986 he published *The Case for Animal Experimentation*, a book well received by many researchers. To everyone's surprise, within a year Fox completely changed his mind and has since argued against animal experimentation. No longer believing that human beings are always more important than animals, Fox has come to believe that the antivivisectionists are morally right in opposing animal experimentation. In the following viewpoint, he explains why he now argues against his previous convictions.

As you read, consider the following questions:

1. According to Fox, what happened to make him change his mind about the moral justification for animal experimentation?
2. In Fox's view, why is it morally wrong to use animals in scientific research?
3. What would happen to human beings if they were to stop using animals as subjects of experimentation, according to the author?

From "Animal Experimentation: A Philosopher's Changing Views" by Michael Allen Fox, *Between the Species*, Summer 1987. Reprinted by permission of the publisher.

The notion of turmoil and radical change within the staid world of academic philosophy must strike many as very strange. After all, aren't philosophers members of one of the oldest establishments, one of the oldest professions? Aren't they concerned with perennial questions—those which bring them into daily contact with Truth, Beauty, and Goodness, to paraphrase a facetious comment made by Sandra Harding (a non-establishment feminist philosopher)? Profound transformations have indeed occurred, however. Many of philosophy's traditional preoccupations still hold sway, but there is also a growing awareness that philosophy cannot divorce itself from the real world. Thus, recent decades have seen the rapid development of fields of "applied philosophy," such as business ethics, environmental ethics, and medical ethics. But of course, it is not "philosophy"—some abstract entity—that undergoes turmoil and radical change but the thought and lives of individual philosophers. Like mine, for instance. Let me explain.

Why I Once Supported Animal Experimentation

In 1975, when Peter Singer published his book *Animal Liberation: A New Ethics for Our Treatment of Animals*, I was readily able to dismiss its unorthodox and polemical thesis that "all animals are equal." Singer, who coined the term "animal liberation," also popularized another, "speciesism," which he defined as "a prejudice or attitude of bias toward the interests of members of one's own species and against those members of other species." He claimed that speciesism is analogous to other forms of oppression, such as racism and sexism. To me, as to most other philosophers at the time, these ideas appeared wrongheaded in the extreme. They were misguided because of course everybody knows only humans matter, ethically speaking. Or so I thought. Animal suffering could and should concern us, because we can empathize with animals, and we wish to avoid causing or permitting suffering because it is better to be kind than to be indifferent or cruel. But basically animals, like the rest of nature, were understood to have no intrinsic value, only instrumental value, that is, use-value or else value relative to the enjoyment or enrichment they bring to our lives.

It seemed easy to write off Singer's arguments, falling back on the comfortable human-centered ethical tradition for convenient counter-arguments. I was intrigued by the way in which Singer forced his readers to confront some of the most fundamental questions of ethics and challenged their most deeply held convictions. One had to ask, for example, what is it that makes something a subject of moral concern? What is a right? What makes something a possessor of rights? Is the capacity to suffer the universal criterion for moral considerability? Most philosophers, sad to tell, did not take the challenge seriously, and many still do not. But many did, and quite a number of philosophers may be found today among the activist membership of the environmental and antivivisection movements.

With some trepidation, but also not a little smugness, I took on the mantle of speciesism. However, Singer's writings unsettled me, and I soon saw that speciesism was untenable. For whatever set of characteristics one might single out that designate our species as deserving of full moral consideration, one can ask whether it would be rational to exclude members of another species that shared all these characteristics (e.g., Martians) from equal consideration just because their physical appearance was different. Clearly this would be absurd. But I could not yet see that this kind of thinking, as well as the hierarchical view of humans as superior to all else in nature, to which I still adhered, were indeed analogous to those specious and loathsome arguments used to promote racism and sexism. (I still disagree with Singer on some important points, but at least I've seen the light on this one.)

I carried on in the same vein for several years, publishing papers, speaking at conferences, and serving as a consultant to various organizations on the subject of the ethics of animal experimentation. All this activity culminated in the 1986 publication of my book *The Case for Animal Experimentation: An Evolutionary and Ethical Perspective*. But much happened to me after that, and the book is now an embarrassment to me, a work so foreign-sounding that when I re-read it, it seems as though it must have been written by someone else. . . .

Abandoning the Anthropocentric Position

I continued on, after the book's appearance, basking in the warmth of the benefits that scholarly publications bring to academics, and in the general praise it received from the scientific community. Then rather suddenly my complacency was derailed. A number of critical reviews made me question my assumptions. One stated that my "philosophical argument is superficial, dogmatic and unconvincing," and went on to point out that "Fox [offers] a curmudgeonly philosophy that begrudges in principle the humane and decent sentiments he would apply in practice." These did not really hit home, however, until a close friend of mine, a woman who is a radical feminist, made me confront the arbitrariness of the patriarchal, hierarchical, human-centered ethical theory I had adopted and defended for so long, and had lacked the courage to examine fully. Like Kant, I was "awakened from my dogmatic slumbers," for which my friend deserves the credit. Naturally, this was quite a jolt, and many personal as well as philosophical doubts rose up in me. I realized that I had had vague misgivings about my arguments for some time but that I had avoided any serious questioning of them.

For several months I mulled this over. I realized that I had to abandon the anthropocentric position that I had taken. I had to face the painful decision to completely revise a new book-length manuscript on environmental ethics which was almost two-thirds complete. I wrote one or two things renouncing my previous book which appeared in print. I did not foresee that the phenomenon of an academic undergoing a change of mind and publicly acknowledging the fact was so rare as to be newsworthy. But before long the media began to cover the "event," and I felt hard put not to have the whole matter turned into a media circus. To attempt to explain myself to myself, and to other interested persons with whom I'd spent many hours discussing animal research over the past few years, I formulated the position at which I have now arrived. A version of this follows.

Why Animal Experimentation *Cannot* Be Justified

On any theory of morality, a basic principle is that we have an obligation to avoid causing harm to others. Whether this is the most fundamental moral principle may be debated, but it is about as important as any that can be formulated. The harm-avoidance principle is sometimes called "the principle of non-maleficence." It applies straightforwardly of course only on the condition that the actual or possible recipients of harm are innocent: it is wrong to harm (injure or damage) those who are innocent of any wrongdoing, but not necessarily wrong to harm those who seek to harm us. It therefore states a *prima facie* obligation.

Now why might it be thought that the principle of nonmaleficence states our most fundamental moral obligation? Some literature on the subject suggests that the reason is that in the scale of things, it is a more serious wrong to cause someone to be worse off than he/she would have been otherwise than it is simply to fail to help him/her. The assumption here is that when one "merely *omits* to perform a morally desirable act, others are usually no worse off than they were before the omission—they have just lost out on some further benefits they might have enjoyed had the action been performed," in the words of Robert Goodin.

Should the principle of nonmaleficence be extended to animals? This question may be met with a question: Can animals be harmed? If they can be, then what reason could there be for not extending the principle to them? But clearly animals *can* be harmed. How can this best be understood? Charles Fried defines "physical harm" as "an impingement upon the body which either causes pain or impairs functioning." Fried, being a legal philosopher, recognizes that harms comprise a broader category of wrongs, including, for example, damage to one's reputation and similar intangibles. Others, like Tom Regan, link harms to having any sort of interest; anything that has at least one kind of interest, namely, an interest in its own welfare, according to this theory, can be harmed. To have an interest in this sense just means that the being in question is capable of faring well or faring ill, and to say that it may be harmed is to say that actions of ours may cause it to fare ill in some significant way. Many experience pain, and some suffer psychologically as well. When we inflict pain or suffering on animals, we harm them. But harm may also result when we confine or socially isolate them, deprive them of the ability to behave in ways natural to their species, or kill them. Are these lesser wrongs when the recipients of our harmful behavior are animals than when they are humans?

"OH, WE JUST GIVE HIM THE CIGARETTE
TO CALM HIS NERVES."

Some have argued that harms caused to animals are of little or no ethical concern. This is because they believe that animals' lives and experiences are of no intrinsic value, or of lesser value than those of humans. But animals are living things, in many and essential respects very much like ourselves. They also possess unique characteristics as much as we do. No species is singularly equipped to survive and dominate. All species have their strengths and weaknesses, and none is inherently superior or inferior to any other. If we choose to celebrate life, then how can we avoid affirming the equal intrinsic value of all organisms?

The Central Issue

Whether or not animals' lives and experiences have intrinsic value, however, does not affect the central issue. For if we agree that their lives may be made either better or worse by us, that they have a welfare or well-being that may be injured by us, then few would disagree that we can harm animals and have an obligation to avoid doing so. Furthermore, it may be argued (and humane scientists would agree) that we have a more positive obligation toward them, namely, to protect or promote their welfare. But we cannot carry out this obligation by first subjecting them to harmful acts.

Perhaps harms are an inevitable part of life. In human society policies and decisions seldom, if ever, benefit everyone equally. Some group or groups always suffer a negative impact. Is it ever morally acceptable or right to benefit from the sufferings or disadvantages of others? I think we feel intuitively that this is wrong. Yet most, if not all of us, do so benefit. Ideally, we would try to address this problem by attempting to compensate in some other way those who lose something when a particular social policy or decision goes into effect. Sometimes this works, sometimes not. To the degree that it does not work, or we do not try to make it work, we have an unjust society.

In addition to the harms that result from the operation of social policies, there are also the direct or indirect harms we cause each other. Here it is more manifest that *we*, not some impersonal bureaucracy, are the agents of harm. For this reason, it is more obvious that, as a rule, we act wrongly when we benefit from the harm we cause. Whether this kind of wrong can be mitigated by compensation, I am not sure, but let us suppose, for the sake of argument, that it can be.

When we require animals to make sacrifices for us, what compensation do we offer them? None. So how can it ever be morally acceptable to benefit from their suffering? When we perform cost/benefit analyses on animal research, if we consider the animals at all, our assessment is primarily in terms of the cost to them versus the benefits for us. Sometimes we consider the benefits for them as well, but generally we justify the research if the benefits for us outweigh, by some arbitrary, human-centered measure, the costs to them. Nor do they have any say in the matter.

What Justification?

What does it mean to seek a justification for using animals as means to our ends? To justify, in this context, is to show that something which appears, *prima facie*, to be wrong is not wrong, or at any rate is less wrong than it seemed to be; it is also (more importantly) to free ourselves from blame or guilt. But if animals are capable of being harmed, are beings that have intrinsic value, and cannot be or are not compensated for the harms we cause them, where is the justification to come from? I see no answer to this question.

Humans are currently the dominant species on earth and exercise a great deal of power and control over nature. But very few believe might makes right, so the fact that we have greater power cannot enter into a justification of our use and treatment of animals. Rather, where other beings are under our power, we should feel obligated to show self-restraint and to act out of mercy and compassion.

We cannot avoid causing harm to other beings in the process of living our own lives. Nor does morality consist in trying to be perfect and pure. But we can adopt an orientation toward minimizing the amount of harm we cause and taking full responsibility for it, seeing it for what it is.

To justify animal experimentation is to start at one end of a continuum. Much of what we do will be morally acceptable (in our eyes), and we will chip away at the extremity where what we do shades into cruelty. I no longer believe that a general moral justification of animal experimentation can be given. Suppose, then, that we begin at the opposite end of the continuum. *No* animal experiments can be morally justified. We act wrongly when we do them. Does this mean that we should all become antivivisectionists or abolitionists? Yes.

What if we refuse to forego the benefits of animal experimentation in spite of the moral argument against it? A way to live with our consciences might be to do only those experiments that are deemed most crucial, to rethink the entire range of questions concerning the "need" for animal experimentation, to seriously seek alternatives at every opportunity, and to commit ourselves to a firm policy of phasing out animal research as rapidly as possible.

A Tentative List of Permissible Experiments

Another way might be to try to define the class of experiments (for which there are at present no alternatives to the use of animals) that *might* be morally justified. A tentative list of these is the following:

1. Experiments that cause no harm (e.g., those that are noninvasive; clinical observations of normal and pathological conditions: field studies; those that utilize alternatives to live animals).
2. Experiments that benefit the individual experimental animals.

3. Experiments in which animals willingly participate, where "willingly" does not mean some trivial "reward" is offered to a previously deprived animal (e.g., ape language learning; dolphin training).
4. Experiments where harm is caused but for which offsetting (compensating) benefits are given to the subjects.
5. Experiments that benefit other animals of the same or different species.
6. Experiments that are life-saving, and where widespread loss of human life is threatened directly by animals (e.g., as disease carriers).

(Classes 4 through 6, however, strike me as doubtful candidates.) . . .

Living Without Animal Experimentation

Would biomedical and behavioral research come to a halt if . . . animal experimentation ceased? Probably not, but this is much too large an issue to get into here. However, suppose it did cease. The human species would doubtless continue to exist, just as it did before animal experimentation began, with a diminished life span and quality of life, to be sure. Yet other institutions, from which humans individually and collectively have benefited—for example slavery—have been abandoned for moral reasons. And many more should be, for similar reasons, such as the oppression of women, children, the elderly, and marginal peoples, and the pursuit of "superiority" in nuclear weapons. I am not arguing here that animal experimentation should be stopped, only pointing out that the fact that stopping it would cause us much inconvenience and even misery is not the end of the matter.

Finally, to be consistent, the argument that benefiting from harms caused to other animals is always wrong should be applied to other parts of one's life, as much as possible. This means giving up animals and animal products for food, clothing, and so on, except when it is absolutely essential to use them. It would also require an entire re-evaluation of one's relationship to nature. It means, in short, nothing less than the search for a whole new way of life. To avoid the negativism of the view that we are always in the wrong in our dealings with the environment, let this be thought of as learning to live in harmony with nature.

"*The collective decision society has made is that the benefits derived from animal research far outweigh the costs.*"

The Case for Animal Research in Psychology

Elizabeth Baldwin

Elizabeth Baldwin is research ethics officer for the American Psychological Association's Science Directorate. In the following viewpoint, she contends that animal research by experimental psychologists is justified because it benefits both humans and animals. Moreover, she argues that current guidelines regulating such research assure the public that sufficient safeguards for the welfare of animals are in place.

As you read, consider the following questions:

1. How did the research community initially respond to attacks by animal rights activists, according to the author?
2. According to Baldwin, in what ways is animal rights literature often misleading?
3. What benefits are derived from psychological research with animals, according to the author?

Excerpted from "The Case for Animal Research in Psychology" by Elizabeth Baldwin, *Journal of Social Issues*, vol. 49, no. 1, pp. 121-31. Reprinted by permission of the author and the Society for the Psychological Study of Social Issues, © 1993.

Animal liberationists do not separate out the human animal. A rat is a pig is a dog is a boy.—*Ingrid Newkirk, People for the Ethical Treatment of Animals*

The shock value of this quote has made it a favorite of those defending the use of animals in research. It succinctly states the core belief of many animal rights activists who oppose the use of animals in research. Although some activists work for improved laboratory conditions for research animals, a survey [by S. Plous] suggests that most activists would like to eliminate animal research entirely. These activists believe animals have rights equal to humans and therefore should not be used as subjects in laboratory research.

The debate over animal research can be confusing unless one understands the very different goals of animal welfare organizations and animal rights groups. People concerned with animal welfare seek to improve laboratory conditions for research animals and to reduce the number of animals needed. These mainstream goals encompass traditional concerns for the humane treatment of animals, and most researchers share these goals. In contrast, the views of animal rights activists are *not* mainstream, since there are few people who would agree with the above quote from Ingrid Newkirk. Indeed, in a 1991 national poll conducted by the National Science Foundation, half the respondents answered the following question affirmatively: "Should scientists be allowed to do research that causes pain and injury to animals like dogs and chimpanzees if it produces new information about human health problems?" These findings are particularly impressive given the explicit mention of "pain and injury" to popular animals such as dogs and chimpanzees. My own position is that animals do not have rights in the same sense that humans do, but that people have a responsibility to ensure the humane treatment of animals under their care. Animals have played a pivotal role in improving the human condition, and in return, society should strive to treat them well. . . .

Framing the Debate

In the 1980s, activists targeted certain researchers or areas of research that they viewed as vulnerable to attack, and researchers were forced to assume a defensive posture. Unfortunately, activists were right about the vulnerability of individual scientists; little or no institutional defense was mounted against these early attacks. The prevailing attitude was to ignore the activists in hopes that they would go away, and thus attract less attention from the public and the press. This passivity left the early targets of animal rights activists in the position of a man asked, "Why do you beat your wife?" No matter how researchers responded, they sounded defensive and self-serving. It took several years for the research community to realize that animal rights activists were not going away, and that the activists' charges needed to be answered in a systematic and serious manner.

This early failure on the part of the research community to communicate its position effectively left the public with little information beyond what was provided by the animal rights activists. Framing the debate is half the battle, and the research community was left playing catch-up and answering the question, "Why do you abuse your research animals?"

Encouraging Violence

Not only have the animal rights movement's most prominent and influential leaders refused to clearly and unequivocally renounce the use of violence, they have encouraged it by acting as spokesmen and paying legal fees and fines on behalf of militant activists convicted of committing crimes in the name of "animal liberation."

Interestingly, the prime targets of animal rights extremists are not authentic abusers of animals—such as gambling promoters who organize illegal dog and cock fights—but medical researchers.

Raymond Wannall, *Human Events*, August 31, 1991.

The research community also faced the daunting task of explaining the use of animals in research to a public whose understanding of the scientific method was almost nil. The most difficult misconception to correct was the belief that every research project with animals should produce "useful" results. Social scientists who have received Senator William Proxmire's "Golden Fleece Award" are well aware of this line of thinking—a line of thinking that displays a complete misunderstanding of how science works, and ignores the vast amount of basic research that typically precedes each "useful" discovery.

It is difficult for scientific rationales to compete with shocking posters, catchy slogans, and soundbites from the animal rights movement. The most effective response from the scientific community has been to point out innumerable health advances made possible by the use of animals as research models. This approach is something that most people can relate to, since everyone has benefited from these advances.

The early defensive posture of scientists also failed to allay public concerns about the ability of researchers to self-regulate their care and use of research animals. Unlike the participation of humans in research (who are usually able to speak in their own defense and give consent), there seemed to be no one in the system able to "speak" for the animals. Or so people were encouraged to believe by animal rights activists. As discussed below, there are elaborate federal regulations on the use of animals in research, as well as state laws and professional guidelines on the care and use of animals in research.

Restoring Trust

Scientists, research institutions, and federal research agencies finally came to realize that the charges being leveled by animal rights activists needed to be publicly—and forcefully—rebutted. Dr. Frederick Goodwin, former administrator of the Alcohol, Drug Abuse, and Mental Health Administration (ADAMHA), was one of the first federal officials to defend animal research publicly, and point out the difference between animal welfare and animal rights. Recently, many more federal officials and respected researchers have publicly spoken on the importance of animal research.

Countering Misinformation Animal rights literature often uses misleading images to depict animal research—images such as animals grimacing as they are shocked with electricity. These descriptions lead readers to believe animals are routinely subjected to high voltage shocks capable of producing convulsions. Such propaganda is far from the truth. In most cases, electric shock (when used at all) is relatively mild—similar to what one might feel from the discharge of static electricity on a cold, dry day. Even this relatively mild use of shock is carefully reviewed by Institutional Animal Care and Use Committees before being approved, and researchers must demonstrate that alternate techniques are not feasible. Stronger shock *is* used in animal research, but it is used to study medical problems such as epilepsy (a convulsive disorder). It is also used to test the effectiveness and side effects of drugs developed to control such disorders. It is not within the scope of this viewpoint to refute the myriad charges issued against animal research in general, specific projects, and individual researchers. Suffice it to say that such allegations have been persuasively refuted by D.C. Coile and N.E. Miller; D. Feeney; D. Johnson; and K. McCabe.

Benefits to Animals Animal rights activists often fail to appreciate the many benefits to animals that have resulted from animal research. Behavioral research has contributed to improvements in the environments of captive animals, including those used in research. The list of benefits also includes a host of veterinary procedures and the development of vaccines for deadly diseases such as rabies, Lyme disease, and feline leukemia. Research in reproductive biology and captive breeding programs are also the only hope for some animals on the brink of extinction.

Regulations and Guidelines It is clear that many people concerned about the use of animals in research are not aware of the elaborate structure that exists to regulate the care and use of animals in research. This system includes federal regulations under the Animal Welfare Act, Public Health Service (PHS) policy, and state laws that govern the availability of pound animals for research.

The Animal Welfare Act

The Animal Welfare Act, most recently amended in 1985, is enforced by the U.S. Department of Agriculture's (USDA) Animal and Plant Health Inspection Service (APHIS). The regulations connected with this law include 127 pages of guidelines governing the use of animals in research. They also include unannounced inspections of animal research facilities by APHIS inspectors who do nothing but inspect research facilities. Their inspections are conducted to ensure compliance with regulations that include everything from cage size, feeding schedules, and lighting to exercise requirements for dogs and the promotion of psychological well-being among nonhuman primates.

In addition to APHIS inspectors who make unannounced inspections of animal research facilities, there are local Institutional Animal Care and Use Committees (IACUCs) that review each proposed research project using animals. Research proposals must include a justification for the species used and the number of animals required, an assurance that a thorough literature review has been conducted (to prevent unnecessary replication of research), and a consideration of alternatives if available. IACUCs are also responsible for inspecting local animal research facilities to check for continued compliance with state protocols.

Each grant proposal received by a PHS agency (National Institutes of Health and the Centers for Disease Control) that proposes using animals must contain an assurance that it has been reviewed by an IACUC and been approved. IACUCs must have no less than five members and contain at least one veterinarian, one practicing scientist experienced in research involving animals, one member who is primarily concerned in nonscientific matters (e.g., a lawyer or ethicist), and one member who is not affiliated with the institution in any way and is not an immediate family member of anyone affiliated with the institution.

Beyond federal animal welfare regulations, PHS policy, and the PHS guidelines, there are professional guidelines for the care and use of research animals. Examples include the American Psychological Association's (APA) *Ethical Principles of Psychologists* (1990) and *Guidelines for Ethical Conduct in the Care and Use of Animals* (1993), and the Society for Neuroscience's handbook (1991).

The APA also has a Committee on Animal Research and Ethics (CARE) whose charge includes the responsibility to "review the ethics of animal experimentation and recommend guidelines for the ethical conduct of research, and appropriate care of animals in research." CARE wrote the APA's *Guidelines for Ethical Conduct in the Care and Use of Animals*, and periodically reviews it and makes revisions. These guidelines are widely used by psychologists and other scientists, and have been used in teaching research ethics at the undergraduate and graduate level. The APA's Science Directorate provided support for a conference on psychological well-being of nonhuman primates used in research, and published a volume of proceedings from that conference. The APA also helps promote research on animal welfare by membership in and support for such organizations as the American Association for the Accreditation of Laboratory Animal Care (AAALAC).

AAALAC is the only accrediting body recognized by the PHS, and sets the "gold standard" for animal research facilities. To receive AAALAC accreditation, an institution must go beyond what is required by federal animal welfare regulations and PHS policy. AAALAC accreditation is highly regarded, and those institutions that receive it serve as models for the rest of the research community.

Not a Self-Regulating System

Even with all these safeguards in place, some critics question the ability of the research community to self-regulate its use of animals in research. The system can only be considered self-regulating, however, if one assumes that researchers, institutional officials, members of IACUCs (which must include a member not affiliated with the institution), USDA inspectors, animal care and lab technicians, and veterinarians have identical interests. These are the individuals with the most direct access to the animals used in research, and these are the specialists most knowledgeable about the conditions under which animals are used in research.

In several states, animal rights activists have succeeded in gaining access to IACUC meetings where animal research proposals are discussed. On the whole, however, research institutions have fought—and are still fighting—to keep these meetings closed to the general public. There is a very real fear among researchers that information gleaned from such meetings will be used to harass and target individual researchers. Given the escalating nature of illegal break-ins by such organizations as the Animal Liberation Front, this is a legitimate concern. Indeed, on some campuses "reward posters" offer money to individuals who report the abuse of research animals.

Even though IACUC meetings are generally closed to the public, the elaborate system regulating animal research is by no means a closed one. The most recent animal welfare regulations were finalized after five years of proposals recorded in the *Federal Register*; comments from the public, research institutions, professional associations, animal welfare groups, and animal rights groups; the incorporation of these comments; republication of the revised rules; and so forth. Neither researchers nor animal rights groups were entirely pleased with the final document, but everyone had their say. Although certain elements of the regulatory system rely on researchers, it is hard to imagine a workable system that would fail to use their expertise. The unspoken assumption that researchers cannot be trusted to care for their research animals is not supported by the records of APHIS inspections. Good science demands good laboratory animal care, and it is in a researcher's best interest to ensure that laboratory animals are well cared for.

The Benefits of Behavioral Research with Animals

The use of animals in psychological and behavioral research was an early target of animal rights activists. This research was perceived as a more vulnerable target than biomedical research, which had more direct and easily explained links to specific human health benefits. Psychological and behavioral research also lacked the powerful backing of the medical establishment.

There is, of course, a long list of benefits derived from psychological research with animals. These include rehabilitation of persons suffering from stroke, head injury, spinal cord injury, and Alzheimer's disease; improved communication with severely retarded children; methods for the early detection of eye disorders in children (allowing preventive treatment to avoid permanent impairment); control of chronic anxiety without the use of drugs; and improved treatments for alcoholism, obesity, substance abuse, hypertension, chronic migraine headaches, lower back pain, and insomnia. Behavioral research with nonhuman primates also permits the investigation of complex behaviors such as social organization, aggression, learning and memory, communication, and growth and development.

The nature of psychological and behavioral research makes the development and use of alternatives difficult. It is the behavior of the whole organism, and the interaction among various body systems, that is examined. Computer models may be used, but "research with animals will still be needed to provide basic data for writing computer software, as well as to prove the validity and reliability of computer alternatives," according to the U.S. Congress's Office of Technology Assessment. The alternative of using nonliving systems may be possible with epidemiologic databases for some behavioral research, but chemical and physical systems are not useful for modeling complex behaviors. Likewise, in vitro cultures of organs, tissues, and cells do not display the characteristics studied by psychologists.

The Benefits Outweigh the Costs

Research psychologists have been asked to eschew emotionalism, and bring logic and reason to the debate over animal research. This is certainly the style most researchers are comfortable with—yet they have also been advised by B.J. Culliton to quit trying to "apply logic and reason in their responses [to animal rights activists]." Culliton warns that while "animal rights people go for the heart, the biologists go for the head" and are losing the public in the process.

Which path is best? A reasoned approach draws high marks for civility, but will it help scientists in their trench warfare with animal rights activists?

Do animals have rights that preclude their use in laboratory research? I, and the psychologists I help represent, would say no. But researchers do have responsibilities to the animals they use in their research. These responsibilities include ensuring the humane care of their research animals, using the minimum number of animals necessary, and seeing to it that all laboratory assistants are adequately trained and supervised. As stated in the APA's *Ethical Principles*, "Laws and regulations notwithstanding, an animal's immediate protection depends upon the scientist's own conscience."

Researchers and others concerned with animal welfare can engage in a useful dialogue as standards of care and use evolve. This dialogue has proven fruitless with animal rights activists, though, since they seem unwilling to compromise or consider other viewpoints. What is the middle ground for a discussion with someone whose goal is the elimination of all research on animals?

The collective decision society has made is that the benefits derived from animal research far outweigh the costs. As public opinion polls indicate, most people are willing to accept these costs but want assurances that animals are humanely cared for. Yes, I'm "speciesist" in the eyes of Ingrid Newkirk—I will never believe my son is a dog is a pig is a rat.

"Not all basic research ought to be sanctified by the 'right to know.'"

The Case Against Animal Research in Psychology

Bernard E. Rollin

Bernard E. Rollin is professor of philosophy, physiology, and bio- physics, and director of bioethical planning at Colorado State University. In the following viewpoint, he argues that psychologists who experiment on animals often fail to think through the moral integrity of their research. Because they lack a clear theoretical understanding of their work, Rollin contends, such researchers cause extensive suffering for trivial and useless purposes.

As you read, consider the following questions:

1. What dilemma does Rollin pose to researchers when discussing the morality of their work?
2. According to the author, why is psychological experimentation involving animals useless?
3. What are some examples of "stupid and useless" psychological research described by Rollin?

Reprinted from *Animal Rights and Human Morality* by Bernard E. Rollin; ©1992 by Bernard E. Rollin. Reprinted by permission of Prometheus Books, Buffalo, New York.

Rather than chronicle random cases that illustrate the pernicious nature of a theoretical research from a variety of scientific fields, it is perhaps better to focus upon the field most consistently guilty of mindless activity that results in great suffering. This is the field of experimental, behavioral, comparative, and sometimes physiological psychology. Nowhere are researchers further removed from theory, nowhere are researchers less engaged in trying to develop a picture of some aspect of the world, nowhere are researchers less able to discuss intelligently the significance of their experiments, nowhere are researchers less concerned with the morality of what they do. Robert Paul Wolff once remarked that what is most wrong with contemporary science is that scientists totally lack perspective—each individual researcher sees himself as throwing a little piece of dung onto the giant dung heap, and somehow, eventually, there will stand a cathedral! I recall one of my students who was a psychology graduate student being particularly shocked by a nasty piece of animal research and asking the researcher what the significance of that experiment was. Without blinking an eye, the psychologist replied, "That is for future researchers to decide."

A Moral Question for Psychologists Using Animals

Since I have become interested in animal rights, I often argue with psychologists about the morality of what they are doing. When they are not too defensive to engage in dialogue, I pose the following dilemma to them: "A good deal of your research is on mice and rats, studying behavior and learning, utilizing pleasure and pain to condition the animals. Clearly, you are not interested in the mind of the rat for its own sake. You study these animals because they are relevantly analogous to human beings, because rat behavior is a good model for human behavior. The dilemma is this: Either the rats are relevantly analogous to human beings in terms of their ability to learn by positive and negative reinforcement (i.e., pleasure and pain), in which case it is difficult to see what right you have to do things to rats that you would not do to human beings, or the rats are not relevantly analogous to human beings in these morally relevant ways, in which case it is difficult to see the value in studying them!" I have never received an adequate response to this question; in fact, I have rarely received any response at all. The only semblance of an answer is something like "Well, we're stronger than rats," or "We're not allowed to do it to people," both of which are obviously morally irrelevant.

On one occasion, when a psychologist justified his behavior on the grounds that he was "stronger" than the rats, I must confess to responding with a most unphilosophical counterargument. Being a weightlifter, I picked him up by his lapels and snarled, "Well, I'm stronger than you are—how about I run you through a maze?" (I don't know whether he got the point, but I certainly enjoyed it!)

Obviously, then, there is a clear moral problem associated with psychological research. But there are also deep conceptual problems associated with parts of the field, one of which is implicit in the dilemma, namely, what is the value of studying animal learning and responses? What theory connects rats and humans? Does psychology have a theory at all? Consider the work of B.F. Skinner, certainly the most revered of contemporary behavioral psychologists, who operated in the behaviorist tradition, a tradition which dominated American psychology for many years and is still very influential. Does Skinner's lifetime of research give us a clearer understanding of the human mind? No! Skinner, like other behaviorists, loathes even talking about the mind, which for them is an imprecise, unmeasurable, mystical notion. Does it give us an understanding of the processes underlying human or animal behavior? Again, it does not. In a brilliant and readable article entitled "B.F. Skinner—the Butcher, the Baker, the Behavior-Shaper," my friend and colleague Dr. Richard Kitchener has demonstrated, I think conclusively, that Skinner was not doing pure science or basic research at all. Nothing in what Skinner does, Kitchener points out, helps us to understand the workings of nature. He discovers no laws and generates no theories. Behavioral psychology, says Kitchener, is "cookbook knowledge"; it is "generalizations from practice and trial and error experimentation . . . very similar to the kind of knowledge one finds in certain trades or crafts." Skinner himself, Kitchener points out, admits that psychology "is not concerned with testing theories, but with directly modifying behavior." In *Beyond Freedom and Dignity*, Skinner talks constantly of "behavioral technology."

This development of techniques for molding the behavior of animals and men is therefore not science. It tells us nothing new about the world, it does not help us to understand either ourselves or animals. It is no more science than a book on how to play tennis, or a guide to improving one's golf swing, or a book on how to raise and train a goldfish! True, these all count as knowledge, but not as scientific knowledge—rather as skills, or manipulatory techniques. In Skinner's case, as in his predecessor John Watson's case, the goal is developing the technique of manipulating and controlling human behavior, as Skinner amply demonstrates in works like *Beyond Freedom and Dignity* and *Walden Two*. The point is that this is not basic research helping us to understand the universe, advancing the frontiers of knowledge in a "value-free" way. Since no theoretical understanding of the world is gained, this research amounts to looking for ways of molding human beings, surely a value question of the first magnitude. And surely this does not count as pure science, protected by the value of free inquiry. There are grave social dangers in developing such methods under government aegis, as military abuse of psychedelic drugs has demonstrated, and this surely ought not be done without a good deal of social discussion and control.

The Power of Choice

Unlike our fellow creatures, who are driven by instinct, human beings have the power of choice. We can choose whether to be cruel or compassionate. We can choose to support a scientific agenda that advances human progress with the context of ethical considerations, or we can choose to allow scientists to decide for us what is morally right or wrong. The right choice seems clear.

National Anti-Vivisection Society, *Expressions 2*, 1994.

Besides the potential pernicious consequences for human beings, the lack of theory, the empirical dabblings, and the trial-and-error approach that characterizes behavioristic psychology are extremely mischievous from the point of view of animal suffering. Suffering is essential to psychological research in a way that is unparalleled in all other research, except research on pain, anesthetics, and analgesics. A basic feature of much behavioral psychological research is the use of negative reinforcement (i.e., pain, anxiety, stress, etc.) to condition animal behavior in various ways. It is for this reason that I am so strongly critical of such psychological research. Not only does it not advance our understanding of the world or, for that matter, of the mind (behavioral psychologists hate the word "mind"; they see it as mystical), not only is its *raison d'être* the manipulation of human beings, but it causes incalculable amounts of pain on all sorts of creatures for no apparent benefit. It is extremely revealing and interesting that other scientists who work with animals, even strong defenders of the researcher's right to use animals, often have great contempt for behavioral psychology and point out that by far the most "cruel and useless" experiments are done by psychologists, and that these experiments give *all* researchers a bad name!

There is, furthermore, a good deal of reason to believe that the entire behaviorist enterprise may be misdirected, since some thinkers have argued that human beings (and very likely animals, too) do not learn important things by stimulus-response conditioning. Noam Chomsky, in a series of books and articles, most notably *Rules and Representations*, has argued that the most important cognitive "organs" we possess—like language—are innately programmed and are triggered by experience, not derived from it. If Chomsky is correct, all the conditioning experiments in the world will tell us nothing about the features of the human mind we are most interested in understanding. Researchers like Donald Griffin and many cognitive psychologists see no reason to be hamstrung in their researches into the minds of animals by the archaic straitjacket imposed by behaviorism. It is indeed ironic that although behaviorists have run countless experiments on dogs, cats, and rats in bizarre situations, no attempt has been made to publish work giving any insight at all into the mind of any of these creatures.

Useless Psychological Research Involving Animals

Lest it be thought that we cannot buttress our claims, it is worth citing some salient cases of stupid and useless psychological research, though any reader could make his or her own list today simply by leafing through the journals. These examples were taken from the excellent survey of the *Physical and Mental Suffering of Experimental Animals*, prepared by Jeff Diner at the Animal Welfare Institute, a study that surveys the scientific literature from 1975–1978. A similar list could be constructed today.

• At the Department of Psychology at MIT [Massachusetts Institute of Technology], hamsters were blinded in a study showing that "blinding increases territorial aggression in male Syrian golden hamsters."

• At UCLA [University of California at Los Angeles], monkeys were blinded to study the effects of hallucinogens on them.

• At Harvard, experimenters used squirrel monkeys trained to press a lever under fixed-interval schedules of food or electric shock presentation. The purpose of the experiment was to compare hose biting induced by these two schedules.

• At the University of Maryland, experimenters studied the effect alcohol had on punished behavior in monkeys, i.e., on lever-pressing behavior conditioned by electrical shock.

• At the University of Texas, psychologists studied the effect of foot-shocks in rabbits on brain responsiveness to tone stimuli.

• A particularly bizarre experiment on "learned helplessness" induced by electric shock is worth quoting at length:

> When placed in a shuttle box an experimentally naive dog, at the onset of the first electric shock, runs frantically about, until it accidentally scrambles over the barrier and escapes the shock. On the next trial, the dog, running frantically, crosses the barrier more quickly than on the preceding trial. Within a few trials the animal becomes very efficient at escaping and soon learns to avoid shock altogether. After about 50 trials the dog becomes nonchalant and stands in front of the barrier. At

the onset of the signal for shock, he leaps gracefully across and rarely gets shocked again. But dogs first given inescapable shock in a Pavlovian hammock show a strikingly different pattern. Such a dog's first reactions to shock in the shuttle box are much the same as those of a naive dog. He runs around frantically for about 30 seconds, but then stops moving, lies down, and quietly whines. After 1 minute of this, shock terminates automatically. The dog fails to cross the barrier and escape from shock. On the next trial, the dog again fails to escape. At first he struggles a bit and then, after a few seconds, seems to give up and passively accepts the shock. On all succeeding trials, the dog continues to fail to escape.

Learned helplessness is supposedly justified as a model of human depression, which of course puts us foursquare back into the dilemma we raised earlier. Between the years 1965 and 1969 the behavior of about 150 dogs that received prior inescapable shock was studied. Such research continues to flourish. . . .

• Since 1962, Dr. Roger Ulrich had been inducing aggression in animals by causing them pain. Dr. Ulrich has repudiated his work in a poignant letter to the American Psychological Association *Monitor*, March 1978, which illustrates some of the points we are trying to make:

> When I finished my dissertation on pain-produced aggression, my Mennonite mother asked me what it was about. When I told her she replied, "Well, we knew that. Dad always warned us to stay away from animals in pain because they are more likely to attack." Today I look back with love and respect on all my animal friends from rats to monkeys who submitted to years of torture so that like my mother I can say, "Well, we knew that."

Ulrich is not the first psychological researcher to draw back from earlier activities. Richard Ryder, once an experimental psychologist, is now one of the most eloquent spokesmen for laboratory animals in Britain. Curiously, some years ago, Professor Harry Harlow stated in the *Journal of Comparative and Physiological Psychology* that "most experiments are not worth doing and the data obtained are not worth publishing." Harlow should know; it will be recalled that he is the man who forcibly removed baby monkeys from their mothers and substituted wire surrogate mothers, or other surrogate mothers that spike, chill, eject, or otherwise harm the infant. Harlow then concludes that the monkeys do not develop normally! It is a pity that he did not read his own statement with greater care. A scientist friend of mine who worked with Harlow, and has recently experienced a gestalt shift, can no longer understand how he was able to do that sort of work. . . .

In a particularly vicious piece of irony, until forbidden to do so by the new federal legislation, psychological researchers (who were agnostic about animal consciousness) were wont to do brain surgery on animals using paralytic drugs (which are not anesthetics) because they wanted the animal "conscious."

There is little point in continuing to chronicle atrocities—this has been done well by others: Diner, Dallas Pratt, M.D., in his *Painful Experiments on Animals*, Richard Ryder in *Victims of Science*, Peter Singer in *Animal Liberation*. We are interested only in pointing out that not all basic research ought to be sanctified by the "right to know." There are certain things studied in the name of research that we already know; there are others we do not need to know, most notably in the field of psychology. Projects such as the ones described above should not be funded; public pressure should be brought to bear on government to achieve this result. This sort of research makes all research look bad, is methodologically suspect, cannot be extrapolated to humans, belabors the obvious, and can result in no conceivable benefit to human beings. Lest the reader think that this is the radical statement of an unsympathetic outsider, it is valuable to point out that Dr. Alice Heim, chairperson of the psychological section of the British Association for the Advancement of Science, and a scientist who has been described by the London Times as "one of Britain's most distinguished psychologists," said the same thing in an address in which she discussed animal experimentation. Diner quotes the speech, where she raised the question as follows:

> With respect to animal experimentation, two issues arise: First, how important and informative are the ends? Secondly . . . to what extent is it permissible to use means which are intrinsically objectionable. . . . [By that I mean] those experiments which demand the infliction of severe deprivation, or abject terror, or inescapable pain—either mental or physical—on the animals being experimented upon. . . . It is abundantly clear that such experiments involve the subjects in prolonged and intense suffering—but "suffering" is not of course a behavioral concept. One can read endless accounts of such work and very rarely come across the word "suffering" or "disappointment" and, literally, never meet the word "torture." Yet surely torture may be defined as the infliction of severe pain, often as means to an ulterior end.

Dr. Heim concludes that "some knowledge is too trivial to be valuable in any sense, [and] the acquisition of some items of knowledge is to be deprecated because they are acquired at such cost." She believes that psychology can proceed without torture and infliction of such pain. Further, she cites addiction research, tumors, and neurosis as areas that ought to be studied in humans and not induced in animals, both for moral reasons and because of the lack of analogy between humans and experimental animals.

"I strongly feel that we, as the responsible adults in a society, should be encouraging students to try dissections."

The Case for Dissection

Susan Offner

In the following viewpoint, Susan Offner argues that students need to dissect animals so they may experience firsthand how tissues, muscles, and organs of mammals are constructed. The sense of discovery dissection provides, she contends, is not available by so-called alternatives to dissection. Offner believes that dissection, properly taught, can be a positive experience for most students. Offner teaches biology at Milton High School in Milton, Massachusetts.

As you read, consider the following questions:

1. Why is it important, according to Offner, for students to study real specimens in biology classes?
2. According to the author, how should biology teachers respond to students who object to dissection?
3. On what basis does Offner oppose laws that require teachers to exempt students from dissecting?

Excerpted from "The Importance of Dissecting in Biology Teaching" by Susan Offner, *American Biology Teacher*, March 1993. Reprinted with permission.

I write as an enthusiastic advocate of dissection in the high school biology classroom. Dissection has long been a mainstay of the high school biology curriculum. There is good reason for this.

First, what does dissection teach? Dissection provides concrete, hands-on learning experiences with anatomy, one of the most basic of sciences. Dissection takes many of the things students have heard about and read about and gives them firsthand experience in seeing them. There is no other way to do this.

I can still remember my first dissection of a mammal. It was a mouse, and I thought it was "yucky" and I didn't want to touch it. But, being too proud to admit this to my teacher, I cut it anyway. What ensued was a tremendous explosion of consciousness and understanding. All the things I had been learning were suddenly real. It was a profound experience. But it was something more. By confirming all the things I had been taught, it helped me understand that the world was a rational place, and that knowledge and understanding can come from serious study of real specimens and real data. Every year, I see this same kind of learning occur in my own students. This is what teaching is all about.

Did you know that pigs have three bronchial tubes, one going into the left lung and two going into the right lung? You can find that out if you dissect a fetal pig. Sheep also have three bronchial tubes, one going into the left lung and two going into the right lung, just like the pig. Look at a sheep pluck. In both the pig and the sheep, the right lung is considerably larger than the left lung, and presumably the presence of the second right bronchial tube is necessary to fully aerate the larger right lung. What a nice example of form being related to function!

Did you know that the largest invertebrate brain is about the size of a head of a pin? Look at the brain of a crayfish, one of the most complex of invertebrates, and that's what you'll find. . . .

Year after year, I find students who passed paper-and-pencil tests on these and similar facts who are astonished to find them in a real specimen. This highlights the need for dissection. The learning that occurs in a dissection is qualitatively different from the learning that occurs in a lecture or paper-and-pencil setting. No model, no video, no diagram and no movie can duplicate the fascination, the sense of discovery, wonder and even awe that students feel when they find real structures in their own specimens. When students know a specimen is real, their attention is heightened, and the information they learn is somehow registered as "real." It is a more profound and permanent kind of learning that cannot be obtained in any other way.

I have spoken with many people who are looking for so-called "alternatives to dissection." They produce long lists of "objectives" that they claim cover the purposes of dissection, and then they try to show that you can achieve these paper objectives without actually dissecting. My answer to them is simple: You can have a student regurgitate on a paper-and-pencil test that a mammal's lungs are spongy, but there is no way that student will understand what spongy means unless they see a real lung.

I will add a point that is not to be taken lightly. The overwhelming majority of classroom teachers I know do dissections and consider them to be a vital part of their course.

A Valuable Part of Education

The use of dissection in the secondary school should be well-planned and educationally sound before being implemented. . . . For those entering the health professions, the experience of dissection is invaluable. It should be the responsibility of the education system to provide these pre-college opportunities.

Terry Keiser and Roger Hamm, *The Science Teacher*, January 1991.

I am distressed with the amount of time and energy spent looking for "alternatives to dissection." The alternative to dissection is ignorance, and let us never forget that ignorance comes at a terrible price. There was a time in history when dissection was forbidden, when even medical students and doctors could not see the insides of animals. We call those times the Dark Ages. They were not a time of respect for life. They were a time of ignorance, and along with the ignorance came tremendous insensitivity and cruelty. In the absence of real medical knowledge and understanding, superstition prevailed and all kinds of grotesque mutilations were performed in the name of science. One of the most important lessons to come out of the Dark Ages is that love of and respect for life come from knowledge and understanding and not from ignorance and its invariable handmaidens, fear and superstition. If this sounds farfetched, imagine what this country would be like if nobody had dissected in the last 10 years. . . .

Of course, there should be guidelines for dissection. We must never lose sight of the fact that every time a student dissects, an animal has been sacrificed for the purpose of that student's education. I always remind students of this. They are surprised and moved by the fact that we take their education so seriously.

Any animal being dissected should be treated respectfully. The classroom should reflect a seriousness of purpose. A good teacher will tailor the lesson to the ability of the students. Normally, there should be no more than two students to a specimen. However, in classes where students are more easily distracted, sometimes a demonstration by the teacher is more appropriate. It is important for the teacher to be thoroughly familiar with the dissection. The teacher should visit each group at least once during each period and should be available to answer questions. This assures that students will actually find what they are looking for.

Endangered species should not be used in the classroom, nor should they be sold by biological supply companies.

A good general biology laboratory program should also have labs other than dissections, reflecting the fact that there are many topics other than anatomy that should be covered in a biology class.

Some people say that it is all right for students planning careers in science to dissect, but that dissection is not necessary for the vast majority of high school students who are not planning to be scientists. I disagree. Science education serves two purposes. The first is to train the very small number of students who will be the scientists of the next generation. The second, equally important purpose, is to ensure a high level of scientific literacy in the general population. Dissection is a vital part of this education.

There is the question of what a teacher should do with a student like Jenifer Graham. Jenifer says that dissection is against her ethical principles. She says she loves animals and is a vegetarian and wears plastic instead of leather. First, students like Jenifer are extremely rare. I have been teaching for 20 years and have never had a student who did not want to dissect based on ethical principles. I have spoken with many other longtime teachers who also have never had such a student. So we are dealing with a tiny minority of students, and a problem that most individual teachers will never encounter. My feeling is that Jenifer should be given some kind of alternate assignment without penalty to her grade, with the understanding that the alternate assignment will not teach her what a dissection would. This is a big, beautiful country and there is room in it for all kinds of people. I would want Jenifer to feel comfortable in my class, but at the same time, I would want her ideas to have to compete in the marketplace of ideas. I respect the fact that she sees herself as an animal lover. However, there are many ways to love animals. As a biologist, I think that the best way to love animals is to preserve the Earth as a planet that will continue to support a rich variety of life for many years to come. Toward this end, I think you are being kinder to animals if you wear leather that will biodegrade as opposed to plastic which will pollute the planet until the sun swallows it some 3 billion years from now.

Finally, I would like to add a caution about laws that have been proposed in various state legislatures that would require a teacher to excuse a student from dissection. We should strongly and unequivocally oppose such laws. Some educators are confused about this. They see no harm in a law that seemingly only requires us to do what we already do. However, these laws are far more dangerous. By *requiring* a teacher to exempt a student from dissecting, these laws threaten to throw entire dissection programs into chaos. Imagine, for example, the ads that animal rights groups could take out in local newspapers saying, "You Don't Have to Dissect. It's the Law!"

One bill proposed, and fortunately defeated, in Massachusetts in 1991 and 1992 says that teachers must notify students that they "have the option of being excused from this activity and that no penalty shall result from the student's decision to not perform said dissection." Think about the effect of such a statement in a classroom. You are telling teenagers that the class will be dissecting, but that if they don't want to dissect, they don't have to. This particular bill is remarkable for the lack of requirements it puts on the student. The student does not have to give a reason, does not have to bring in a note from a parent, does not have to discuss the matter with the teacher. Any student can simply say, for any reason or for no reason, that he or she doesn't feel like dissecting, and the teacher must comply with the request. You can imagine how disruptive this would be. Further, I tried to think of an appropriate requirement for the student. If you required a note, the teacher would have to approve the note. Such bills are inappropriate, among other reasons, because they are trying to legislate judgment calls which should properly be made by the teacher on an individual basis. The long-term effect of such bills would be to make dissection so difficult and disruptive that people would slowly stop doing it.

Such bills would also send a confusing message to students. Many students feel squeamish about dissection. I did when I was starting to study biology. Of course, at that time, I didn't know what I could learn from a dissection. I am eternally grateful that my biology teacher, and the responsible adults I knew at the time, told me to "try it." People feel squeamish or funny about many new experiences in life. Some babies do not want to take their first bite of solid food; some people are afraid to fly in airplanes. It is the role of responsible adults in such situations to encourage them to "try it," knowing it is a safe and productive activity. I strongly feel that we, as the responsible adults in a society, should be encouraging students to try dissections. . . .

Further, I can't help thinking that such bills, if passed, would be yet another factor in discouraging women from going into science. It is not too hard to imagine situations in which it would be "cool" for girls to not want to dissect. It would be a real disservice to these young women to give them this easy way out.

"Blanket requirements that dissection should be a rite of passage through middle or senior high have no place in our educational system."

The Case Against Dissection

F. Barbara Orlans

F. Barbara Orlans holds degrees in anatomy and physiology and is currently on the staff of the Kennedy Institute of Ethics at Georgetown University in Washington, D.C. Orlans argues in the following viewpoint that schools ought to seek out alternatives to dissection not only because the practice requires the unnecessary annual destruction of millions of animals, but also because many students, parents, and communities find dissection morally offensive.

As you read, consider the following questions:

1. According to Orlans, why do many people find dissection morally offensive?
2. In Orlans's view, does dissection encourage students to enter careers requiring the study of biological organisms?
3. Why, as the author reports, does the National Association of Biology Teachers urge instructors to consider alternatives to dissection?

F. Barbara Orlans, "The Case Against Dissection," *Science Teacher*, January 1991. Reprinted with permission from NSTA Publications, National Science Teachers Association, 1840 Wilson Blvd., Arlington, VA 22201-3000.

The case against animal dissection in biology education rests on several concerns—unnecessary slaughter of living creatures, the moral revulsion over the killing and the desecration of dissection, the suffering of animals before they are put to death, and the domination of the curriculum by dissection at the expense of other important aspects of biology.

The Number of Animals Killed Annually for Dissection

Millions of animals are killed every year for dissection. No one knows for sure how many, but a 1988 estimate of dissection-related frog deaths gave evidence of around 3 million each year. Environmentalists are concerned that the whole population of native frogs in the United States is becoming so seriously depleted by the large-scale trade in frogs that some species are threatened with extinction. I know of no estimates of the number of pigs, dogs, cats, and other animals killed.

Why People Are Morally Offended

An increasing number of people consider dissection to be morally offensive because it involves such unnecessary killing. Moreover, there is strong evidence that the act of dissection can be emotionally disturbing for some students. They recoil at the prospect of handling a dead body. Some view the cutting up of a body as a desecration; even watching it being done is unpleasant. They have been taught to be kind and caring toward animals, not to kill them.

Other students may become desensitized. Heavy exposure to dissection can harden attitudes toward animal suffering and foster disrespect for animal life. The killing of millions of animals each year for teenagers' education fosters the impression that animal life is cheap. In times when we are struggling to reduce violence in our society, the practice of harming and killing sentient creatures to conduct an "educational exercise" seems out of place.

People are concerned not only about the taking of life, but also about the pain and suffering that the animal may experience on the way to the dissection table. Pain and suffering can occur as part of the capture, handling, confinement, transportation, and method of killing. For instance, frogs typically suffer considerably when they are captured from the wild for sale to schools. Often they are held for several days in overcrowded collecting sacks where they may suffer dehydration and contract disease.

Some methods of animal handling and of death are especially inhumane. Recent accusations aimed at a major biological supply house allege that captive, live cats are handled very roughly and appear to be killed without compliance with recognized humane standards.

Dissecting Cats and Dogs

Cat and dog dissection in high schools arouses especially strong objection because these species are high on the phylogenetic scale. Objections are least with an insect, greater with a frog, and greatest of all with a cat or dog. This is because cats and dogs have a high level of sentience, and also, our sense of kinship is greatest with these animals as they are frequently kept as pets.

Students Do Not Learn More Through Dissection

A growing body of evidence shows that students who use alternatives learn as much as those who dissect. In a 1988 study, student test scores improved significantly when students were taught anatomy by lecture rather than by dissection.

Ethical Science Education Coalition, "Dissection Fact Sheet," undated.

Occasionally, teenagers are instructed by their teachers to take dead cats home and do the dissection there rather than in school. This raises even stronger objections in the community, and with good reason. In a home, not only the student but younger siblings and other family members are exposed to practices that have no rightful place outside a laboratory. Such practices are not only offensive but can bring science into disrepute by fostering an incorrect view that scientists are indifferent to the sensitivities of people toward animals.

"Turned Off"

The case is often made that some students are "turned on" to biological studies by dissection but the opposite may be more likely. Very many students are "turned off" from biology as a career and as a subject of study because of their dislike of dissection. Furthermore, when I have asked the few "turned on" people if they could not just as well have been drawn to the biological sciences by the study of living organisms that were not harmed, they invariably say "yes."

The Increasing Number of Dissections

The growth of dissection over the years has gotten out of hand. When dissection was first introduced in the 1920s (at a time when books were poorly illustrated and before the development of visual aids and films) one dissection in an upper grade level was the norm. By now, multiple dissections are the norm despite the availability of alternatives. Dissections are practiced not only in high schools but have extended down to elementary schools. At the local high school in my neighborhood, students do four vertebrate dissections before graduating (frog, fetal pig, cat, and dog).

The current over-reliance of some teachers on dissection comes at the expense of other laboratory studies. While instruction in mathematics and other sciences has kept pace with advances in knowledge and broadening of perspectives, one wonders whether, in some respects, instruction in biology is not overly preoccupied with anatomical structure and memorization of details that soon will be forgotten. A recent survey of middle and senior high school teachers in Ohio showed that for many middle and high school teachers, dissection of dead animals is the only way they use animals. How can biology be taught properly if the students never study anything living? In the word *biology*, "bio" means life.

Using Alternatives

Isn't it time for the curriculum to be brought more into keeping with the subject that is being taught? Cannot the lessons from dissection be learned without killing animals? Are not alternatives available? Many think so, including the National Association of Biology Teachers [NABT]. Their official 1990 policy on the use of animals in the classroom states that NABT has taken note of the increasing objections being made about dissection by students, parents, and communities and advises that "teachers [should] carefully consider alternative ways to achieve the objectives of teaching" without resorting to the "more traditional practices" of dissection. This policy also states that laboratory activities "should not cause the loss of an animal's life." To back up these statements, NABT has recently published an excellent monograph that includes many lesson plans for alternatives to dissection. (Obtainable from NABT, 11250 Roger Bacon Drive, Suite 19, Reston, VA 22090.)

There is a place for dissection in the training of mature students who have made a career commitment where dissection can assist in the acquisition of necessary knowledge and skills. But even here, there should be a provision for conscientious objection, as provided in several leading medical and veterinary schools. Blanket requirements that dissection should be a rite of passage through middle and senior high have no place in our educational system.

"I believe that it is ethically justifiable to carry out certain types of experimentation with [chimpanzees], as it is also with humans."

Primate Research Is Justified

Alfred M. Prince

Alfred M. Prince is a physician and researcher at the Liberian Institute for Biomedical Research in Robertfield, Liberia. In the following viewpoint, he defends his experimentations on chimpanzees in research for vaccines for hepatitis B, hepatitis C, and onchocerciasis. After indicating how his institute obtains chimpanzees, Prince describes their care and use in medical experiments. He compares such research with an imaginary scenario involving human children and concludes that both are justifiable.

As you read, consider the following questions:

1. According to Prince, how has his institute obtained chimpanzees?
2. As Prince describes the arrangements, under what conditions are the chimpanzees housed?
3. What imaginary scenario does the author create in order to compare his experiments on chimpanzees with similar possible research on children?

Alfred M. Prince, "Is the Conduct of Medical Research on Chimpanzees Compatible with Their Rights as a Near-Human Species?" *Between the Species*, Winter 1993. Reprinted by permission of the publisher.

Many animal rights activists consider that all research carried out with animals is indefensible. This would apply especially to research with chimpanzees. I assume that chimpanzees are the closest relatives to humans and that they deserve ethical considerations which are similar to those accorded humans. Nevertheless, I believe that it is ethically justifiable to carry out certain types of experimentation with this species, as it is also with humans. I welcome the opportunity to defend this position here.

The Use of Chimpanzees at Vilab II

My laboratory, Vilab II, has been carrying out research with chimpanzees in Liberia since 1975. The research, none of which affects the health or well-being of the animals, is directed toward the development of vaccines for prevention of three major human diseases: hepatitis B, hepatitis C, and onchocerciasis (river blindness). Chimpanzees are the only nonhuman animal species susceptible to these infections.

We originally acquired chimpanzees by humane capture using anaesthetic darts in a recently logged forest destined for agricultural exploitation. The animals in this region were thus severely threatened, since Liberian farmers do not hesitate to shoot chimpanzees which forage on their crops. Later, we acquired animals who had been held in Liberian or expatriate families as pets, and whose owners could no longer care for them as they emerged from the "cute" and easy to handle juvenile stage. These animals had no future, since humane facilities for housing and care of adult chimpanzees are not available in Liberia, except at Vilab II. Recently, colony born animals have more than satisfied our requirements for additional animals.

Because of our awareness of the near human needs and nature of chimpanzees, a major emphasis of our laboratory has been to maintain animals under conditions which satisfy their physical and emotional needs to a maximal extent. Briefly, this has involved our requirement that animals never be housed alone, that they be housed in large outdoor cages from which they can hear and observe many other animals, that foraging type enrichment devices be provided, and finally that after studies are completed, the animals are socialized into progressively larger groups leading ultimately to the release of groups of 20–30 animals on to 12–30 acre islands in nearby rivers where they are maintained in a free living state with moderate food supplementation. The success of our approach was shown by the extraordinary fertility of the released animals. Of 90 animals released on 5 islands, all females of breeding age were either pregnant or carrying babies in 1990.

An endowment fund has been established which we hope will ultimately assure the indefinite survival of the island groups.

115

These groups will provide opportunities for behavioral studies, and if safe and secure national parks become established in the region, they could provide a source of animals for restocking of wild chimpanzee populations.

An Ethical Defense

Has the Vilab II experience been ethically defensible? I believe that it has. First, the animals acquired had little or no future, and now have a safe and assured life in which they can live out their lives under natural conditions. Second, their contribution to research has been an essential one: vaccines have been developed with their help for hepatitis B, and are in the process of being developed for hepatitis C and onchocerciasis, diseases which cause untold human suffering. The experiments carried out with chimpanzees involve challenging putatively immunized animals with live virus or infective larvae. This cannot be done with humans because it entails a risk of death or serious illness. Fortunately, the immune systems of chimpanzees are more effective than ours, and as a result, they have never developed overt illness as a result of these infections. Thus, these important studies can be humanely done in the chimpanzee model. Furthermore, this can be done under conditions which benefit the animals and provide them with a secure and humane future.

Using Captive-Bred Primates

I think we haven't reached the point where we say: We cannot use animals in research. But if we are to use primates in that way, I think we should use only the ones bred in captivity and increase those breeding colonies. We must not keep trapping animals out of the wild, because there aren't too many of them left there.

Let the remnants of the wild populations stay in the wild. That decision would be a good one for responsible 'stewards' to make.

Deborah Blum, *The Animal Welfare Institute Quarterly*, Winter 1995.

If chimpanzees are to be afforded the same ethical considerations as are humans, then it can be legitimate to ask whether similar research could be ethically done with humans. Consider the following imaginary scenario: During a famine in the Sahel, an epidemic of meningococcal meningitis is decimating the starving children of the region. A medical research team wishes to evaluate vaccines which might halt this and other similar epidemics. The studies have to be done in children, since adults are already immune as a result of past epidemics. They therefore set up camps in which orphaned children can be well housed and fed and in which the vaccines can be tested. Because of the age and limited education of the children, obtaining meaningful informed consent is not feasible. Without this project, these children will be in serious danger of starving to death. If illness occurs during the vaccine trials, prompt treatment will be available to avert serious sequelae. It is planned that after the completion of the trials, the children will be returned to their villages in good health, and with sufficient support to provide for their subsistence and an elementary education.

Is the above an ethical project? Are these children being "used"? They are. However this is providing benefit both to the subjects of the trials and to society as a whole, and without unacceptable risk to the subjects themselves. I believe that this imaginary scenario describes an ethically defensible medical research project. However, I recognize that this conclusion, and the project itself, would be controversial. I think that this imaginary project shares essential similarities with the Vilab II chimpanzee research project, and that both can be justified on similar grounds.

"No imprisoned chimpanzee today receives what I would regard as optimum living conditions and proper treatment."

Primate Research
Is Not Justified

Geza Teleki

Geza Teleki is chairman of the Committee for Conservation and Care of Chimpanzees in Washington, D.C. He is currently attempting to establish a new national park for chimpanzees in Sierra Leone. In the following viewpoint, Teleki describes the decline of the chimpanzee population, the conditions under which confined chimpanzees live, and the plight of such animals in medical laboratories. Teleki argues that chimpanzees are close living relatives to humans, and as such they are individuals with rights to freedom and self-determination.

As you read, consider the following questions:

1. In Teleki's estimate, how precipitous is the decline of the chimpanzee population?
2. What is the plight of the confined chimpanzee as Teleki describes it?
3. What evidence does the author provide to support his view that medical scientists are the strongest opponents of legislation designed to protect chimpanzees?

In their wilderness retreats, free chimpanzees are under assault by waves of humans bearing hoes, saws and guns. Few chimpanzee communities in Africa are today safe from human encroachment and persecution. The national population estimates ring alarm bells. In the twenty-five nations encompassing the historical range of the species, four contain no chimpanzees and fifteen others retain less than 5,000 chimpanzees apiece. Survival is not assured even in the six remaining nations where populations are still relatively intact, due to recent sales of extensive timber concessions.

The Decline in Chimpanzee Populations

During the early 1980s a survey of Gabon, containing some of the best habitats, yielded an estimate of about 64,000 free chimpanzees. Biomedical scientists, whose interest in these apes has always been a consuming one, promptly cited Gabon as proof that Africa still has a 'plentiful supply' of free chimpanzees available for 'harvesting' to save human lives. But by April of 1988 the surveyors, Caroline Tutin and Michel Fernandez, stated that 'in the five years since completion of the census the situation has changed' so much that 'by 1996 the chimpanzee population of Gabon will be reduced by at least 20% as a result of habitat alteration caused by selective logging'. Other major population nucleuses in Cameroon and Zaïre are similarly threatened by rapid change.

The Plight of Confined Chimpanzees

In their prison settings, confined chimpanzees continue to suffer abusive treatment, social isolation, mental deprivation, emotional trauma and the like. I estimate that between 4,000 and 5,000 chimpanzees exist worldwide in medical institutions, zoological exhibits, roadside menageries, entertainment compounds and the homes of pet owners. Conditions of confinement may vary but it is a clear truth, in my mind, that no imprisoned chimpanzee today receives what I would regard as optimum living conditions and proper treatment.

The plight of chimpanzees in medical laboratories causes me the greatest concern. In the United States, where captive census data are most readily available, about 2,000 of 3,000 confined chimpanzees exist in biomedical facilities. It is indeed a sad statement on human values that the very institutions which proclaim a dedication to alleviating suffering and pain in humans cause so much distress to chimpanzees. And it is equally perplexing that medical scientists are the most dedicated opponents to the enacting of legislation designed to better protect free chimpanzees and improve the treatment of confined chimpanzees. I rest my case on two examples of this remarkably inconsistent position.

First, after several conservation groups petitioned the US Department of Interior's Fish and Wildlife Service to place chimpanzees on the endangered list under the Endangered Species Act, the government received 54,212 letters of support and only nine letters of dissent in 1988. Supportive letters included many from a wide range of institutions, but no biomedical facilities, while opposing letters included eight from biomedical research centres and one from a circus. Acting on behalf of the medical community, the government's National Institutes of Health mounted an intensive lobbying campaign to convince Congress that endangered status was not warranted due to presence of an 'ample supply' of chimpanzees in Africa. Because the

---

A Declaration on Great Apes

We demand the extension of the community of equals to include all great apes: human beings, chimpanzees, gorillas and orangutans.

"The community of equals" is the moral community within which we accept certain basic moral principles or rights as governing our relations with each other and enforceable at law. Among these principles or rights are the following:

1. *The Right to Life*
   The lives of members of the community of equals are to be protected. Members of the community of equals may not be killed except in very strictly defined circumstances, for example, self-defense.

2. *The Protection of Individual Liberty*
   Members of the community of equals are not to be arbitrarily deprived of their liberty; if they should be imprisoned without due legal process, they have the right to immediate release. The detention of those who have not been convicted of any crime, or of those who are not criminally liable, should be allowed only where it can be shown to be for their own good, or necessary to protect the public from a member of the community who would clearly be a danger to others if at liberty. In such cases, members of the community of equals must have the right to appeal, either directly or, if they lack the relevant capacity, through an advocate, to a judicial tribunal.

3. *The Prohibition of Torture*
   The deliberate infliction of severe pain on a member of the community of equals, either wantonly or for an alleged benefit to others, is regarded as torture, and is wrong.

The editors of and contributors to *The Great Ape Project: Equality Beyond Humanity*, eds. Paola Cavalieri and Peter Singer, 1993.

figures collected from thirty-nine field scientists could not be easily disputed, some members of the biomedical community attacked the credibility of the field experts instead.

Second, five years after the US Senate passed amendments in 1985 requiring laboratories to provide 'a physical environment adequate to promote the psychological well-being of primates', the US Department of Agriculture proposed new regulations under the Animal Welfare Act. The delay was caused by medical opposition on an unprecedented scale. The regulations were revised many times in public reviews that produced some 12,000 letters to the US Department of Agriculture. One round of proposals published on 15 August 1990 yielded 1,372 institutional criticisms plus an uncounted number of personal objections from the medical research community. Tremendous lobbying pressure was directed at Congress to press the US Department of Agriculture into submission. Capitulation occurred by 15 February 1991. The final regulations adopted wholesale the minimum standards of maintenance and care set many years ago by the government's National Institutes of Health. For instance, the recommended cage size for permanently confining a single adult chimpanzee remained at a meagre 5 x 5 x 7 feet and even infants were not guaranteed social housing. . . .

A Kindred Species

My work on chimpanzee survival and well-being issues these past years has yielded some insights but no simple solutions to this terrible situation. I do believe, however, that every chimpanzee has rights to the freedom and the self-determination we so highly value for ourselves. And because I see chimpanzees as individuals, some of whose experiences and memories I share, I feel a moral obligation to respect the members of a kindred species.

Looking at chimpanzees from where I stand, eye to eye, not down my sharper human nose, I consider it sheer arrogance to perpetuate the anthropocentric views established by my ancestors simply because that was the collective human impulse. As Pogo once said in a memorable cartoon: 'We have met the enemy and they are us.'

Periodical Bibliography

The following articles have been selected to supplement the diverse views presented in this chapter. Addresses are provided for periodicals not indexed in the *Readers' Guide to Periodical Literature*, the *Alternative Press Index*, or the *Social Sciences Index*.

Stephen Baier — "The Impact of Animal Rights on the Use of Animals for Biomedical Research, Product Testing, and Education," *American Biology Teacher*, March 1993. Available from 11250 Roger Bacon Dr., Suite 19, Reston, VA 22090.

Mark Bekoff et al. — "Animals in Science: Some Areas Revisited," *Animal Behaviour*, September 1992. Available from 24–28 Oval Rd., London NW1 7DX, U.K.

Mark Bernstein et al. — "Is Justification of Animal Research Necessary?" *JAMA*, March 3, 1993. Available from 515 N. State St., Chicago, IL 60610.

Lynda Birke and Mike Michael — "Views from Behind the Barricade: Animal Rights Campaigners Have Left Researchers Feeling Under Siege," *New Scientist*, April 4, 1992. Available from IPC Specialist Group, King's Reach Tower, Stamford St., London SE1 9LS, U.K.

Alan Bowd and Kenneth Shapiro — "The Case Against Laboratory Animal Research in Psychology," *Journal of Social Issues*, Spring 1993.

Bill Breen — "Why We Need Animal Testing," *Garbage*, April/May 1993.

Paul Cotton — "Animals and Science Benefit from 'Replace, Reduce, and Refine' Effort," *JAMA*, December 22, 1993.

Carolyn Fraser — "The Raid at Silver Springs: A Reporter at Large," *New Yorker*, April 19, 1993.

R.G. Frey — "Medicine and the Ethics of Animal Experimentation," *World & I*, April 1995. Available from 3600 New York Ave. NE, Washington, DC 20002.

Helen Gavaghan — "Animal Experiments: The American Way," *New Scientist*, May 16, 1992.

Wayt Gibbs — "Teaching Science: The Dissection Dilemma," *Scientific American*, September 1993.

Philip Hilts

"Research Animals Used Less Often," *New York Times*, March 3, 1994.

Stephen Labaton

"Judge Orders Rule Tightened to Protect Animals in Research," *New York Times*, February 26, 1993.

John Maddox

"The Kinship of Apes and People," *Nature*, July 15, 1993.

Susan Miller

"Moderates Bury the Hatchet over Animal Rights," *New Scientist*, November 27, 1993.

Juliana Texley

"Doing Without Dissection," *American School Board Journal*, January 1992. Available from 1680 Duke St., Alexandria, VA 22314.

Gail Vines

"Planet of the Free Apes?" *New Scientist*, June 5, 1993.

David Wiebers et al.

"Animal Protection and Medical Science," *Lancet*, April 9, 1994. Available from 46 Bedford Square, London WC1B 3SL, U.K.

Should Animals Be Used for Food and Other Commodities?

ANIMAL
RIGHTS

Chapter Preface

Many animal rights activists become vegetarians as a way of combating the use of animals for food and protesting what they view as the inhumane treatment of farm animals. In a brochure advocating vegetarianism, the animal rights organization People for the Ethical Treatment of Animals (PETA) states:

> Approximately 92 million animals are slaughtered for human consumption in the United States every week. . . . Most of these animals are raised on "factory farms," where they are kept cruelly overcrowded or confined to small cages or stalls. Animals are dehorned and debeaked, have their tails docked, and are otherwise mutilated without painkillers. They are denied comfort, exercise, companionship, natural diets, and other basic needs.

As a further incentive to adopt the vegetarian lifestyle, PETA argues that human beings do not need to eat meat to obtain the nutrition necessary to sustain a healthy body: "The human body can easily obtain all necessary proteins, minerals, carbohydrates, vitamins, and other nutrients from vegetables, grains, legumes, and fruits."

Others disagree with the arguments of those who advocate vegetarianism. The agricultural industries, for example, dispute the charge that modern farming techniques are cruel. The Animal Industry Foundation, responding to accusations that farm animals are raised on "'factory farms,' confined in crowded, unventilated cages and sheds," states:

> Animals are generally kept in barns and similar housing, with the exception of beef cattle, to protect the health and welfare of the animal. Housing protects the animals from predators, disease, and bad weather or extreme climate. . . . Modern animal housing is well ventilated, warm, well-lit, clean and scientifically designed for the specific needs of the animal.

Furthermore, meat eaters contend that meat is a beneficial—even essential—component of the human diet. "Nutritionally," writes Daryn Eller, "meat packs a wallop: It provides abundant amounts of crucial vitamins and minerals, including B vitamins, iron, and zinc."

The merits of meat eating and vegetarianism are debated in the following chapter on the use of animals as commodities.

"The food production miracle in this country did not come about at the sacrifice of animal welfare."

Modern Farming Is Humane

Steve Kopperud

Steve Kopperud is president of the Animal Industry Foundation and senior vice president of the American Feed Industry Association, both of which are located in Arlington, Virginia. In the following viewpoint, Kopperud assures farmers, cattlemen, and livestock and poultry processors that they can take justifiable pride in their professions. Unwilling to seek a compromise with the animal rights movement, Kopperud urges his audience to direct its efforts toward increasing research, improving production practices, and countering current misinformation about animal agriculture.

As you read, consider the following questions:

1. Why does Kopperud believe that animal agriculturalists should admit that improvements can be made within their profession?
2. How does the author support his contention that animals are treated humanely by cattlemen, poultry producers, and meat processors?
3. Why, in Kopperud's estimate, is it self-defeating to attempt dialogue with members of the animal rights movement?

"So What's the Beef About Animal Rights?" by Steve Kopperud, *Agricultural Engineering*, May 1993. Reprinted with permission.

True or false: There's no room for improvement in animal agriculture. Livestock and poultry production is perfect, thank you, a model by which all other industries should be judged. Right? Yeah, and those guys from the government are here to help you.

For those in animal agriculture involved in countering animal rights propaganda, two questions are invariably asked by the public at some point in any discussion about the legitimacy of the animal rights philosophy:

- Are you saying that farming and ranching are perfect?
- Isn't there a "moderate" animal rights group you could work with?

After 10 years working the animal rights issue, the answers—at least to me—are obvious: No, and we haven't found one yet, but we're still looking.

Ripe for Propaganda

Animal agriculture is definitely two things, and for some, they may at first appear to be contradictory. First, U.S. livestock and poultry producers are the best in the world, the model by which other industrialized and developing countries pattern their industries. Second, there is, and likely always will be, room for improvement.

If anyone in animal agriculture stood before an audience and attempted to convince them otherwise, they'd be silly. That message ignores the basic nature of the industry. There is no one tougher on a new system or product than a farmer. If the animals don't prosper, the farmer doesn't prosper, and the system is dumped in a heartbeat.

There are bad players in farming and ranching, just as there are bad players in animal rights, politics or journalism. However, to paint an entire industry with a brush dipped in the sins of one, or even a handful of producers, is unfair. Increasingly, the good players are working to either improve the bad guys or get them out of the business. All it takes is one bad apple.

Unfortunately, the public is ripe for this type of propaganda. Now two or three generations away from the farm, the average urban consumer does not relate to life on the farm. If anything, they hold an overly romantic notion of rural life. They see farming as the last bastion of solid values left in America, but at the same time, prod a yuppie and you'll likely find a notion that folks out there in the country aren't quite as sharp as go-getters in the city.

Even President Clinton's chief science advisor has fallen for the message. In a recent Associated Press interview, he was adamant that he did not eat veal, because the animals were "force fed . . . raised in a cage." This man is a physicist who used to raise cattle.

This is why farmers must begin to market themselves and their contribution to the urban quality of life as actively as they market their products. Consumers must be reassured their collective confidence in farmers and ranchers and the products they produce is not misplaced.

The Miracle of Ag Production

Consumers have to understand the sheer miracle of modern livestock and poultry production in this country. This is not an overstatement. Consider the following:

• Less than 2.5 percent of the U.S. population farms, the lowest percentage of *any country in the world, including Western Europe.* Yet this group feeds 250 million Americans and maintains an export market that is one of the only positive contributors to the U.S. balance of trade.

Reprinted by permisssion of Chuck Asay and Creator's Syndicate.

• U.S. livestock and poultry producers *do not receive direct federal subsidies* for their work. So-called welfare systems adopted by some European countries include massive government indemnification to farmers to offset increased costs of production and subsequent reduction of farm income.

• U.S. producers raise for consumption more than 5 billion

128

animals yearly, and by USDA [U.S. Department of Agriculture] reckoning, *less than one-tenth of 1 percent are not certified for human consumption.*

• American pay less than 11 percent of their disposable income for food, *less than any nation in the world.*

Increased Awareness of Animal Welfare

If farmers routinely abused animals, or raised animals in environments unsuitable for healthy growth, the death loss among production animals would be astronomical, you'd have one heck of a lot of bankrupt farmers, and food costs would be closer to 20 to 25 percent of disposable income based simply on supply and demand.

The food production miracle in this country did not come about at the sacrifice of animal welfare. If anything, science, engineering and producer experience have combined to provide the most advanced animal production systems in the world. U.S. animal disease rates are lower, birth rates are higher and farm income is relatively higher than elsewhere.

And much the same can be said for the population that consumes the meat, milk and eggs from these animals.

If there is a positive effect of the animal rights movement in the United States, it is greater introspection and analysis by producers. Not to appease some sign-waving activist, but because there is the understanding that production practices and the product they sell is under increased public scrutiny.

Farmers are learning to challenge the traditional. They know that just because they were taught to do it one way, does not mean there is not a better way that can be adopted to possibly benefit the animal, and increase their efficiency and profit. National groups, notably the National Pork Producers Council, the Animal Industry Foundation, the American Veal Association and Southeastern Poultry & Egg Association collectively spend more than $1 million in production research. This doesn't count the millions in federal and private corporate dollars spent on the same goal. If there's a better way, this industry will find it.

Refuting Ethical Vegetarianism

Consumers also must understand that the farmer-as-cruel message of the animal rightist has taken a backseat to a repackaged, 1990s kind of attack. The major push today is that animal agriculture is environmentally unsound, and food products from these systems are unsafe—and potentially lethal—for you and your family.

This is the newly constructed philosophy of "ethical vegetarianism," a lifestyle that rids you of the guilt of avoiding environmental, food safety and animal cruelty crusades. If you care about the planet, your children's health and the animals, you'll go vegetarian. Interestingly, despite the movement's efforts, the vegetarian community reports less than 3 percent of American are true vegetarians, a figure that has not changed in 20 years.

Using propaganda, pseudoscience and outright scare tactics, the movement is attempting to frighten Americans away from meat, milk and eggs. Armed with a little knowledge of food safety, activists routinely stand before audiences and talk about salmonella, E. coli and other microbial contamination, but never mention that salmonella is found on *all foods*, including fruits and vegetables, or that E. coli contamination is more common in water than on meat.

The Benefits of Housing

Myth. Farm animals are routinely raised on "factory farms," confined in "crowded, unventilated cages and sheds."

Fact. Animals are generally kept in barns and similar housing, with the exception of beef cattle, to protect the health and welfare of the animal. Housing protects animals from predators, disease, and bad weather or extreme climate. Housing also makes breeding and birth less stressful, protects young animals, and makes it easier for farmers to care for both healthy and sick animals.

Modern animal housing is well ventilated, warm, well-lit, clean and scientifically designed for the specific needs of the animal, such as the regular availability of fresh water and a nutritionally balanced feed.

Animal Industry Foundation, *Animal Agriculture: Myths and Facts*, 1988.

We're asked why, if the livestock and poultry industry is responsible, do these groups continue their protests? There is the objective analysis, recognizing the philosophy held by many activists that says there is no moral justification of animal exploitation. This is an honestly held belief system. These are the true vegans, those who live their lives by their beliefs, allowing no animal products of any type to touch them. They will work to "liberate" animals as part of that belief system.

But there is the cynical analysis that also recognizes that this movement has become big business. It is no longer rag-tag activists with a cause, but it is now multimillion-dollar organizations with sophisticated public relations and advertising programs. It is groups with warehouses full of merchandise and publications that are sold to the public. It is previously anonymous activists who now get "Today" show appearances and guest shots on "Entertainment Tonight." This is heady stuff, almost addictive, and not easy to walk away from.

Is there a "compromise" that can eventually be reached? The very makeup of the animal rights movement argues against it. If you understand that in the United States there are about 400 hard-core animal rights groups, and that no one group is the acknowledged leader of the movement, you have to ask the question: "To whom do we talk?" And with a movement that believes what you do for a living is morally wrong, it's difficult to even discuss the issue, let alone find common ground. How do you compromise with an organization that has the ultimate goal of putting you out of business?

Is there a more moderate part of the true "welfare" community with which animal agriculture could deal? There have been discussions with some groups, but they generally ended up as lectures—telling farmers what's wrong and how they want them to fix it.

There's also a dilemma: If you address the concerns of one faction, altering what you do so that one group is satisfied, how then do you deal with the next group and the next? Ultimately, what good has been achieved when the serious public attacks come from the abolitionists?

It seems to many in animal agriculture that the prudent use of resources and expertise is to direct efforts toward remaining progressive, ensuring the industry continues to evolve in both practice and philosophy. To spend time, effort and limited dollars trying to appease a minority viewpoint, however vocal, is self-defeating.

The Need to Speak Up

If you support farmers and ranchers, if you wish to continue to consume meat, milk and eggs, then you must do your homework and learn where they come from and who are the people who provide your food. You must be willing to counter the misinformation as you encounter it, whether it's a letter to the editor, a misinformed activist on a TV talk show, or a grocery store chain that pushes "natural" foods by bashing commercially raised products.

Engineers who understand the system, who understand the players and whose livelihoods are directly or indirectly linked to the success of modern livestock and poultry production need to speak up. You have the educational and professional credentials, which give you credibility with the public.

Your expertise is needed in helping farmers to remain progressive and dynamic. Your support is needed in getting messages to the public, letting them know things are okay down on the farm—and getting better.

"People have started asking questions about the way food-producing animals are raised and slaughtered."

Modern Farming Is Inhumane

Laura Ten Eyck

In the following viewpoint, Laura Ten Eyck criticizes the way many animals live and die within the confines of hatcheries, farms, and animal factories designed to intensify meat, poultry, and milk production. Convinced that too many animals suffer acutely within such animal factories, Ten Eyck urges consumers to purchase only those animal products produced by small-scale farmers who practice humane animal husbandry. Laura Ten Eyck is a contributing editor for *Animals*, a bimonthly magazine published by the Massachusetts Society for the Prevention of Cruelty to Animals.

As you read, consider the following questions:

1. According to Ten Eyck, how has livestock husbandry gone awry in the egg industry?
2. As Ten Eyck describes the process, what in her opinion is inhumane about the way animals are slaughtered?
3. What recommendations does the author make for consumers who find her observations truthful?

Excerpted from "Thought for Food" by Laura Ten Eyck, *Animals*, March/April 1995; ©1995 by the MSPCA. Reprinted by permission of the Massachusetts Society for the Prevention of Cruelty to Animals.

Unable to confront the harsh treatment farm animals endure, people don't allow themselves to think about where the meat on their plates comes from. "We have built-in distancing devices," says Jim Mason, coauthor of *Animal Factories*. "There's a reason you don't see Connie Chung and Tom Brokaw going into factory farms. This subject is considered off-limits by the media."

But recently that has begun to change. People have started asking questions about the way food-producing animals are raised and slaughtered. Vegetarians and animal-welfare activists have allied themselves with environmentalists and progressive farmers working to educate the public and to offer humane and environmentally sound alternatives to factory farming.

The Example of the Egg Industry

The egg industry is but one example of how intensive livestock husbandry has gone awry. In industrial-scale hatcheries, all male chicks are destroyed. At some hatcheries, male chicks are thrown into large, heavy-duty plastic bags, where they suffocate. Other poultry producers decapitate the chicks or place them in carbon dioxide chambers, where they asphyxiate. Many hatcheries throw live chicks along with their eggshells into a grinder that pulverizes them into meal used as a protein supplement in animal feed. A decompression chamber in which the male chick explodes is in use at some facilities.

It is questionable whether female chicks fare much better. When full-grown, between four and six laying hens are confined to a cage that allows each one just enough space to sit and lay an egg every day for one to two years. Their beaks and claws are cut off so that they cannot injure each other. Debeaking, done with hot-knife machines, is often carried out improperly by workers who are expected to debeak 15 birds a minute. Tongues are mistakenly cut off. A blade that is too hot causes blisters. A cold or dull blade results in the formation of a painfully sensitive growth that prevents the bird from eating.

Up to 250,000 caged birds will be stacked in a single building that is frequently inadequately staffed. The birds are fed and watered automatically. The cage floors slant so that the eggs roll out onto a conveyor belt. Manure is collected on sheet-metal strips placed beneath the cages, scraped automatically into an enormous pit below, and automatically hauled out of the building. The manure, along with dead chickens, slaughterhouse offal, and animal carcasses that do not pass inspection at the slaughterhouse, is processed and mixed into animal feed, which is then fed back to the birds. The Food and Drug Administration (FDA) has suggested that this practice contributes to the spread of salmonella and other food-borne diseases. Chicken feed also contains drugs intended to boost egg production and stimulate growth, as well as additives to enhance the yellow color of egg yolks.

Because laying hens can hardly move, their bones grow weak and shatter during rough handling when they are ultimately packed into crates and shipped to slaughter. At the slaughterhouse the birds are hung upside down by their feet on a conveyor line that carries them into the killing room. If they are lucky, their heads will be dragged through water charged with electric current before their throats are cut.

Death in the Slaughterhouse

All livestock endure rough handling, pain, and fear at the slaughterhouse and during transport. Any animal destined for sale must be slaughtered at a federally inspected slaughterhouse. The Humane Slaughter Act, enforced by the U.S. Department of Agriculture (USDA), dictates that all livestock, excluding chickens, be rendered unconscious prior to slaughter. But according to Bradley Miller, national director of the Humane Farming Association, the stunning process doesn't always work. "For example, most hog-processing plants zap the pigs with an electric charge," says Miller. "But frequently the charge is not adequate, and because of the speed at which the plant operates, the workers don't have the time to ensure that the animal is knocked out. Still conscious, a hog will be chained by the hind leg and hoisted kicking and screaming. Because the animal is so heavy, its chained leg will become dislocated, causing great pain. The hog's throat will be slit, and theoretically it will bleed to death. But since the animal is still conscious, it tenses up and doesn't bleed out as quickly. Time after time, I've seen hogs go fully conscious into the scalding tank, where they are killed after a violent struggle. It's a terrible, terrible death." And, he adds, the USDA has never prosecuted a violation of the Humane Slaughter Act.

As horrible as slaughter can be, for many farm animals it ends a life of suffering. Laying hens are not the only animals that spend most of their lives in close confinement. Pigs and most veal calves are subjected to confinement so severe that they cannot even turn around. "The crating of pigs and veal calves is one of the cruelest elements of factory farming," says Henry Spira, coordinator for Animal Rights International and its Coalition for Nonviolent Food. "There is no pleasure in their lives from birth to slaughter." Breeding sows are confined to narrow crates in which they are unable to walk or turn around. On some farms, the sow is actually tied to the floor in an attempt to prevent her from crushing any of her piglets. Veal calves are taken away from their mothers at birth and kept chained inside small crates in darkened warehouses for 15 weeks before going to slaughter. In order to ensure that the calves' flesh will be white and tender, their only nourishment is typically an iron-deficient milk substitute that is laden with antibiotics, keeps the animals in an anemic state, and gives them chronic diarrhea.

Additional Suffering

Farm animals often suffer from deformities and health problems brought about by genetic engineering, improper breeding, and hormone manipulation. "Broiler chickens are bred for rapid growth and body bulk," says Mason. "Some broiler chickens' chests are so heavy they can't walk. Instead they must drag themselves around." Most livestock on factory farms are continuously fed subtherapeutic levels of antibiotics that enable the animals to grow despite the harsh conditions. Many scientists fear that human consumption of meat contaminated with antibiotic residues may account for the increasing number of antibiotic-resistant infections in humans.

Manure, dead animals, slaughterhouse offal, and the carcasses of animals unfit for human consumption, such as those with cancer, are fed not just to chickens but to all livestock, even strictly herbivorous animals like cattle and sheep. "We're turning cows into cannibals," says Howard Lyman, director of the Eating with Conscience campaign, sponsored by the Humane Society of the United States (HSUS). Dangerous heavy metals build up in manure, bones, and internal organs, such as kidneys and livers, and are then recycled back through livestock as feed. Disease organisms that survive in animal tissue processed into feed can infect the livestock. . . .

What Can Consumers Do?

What can individual consumers do to protect themselves, the animals, and the environment from a system of food production gone haywire? In the United Kingdom, the Royal Society for the Prevention of Cruelty to Animals has launched its Freedom Food Campaign, a labeling program that informs consumers the food they are buying was produced under high animal-welfare standards. In this country, HSUS's Eating with Conscience campaign, launched in the fall of 1994, recommends the three Rs—refine, reduce, and replace—encouraging consumers to refine their diets by buying only animal products that have been raised humanely, reduce their consumption of animal products, and replace animal products with other foods.

Replacing meat and other food derived from animals, such as dairy and eggs, is the only surefire way of guaranteeing that you are not inadvertently encouraging factory farming. Many, however, are not prepared to eliminate meat, dairy products, and eggs from their diets entirely. If this is how you feel, your best bet is to significantly reduce the amount of meat and other animal products in your diet. Try eating meat only three times a week or less. And when you do eat animal products, eat only those from animals raised humanely.

Eggs laid by so-called free-ranging chickens—as opposed to eggs laid by caged hens—were one of the first humane animal products to catch on in the marketplace. "NestEggs was the earliest and largest humane egg-production effort," says Kevin Morrisey, program officer for Food Animals Concerns Trust (FACT). Just 11 years ago, FACT developed criteria for humane egg production and contracted with farmers to produce eggs according to their standards: laying hens would roam free within large, open buildings, and they would have access to whole-grain unmedicated food, fresh water, nesting boxes, and scratching and dust bath areas. The project took off. Today over 1 million dozen eggs produced under the NestEggs label are sold annually. FACT's standards are strict. But, warns Gus W. Thornton, president of the Massachusetts Society for the Prevention of Cruelty to Animals, "just because an egg facility does not use battery cages does not mean there may not be significant problems for the hens if the facility is crowded and not properly managed.". . .

Meat Machines

Over 95% of all animals killed die for the meat market—a total of 5 billion a year in the U.S. alone. The overwhelming majority of them are now raised in intensive confinement, factory farms, where they are subjected to severe physical and psychological deprivation, unable to satisfy their most basic needs. Crammed into tiny cages with artificial lighting and fed drugs to keep them alive until slaughter, farm animals are treated as nothing more than meat machines.

Trans-Species Unlimited, flyer, undated.

Humanely raised meat and animal products are found in health-food stores, food co-ops, gourmet groceries, and natural-food markets. "The natural-food market is the fastest-growing niche in the supermarket industry," says John Nicholson, meat coordinator for the Massachusetts-based Bread & Circus Whole Foods Market, one of the nation's largest natural-food chains. But supplying customers with humanely raised animal products is a tough job. "Normally vendors are pounding on our door trying to get us to carry their product," says Nicholson. "But with humanely raised meat we have the opposite problem. We have to go and seek the products out. The demand is there but the supply is not."

If you live in a rural or suburban area that does not have natural-food markets, try going to a local farmer's market or heading out to visit family-run farms. Talk to the farmers. Small-scale farmers are the original entrepreneurs and are highly attuned to the development of new markets. Chances are, if they understand what you want, they will do their best to provide it. In addition, talk to the manager of your supermarket. Some large grocery chains have begun to carry humanely raised animal products at the consumer's request. "It doesn't take much of a squeak to get the wheel oiled," says HSUS's Lyman. If the stores near you don't carry products specifying that they are from humanely raised animals, look for those that are certified as organically raised. Organic feeding and humane conditions usually go hand in hand.

"Money is the most powerful thing in the world," says Lyman. "Every time you pick up your fork, you are making a decision about the way the food you eat is produced. Every time you're at the grocery store and you open your wallet and pull out your money to buy meat, you are either supporting a factory farm or a farm that raises livestock humanely."

"As more people have become aware of the cruelties of meat production, vegetarianism is rapidly gaining in popularity."

The Case for Vegetarianism

People for the Ethical Treatment of Animals

People for the Ethical Treatment of Animals (PETA), founded by Ingrid Newkirk and Alex Pacheco in 1980, with over 300,000 members, is the largest and most well-known animal-rights organization in the United States. In the following viewpoint, PETA summarizes the case for vegetarianism, asserting that meatless meals benefit one's health, alleviate animal suffering, protect the environment, and help provide additional food resources for human consumption.

As you read, consider the following questions:

1. As PETA describes them, what are the health benefits that a vegetarian enjoys?
2. Why does PETA consider becoming a vegetarian a moral choice?
3. What ecological arguments does PETA present to support its case for vegetarianism?

From People for the Ethical Treatment of Animals, *Factsheet #5*, "Vegetarianism: Eating for Life," June 1995. Reprinted with permission.

Vegetarianism has been a way of life for many people for centuries, and today nearly 20 million Americans are vegetarians; many more have greatly reduced their meat consumption. Recently, as the link between meat consumption and life-threatening illness has become more apparent, and as more people have become aware of the cruelties of meat production, vegetarianism is rapidly gaining in popularity.

Health Benefits

There is no nutritional need for humans to eat any animal products; all of our dietary needs, even as infants and children, are best supplied by an animal-free diet. Our evolutionary ancestors were, and our closest primate relatives are, vegetarians. Human teeth and intestines are designed for eating and digesting plant foods, so it is no wonder that our major health problems can be traced to meat consumption.

The consumption of animal products has been conclusively linked with heart disease, cancer, diabetes, arthritis, and osteoporosis. Cholesterol (found only in animal products) and animal fat clog arteries, leading to heart attacks and strokes. A vegetarian diet can prevent 97 percent of coronary occlusions. The rate of colon cancer is highest in regions where meat consumption is high, and lowest where meat-eating is uncommon. A similar pattern is evident for breast, cervical, uterine, ovarian, prostate, and lung cancers.

Low-fat diets, particularly those without saturated fat, have been instrumental in allowing many diabetics to dispense with their pills, shots, and pumps. A study of more than 25,000 people over age 21 found that vegetarians have a much lower risk of getting diabetes than meat-eaters.

A South African study found not a single case of rheumatoid arthritis in a community of 800 people who ate no meat or dairy products. Another study found that a similar group that ate meat and other high-fat foods had almost four times the incidence of arthritis as those on a low-fat diet.

Osteoporosis, or bone loss due to mineral (particularly calcium) depletion, is not so much a result of insufficient calcium as it is a result of eating too much protein. A 1983 Michigan State University study found that by age 65, male vegetarians had an average measurable bone loss of 3 percent; male meat-eaters, 18 percent; female vegetarians, 7 percent; female meat-eaters, 35 percent.

In addition to the problems associated with too much fat, cholesterol, and protein, consumers of animal products take in far greater amounts of residual agricultural chemicals, industrial pollutants, antibiotics, and hormones than do vegetarians. The absorption of antibiotics through meat-eating results in antibiotic-resistant strains of pneumonia, childhood meningitis, gonorrhea, salmonella, and other serious illnesses.

Approximately 9,000 Americans die annually from food-borne illness and an estimated 80 million others fall ill. The U.S. Department of Agriculture estimates that up to 40 percent of the poultry sold in this country is infected with salmonella bacteria.

BORN LOSER

The Born Loser reprinted by permission of Newspaper Enterprise Association, Inc.

Meat contains 14 times as many pesticide residues as plant foods, dairy products, more than five times as many. Fish is another source of dangerous residues. The EPA estimates that fishes can accumulate up to nine million times the level of cancer-causing polychlorinated biphenals (PCBs) found in the waters in which they live. Ninety-five percent of human exposure to dioxin, a "probable" cause of cancer and other health risks, comes through meat, fish, and dairy consumption.

Vegetarian Ethics

Human beings must consider what impact our actions have on the lives of others. To limit moral consideration to humans only is no more logical or justifiable than limiting concern to white people only or to men only; speciesism, like racism and sexism, is wrong because all animals contribute to the ecosystem and are capable of suffering. We do not need to eat meat, drink cows' or goats' milk or eat eggs to survive. Because today's system of mass production of these "products" causes pain, distress and ultimately death to the billions of animals from whom they are taken each year, we are ethically bound to renounce them.

Ecological Arguments

More than 4 million acres of cropland are lost to erosion in the United States every year. Of this staggering topsoil loss, 85 percent is directly associated with livestock raising, i.e., overgrazing.

Throughout the world, forests are being destroyed to support the meat-eating habits of the "developed" nations. Between 1960 and 1985, nearly 40 percent of all Central American rain forests were destroyed to create pasture for beef cattle. The rain forests are the primary source of oxygen for the entire planet; the very survival of the earth is linked to their survival. The forests also provide ingredients for many medicines used to treat and cure human illnesses, and these resources have yet to be explored for their full potential.

Much of the excrement from "food" animals (which amounts to 20 times as much fecal matter as human waste) flows unfiltered into our lakes and streams.

The production of one pound of beef requires 2,500 gallons of water. It takes less water to produce a *year's* worth of food for a pure vegetarian (a vegan; one who consumes no meat, eggs, or dairy products) than to produce a *month's* worth of food for a meat-eater.

Humanitarian Concerns

Raising animals for food is an extremely inefficient way to feed a growing human population. The U.S. livestock population consumes enough grain and soybeans to feed more than *five times* the entire U.S. population. One acre of pasture produces an average of 165 pounds of beef; the same acre can produce 20,000 pounds of potatoes.

If Americans reduced their meat consumption by only 10 percent, it would free 12 million tons of grain annually for human consumption. That alone would be enough to adequately feed each of the 60 million people who starve to death each year.

Be Healthy and Humane

When you consider the serious health risks of a meat- and dairy-based diet, the environmental devastation caused by animal agriculture, the huge waste of resources in a world faced with chronic human starvation, and the violence to and suffering of billions of animals kept cruelly confined on "factory farms," the switch to vegetarianism makes perfect sense.

"The new thinking is that meat fits into a healthy diet, as long as you strive for balance."

The Case for Eating Meat

Daryn Eller

In the following viewpoint, Daryn Eller argues that meat provides many vitamins and minerals that are more readily absorbed than those supplied by vegetables. Noting that more low-fat meats are now available, he recommends that consumers—especially women—include meat and milk, along with vegetables, in their daily intake of food in order to maintain a healthy body. Daryn Eller writes about fitness and nutrition for numerous national magazines.

As you read, consider the following questions:

1. Why does Eller stress that it is important for women to eat meat?
2. According to the author, what are the benefits of eating meat?
3. Why, in Eller's estimate, is it important to eat both meat and vegetables?

Daryn Eller, "Should You Eat Meat?" *Redbook*, March 1994. Reprinted by permission of the author.

Enjoying a juicy hamburger has begun to seem like a reckless act—all that fat and artery-clogging cholesterol! But few people have given up meat entirely. What's more, sales of pork have actually increased, and both beef and lamb sales are holding steady. And nutrition experts say that's just fine—the new thinking is that meat fits into a healthy diet, as long as you strive for balance.

What's So Good About Meat?

Certain kinds of meat are leaner now than they used to be, thanks to new breeding and feeding programs. Pork had 31 percent less fat in 1990 than in 1983, according to a University of Wisconsin study. Many beef producers are studying cows' genetic traits so they can select for those that produce tender meat without the extra fat, reports Eric Hentges, Ph.D., director of nutrition research for the National Livestock and Meat Board. The beef industry is even providing financial incentives to breeders who produce leaner animals.

Nutritionally, meat packs a wallop: It provides abundant amounts of crucial vitamins and minerals, including B vitamins, iron, and zinc. You can get zinc and iron from seafood and poultry, but meat generally weighs in with more. Women in particular, who lose iron due to their menstrual cycle, may benefit from meat's high dose of the mineral.

Many plant foods are mineral-rich, too, but most of the minerals they contain aren't as readily absorbed by the body as those found in animal foods. Meat has the edge over vegetables because it contains stearic acid, which aids in the absorption of iron. What's more, stearic acid helps make *any* iron in your meal—including that contained in vegetables—more absorbable, explains Phyllis Johnson, Ph.D., associate director for the Pacific West area of the Agricultural Research Service of the United States Department of Agriculture (USDA).

The Low-Down on Fat

Even the leanest meat isn't low fat—some cuts derive more than 60 percent of their calories from fat, 20 percent of which is saturated (the primary culprit behind high cholesterol levels). According to the American Heart Association (AHA), fat should make up no more than 30 percent of your total calories, and only 10 percent of that should be saturated fat. For women consuming 1,800 to 2,200 calories per day, that's 50 to 60 grams of fat, 20 to 24 grams of which can be saturated.

Since a serving of meat has anywhere from 4 to 9 grams or more of fat, depending on the cut, it may seem that the easiest way to meet the AHA guidelines is to give up meat completely. But it doesn't have to come to that. "What matters most is not how much fat a particular food has but rather how much fat you eat in one day," says Liz Marr, R.D., a Denver-based spokesperson for the American Dietetic Association. A balanced diet is the key. New guidelines from the USDA recommend limiting protein foods—including poultry, seafood, dried beans, eggs, and nuts as well as meat—to two or three servings per day (a serving is two to three ounces).

Not a Vegetarian

I share with many people across the political spectrum a concern that food animals be treated in accordance with basic humanitarian principles.

Those opposed to the torture of innocent, defenseless beasts should not be dismissed as extremists who want animals to have the same rights as humans. I eat meat (though, given present practices, not veal or pork). While I admire vegetarians, I do not share their sacrifice.

Philip D. Oliver, *Los Angeles Times*, February 26, 1993.

Meat shouldn't be your *only* source of protein. The more you vary your protein sources, the greater your chance of getting a variety of nutrients, including some that meat doesn't provide. For example, fish contains cholesterol-lowering fatty acids, and beans are packed with fiber. Both are also very low in fat.

Skinnier Meat

New types of low-fat meat, now available in most supermarkets, are made with safe, natural fat substitutes. But even these may get up to 45 percent of their calories from fat, though that's still less than regular lean ground beef, with 54 percent of calories from fat. A lighter option is Healthy Choice's low-fat ground beef—it contains a fat substitute made from oat flour and gets only 28 percent of its calories from fat.

The way you prepare meat can slim it down, too. Broiling and grilling, for instance, allow fat to drip off during cooking. And since heat causes some fat to migrate into the meat, you can reduce fat content about 20 percent by trimming the external fat *before* cooking.

The Right Balance

No woman can live by meat alone. The USDA recommends eating at least five half-cup servings of produce—two helpings of fruit, three of vegetables—every day, not just to get enough vitamins and minerals but also to help prevent disease. At least one of those servings should be a food rich in vitamin A—sweet pota-toes or carrots, for instance—and one a good source of vitamin C, such as tomatoes or cantaloupe, according to the National Cancer Institute. These vitamins, which aren't found in meat, may help lower the risk of cancer.

Meat also lacks fiber, which helps keep cholesterol levels low and guards against colon cancer. The best sources are whole-grain foods—the USDA recommends 6 to 11 half-cup servings a day. Lastly, you need two helpings of low-fat dairy products to supply calcium for keeping bones strong—one cup of skim milk or yogurt or one ounce of low-fat cheese equals a serving.

"The tenacious pioneers of gene pharming continue to show faith in their living, breathing protein factories."

Farm Animals Should Be Genetically Engineered

Tabitha Powledge

In the following viewpoint, Tabitha Powledge describes the emerging use of animals as bioreactors producing medicines from mammary glands. Such "gene pharming" will become common practice, she contends, when regulatory and economic forces become favorable. Powledge, the founding editor of the *Scientist*, is a freelance writer specializing in life sciences and science policy.

As you read, consider the following questions:

1. What technological procedures, as the author describes them, now make "gene pharming" possible?
2. Why, in Powledge's estimate, will pigs and rabbits be the animals of choice among gene pharmers?
3. According to Powledge, what obstacles must developers overcome for gene pharming to become a profitable industry?

Tabitha Powledge, "Gene Pharming," *Technology Review*, August/September 1992. Reprinted by permission of the author.

A small group of scientists share an odd vision. They look at a pasture dotted with tranquil, grazing farm animals and see the pharmaceutical factories of the future.

Gene Pharming: The Use of Animals as Bioreactors

Katherine Gordon and her colleagues at Genzyme Corp. of Framingham, Mass., reported in 1987 that the milk of their genetically engineered mice contained a human protein that dissolves blood clots, called tissue plasminogen activator (tPA). Media interest in the concept of using animals as so-called bioreactors to produce medicines in their milk or blood—dubbed "gene pharming"—has been enormous ever since. At least four companies have announced that they have made or are working on some seven products in transgenic animals. More research is under way, but also under wraps.

In 1992 scientists, for the first time, reported production of various therapeutic proteins in livestock. Researchers at Pharmaceutical Proteins Ltd. in Edinburgh, Scotland, have enabled three sheep to yield a biologically active protein, human alpha$_1$-antitrypsin. The absence of this protein, a cause of emphysema, is inherited and leads to one of the most common fatal disorders in males of European descent, with more than 20,000 men in the United States affected. Therapy requires 200 grams of alpha$_1$-antitrypsin per year for each patient—a demand the present source, human plasma, cannot meet. One of the sheep produced the highest level yet reported for any foreign protein made in milk, 35 grams per liter, making large-scale production of alpha$_1$-antitrypsin look possible.

At about the same time, scientists from Tufts University and Genzyme reported that genetically engineered goats had produced a long-acting variant of human tPA. This same collaboration has also resulted in transgenic mice that secrete into their milk the gene product believed to cause cystic fibrosis (CF). Genzyme is exploring this protein partly because that may be the only way of getting large enough quantities needed for research on developing therapies for CF, the most common fatal genetic disease in the United States.

But there's a catch to the hubbub over gene pharming. "Although everyone thinks it's a very neat feat of technical facility," says Harvey Bialy, research editor of the journal *Bio/Technology*, "the response of scientists has been almost uniformly skeptical" about the technology's potential for widespread practical use. Although technical hurdles remain, the trickiest part could be getting the economics right.

Animal genetic engineering for medical purposes has already achieved modest success, with, for example, the development of transgenic mice and rats as models for human disease. Altering the genetic makeup of farm animals seems like a natural step, considering that we have bred them to order for thousands of years. But the engineering of these species by recombinant-DNA techniques has been mostly disappointing. The much greater expense and time involved in breeding livestock has led to far less research on these animals, with a concomitant smaller number of successful transgenic offspring. So far, scientists have tended to find that even when foreign genes merge with the old, they fail to bring forth their customary protein product—or result in animals that are freaks.

In some cases, these problems would disappear if the foreign genes confined their work to tissues or organs where they cannot cause toxic effects. And if the target tissue were a renewable body fluid, the fluid could be withdrawn and the gene product extracted. The animal would become a bioreactor, a whole-organism version of the vats that churn out useful molecules from genetically engineered microbes or mammalian cell cultures in today's biotechnology factories. But which fluids? The proteins that would be produced don't find their way into urine unless an animal is sick. And blood has serious drawbacks. Either the costly transgenic animal must be sacrificed to recover the blood, or the extractors must confine themselves to infrequent harvests, taking only what the animal can spare. Most animal biotechnologists believe the public would be repelled by a drug from slaughtered animals.

Still, animal blood may be the best place to manufacture some proteins—especially human hemoglobin, which, as the protein in blood that carries oxygen, could serve as a substitute for whole-blood transfusions. Transfusions of pure human hemoglobin, separated from animal blood, could not only finesse the problem of incompatible blood types, but also, in these AIDS-conscious times, eliminate the risk of disease transmission. So far, one company—DNX Corp., of Princeton, N.J.—has reported that it has genetically engineered pigs to produce human hemoglobin.

Getting Medicine from Elsie the Cow

Nevertheless, when biotechnologists usually conjure up visions of the animal factory, they are thinking about the organ that defines the Order Mammalia—the mammary gland, which is talented at adding the fancy bits of sugar that human proteins often require to work right. And while milk has shortcomings (only adult females make it, and for limited periods), big animals can produce it in large quantities and it can be made chock-full of a desired drug. And milk enjoys good press. Who wouldn't want medicine from Elsie the cow?

To enable an animal to produce a drug in its milk, geneticists first create a hybrid gene. They fuse a human gene that makes a desirable protein (read "drug") to a chunk of animal DNA that targets protein production in the mammary gland. Then they inject the hybrid gene into zygotes (early animal embryos), transfer the zygotes into the wombs of foster mothers, and hope.

Just getting the zygotes is a major challenge. In the most common procedure, scientists treat the adult female animal with hormones to force the ovary to release as many eggs as possible, and then fertilize them while they are still making their way toward the uterus. The resulting zygotes are removed surgically. Transfer to the foster animal has also been surgical.

Producing More Milk

Milk. It's been a staple for ages among children, adolescents and adults. We're told milk helps build strong teeth and bones and healthy bodies.

Over the last several years, scientists have been developing genetically engineered products to help dairy cows produce more milk.

On November 5, 1993, the Food and Drug Administration approved one such product, sometribove (Posilac), Monsanto Co.'s genetically engineered bovine somatotropin (bST).

Genetically engineered, or recombinant, bST is virtually identical to a cow's natural somatotropin, a hormone produced in its pituitary gland that stimulates milk production. The primary difference between the two is that rbST may include additional amino acids. Injecting rbST can increase a cow's milk production by 10 to 15 percent.

Kevin L. Ropp, *FDA Consumer*, May 1994.

But in September 1991, scientists in the Netherlands reported production of transgenic cattle zygotes in the lab instead of in cows. They collected eggs from slaughterhouse ovaries, fertilized them with bull semen that had been frozen, and transferred the zygotes into foster mothers without surgery. The result (from 2,500 eggs that winnowed down to 103 zygotes, which led in turn to just 21 pregnancies) was the world's first transgenic calves. All two of them.

"The whole process is abysmally inefficient at the moment," Alan Smith, research director of Genzyme, concedes. "And that just means it's expensive." At this point, the price tag for a transgenic cow is estimated at $500,000.

To improve the success rate, Genzyme and others are trying to develop ways of screening zygotes before injecting them into females. "At the moment it's just done blind," Smith says. One way might be to culture the injected eggs beyond one or two cells. Because the cells have not yet specialized, a 32-cell embryo can be split and half popped into the fridge while the other half is analyzed for the gene of interest. The scrutinized cells can no longer be used, but "as soon as you've identified the positive ones, then you can put the other half back into animals," which will in turn produce transgenic offspring, says Lothar Hennighausen, who coauthored the first gene-pharming paper with Katherine Gordon and now develops model animal bioreactors at the National Institutes of Health.

While screening zygotes can reduce the cost of making transgenic animals, it cannot ensure the efficient production of desirable drugs. The transferred genes may not always produce proteins during the normal lactation period. In many cases, transgenic animals are producing proteins of interest during pregnancy, which can cause lactation to stop too soon, Hennighausen says.

The answer to getting the gene to produce a protein at the right time relates to the DNA sequences that control the timing of production. Although such sequences have not yet been identified in livestock, they have been found in other species, leading researchers to feel confident that they can also find them in farm animals.

Milking Transgenic Pigs and Rabbits

Still another problem is determining which animal should be used to produce a drug. Attention has focused largely on the three animals humanity has been milking for thousands of years: sheep, goats, and cattle.

Cattle might seem like the obvious first choice. But cash cows are not so easy to come by; compared with the other animals, their gestation and development is longer, close to 40 months from conception to lactation. Because of that, as well as the surgery that's been needed and the simple facts that they eat more food and need more space, transgenic cows are much pricier than the alternatives.

NIH's Hennighausen thinks pigs have been unjustly ignored by most researchers. To make a transgenic pig that expresses a foreign protein in milk costs roughly $25,000, he says, whereas a similar goat costs almost three times as much. Yet a sow with 10 piglets lactates 10 liters of milk every day, far more than a goat. And pigs bear litters of up to a dozen young, instead of the one or two usually produced by sheep, goats, and cattle. DNX estimates that with normal commercial breeding a single transgenic pig could generate a production herd of 100,000 in just three to five years.

Rabbits might even be the animal of choice for some proteins.

Rabbits are small, cheap, bear large litters, have short generation times, and are easy to maintain. A large colony would be a management headache, but just a few rabbits, which each give up to a liter of milk a day, could make drugs—such as the blood-clotting factors VIII and IX, in demand to treat hemophilia—needed only in tiny amounts.

The economics of gene pharming present a paradox. The eventual high-volume production will mean very inexpensive manufacturing costs enabling pharmaceutical firms to make more profit than by producing drugs in other ways. But companies probably won't have sufficient incentive to first make long-term investments in drugs they see as bringing in only marginal gains, says Katherine Gordon, who recently left Genzyme to do consulting. And the markup on new pharmaceuticals is so high that the manufacturing method has little bearing on the retail cost, says Alan Colman, a biologist who helped start Pharmaceutical Proteins.

So the fact that producing a particular protein in milk is—eventually—very cheap isn't a good enough reason to do it. The key is to pick proteins that can't be made in any other way or that can be made only by animal bioreactors in needed volumes. That is why Genzyme has no plans to commercialize its milk-derived tissue plasminogen activator, a protein already produced in adequate amounts from cell culture. And it is why Pharmaceutical Proteins is pursuing human alpha$_1$-antitrypsin (the protein whose absence causes emphysema) and factor IX, which is now available to hemophiliacs only in very limited quantities.

Making Sure Pharmed Drugs Are Safe

Say you've come up with a drug that can only be produced by gene pharming, and you're willing to invest the time and money. You've selected an animal bioreactor and solved the technological problems of getting the transgenic offspring to lactate properly. One last issue remains: purifying the therapeutic proteins from the milk and delivering a safe, consistent drug. After all, milk is also stuffed with other proteins and contains enzymes that break down proteins.

Quality control and assurance are particularly daunting aspects of the purity problem. Living animals present sanitation challenges undreamed of by those who make other recombinant-DNA products. For example, will the valuable beasts be permitted to graze in pastures, or must they be kept indoors? Will they have to eat the same thing all the time in order to ensure form production?

"A problem we have to face is the possible contamination of the product with viruses," acknowledges Colman of Edinburgh's Pharmaceutical Proteins. One that is much on his mind is the virus that causes scrapie, a virulent disease of sheep. Thus, he notes, "we're flying in 600 sheep from New Zealand, which is a scrapie-free island, because we're starting a scrapie-free herd to continue our pharmaceutical work."

The regulatory climate could also be a factor. Some observers think that the U.S. Food and Drug Administration (FDA) might want to look particularly closely at novel production methods involving both genetic engineering and live animals. Regulators might want to ensure that the manufacturing techniques don't affect safety and efficacy. But some think that the FDA will not be much tougher on gene-pharmed products than on drugs now made by recombinant-DNA technology. Authorities might feel comfortable just checking the protein produced by the live bioreactor method, says Gordon. And while the Food and Drug Administration will doubtless look especially closely at the first cases, the agency has been streamlining its process in response to demand for some new drugs. Hennighausen says he can imagine that a protein like the blood-clotting factor VIII or IX would get a friendly reception because of today's limited supplies.

Next Steps for the Animal Bioreactor

Genzyme's mouse milk production of cystic fibrosis transmembrane conductance regulator (CFTR), the protein believed to be defective in cystic fibrosis, opens up the prospect of a new class of therapeutic molecules. All the other molecules produced so far in animal bioreactors are soluble proteins that, in milk, end up drifting around. But CFTR is one of a group of proteins that reside in membrane and are called membrane proteins. These proteins run a kind of shuttle service for crucial chemicals that need to get in and out of the body's cells.

The significance of Genzyme's CFTR production is that scientists previously have been able to produce only small amounts of membrane proteins before they kill the cell medium in which they're growing, according to Smith, the company's research director. Genzyme came up with the idea of sequestering the membrane containing CFTR from other cells. The mammary gland, as it happens, is an excellent place to try that strategy because its membrane engulfs butterfat globules as they bud off from mammary cells. Eventually the membrane floats away from the mammary cells to become part of the cream.

Although Genzyme has not yet shown that the CFTR it has produced has biological activity, it regards membrane proteins as attractive candidates for future work. Of particular interest are the proteins that transport viruses into cells. If such viral transporters can be developed in quantity by animal bioreactors, researchers may be able to use them to figure out specifically how various disease-causing viruses enter cells. Then scientists can develop techniques to prevent the diseases.

In another new area of research, Pharmaceutical Proteins is considering whether animal bioreactors could make products other than drugs. One idea is to target the thriving market in modified milk; livestock mammary glands might, for example, be an interesting place to produce human infant formula for the many babies allergic to beta lactoglobulin, a protein in cow's milk. Milk from a cow without the gene for beta lactoglobulin could trigger no allergic reactions while providing other important proteins. Researchers have still, however, to remove any gene from the DNA of livestock.

Despite such possibilities, investors have not yet stampeded toward the animal bioreactor. The field "hasn't shown huge promise yet," says John McCamant, publisher of the *AgBiotech Stock Letter*. "We're watching it closely, but it needs to be further along before we can get an investment grasp on it."

But the tenacious pioneers of gene pharming continue to show faith in their living, breathing protein factories. The researchers used to find it difficult to convince anybody that they could create animals that produced therapeutic molecules, recalls Harry Meade, who heads Genzyme's animal bioreactor group. "But now there are bioreactors walking around, making a lot of these proteins."

"We have, I believe, a moral obligation to consider what effect is produced on an animal—any sentient creature—by introducing a genetic characteristic that is not a part of its own species history."

Farm Animals Should Not Be Genetically Engineered

Raymond Giraud

In the following viewpoint, Raymond Giraud addresses moral issues that he believes biologists must consider when working with recombinant DNA. In addition to urging genetic engineers to include the suffering of sentient creatures in their scientific calculations, he cautions transgenic researchers not to succumb to corporate or institutionalized greed. Giraud is professor emeritus of French literature at Stanford University in Palo Alto, California.

As you read, consider the following questions:

1. According to Giraud, what are some of the undesirable effects farm animals experience as the result of transgenic technology?
2. In Giraud's opinion, how does Jeremy Rifkin's notion of the "desacralization of nature" help us understand the acceptance of transgenic enterprises?
3. What, broadly speaking, are the ethical options that the author presents?

Excerpted from "Ethical Considerations in the Use of Transgenic Animals" by Raymond Giraud, *Between the Species*, no. 10, Winter/Spring 1994. Reprinted by permission of the publisher.

It is eminently understandable to view the development of transgenic animals as an exciting area of research, a new technology, promising new biologically engineered solutions to many important problems—among them, food and health.

But, like many other areas of modern scientific research and development, the history of biotechnology has also been marked by less altruistic promises: fame, promotion, and, of course, financial reward for individuals, as well as immense potential profits for the institutions that employ them.

For some universities, grants from the National Institutes of Health have become so important in the budget that they have taken the place of the Department of Defense funding that these institutions had come to be heavily dependent on during the Vietnam war. With the new sources of income provided by the biotechnology revolution, in which the creation of transgenic animals is now at the forefront, both individuals and institutions have flung themselves into a race for patents, with the prospect of wealth beyond the dreams of avarice. . . .

Animal Suffering as a Moral Issue

Among the moral issues that I believe biologists might consider encouraging their students to reflect on is, first and foremost, *the pain suffered by the animals.* Many thoughtful ecologists who contemplate our manipulation of animals of other species than our own are troubled by a fear that the evolutionary process will be affected or that Nature's rich array of species will be impoverished. What is often forgotten, however, is that for the individuals of a species, there can also be intense pain and terror, not to speak of the almost inevitable deprivation of life. One might call this an ontogenic concern, as opposed to the predominantly phylogenic concern of ecologists. These hurts and deprivations are far from being negligible, as, for example, when medical researchers take a blow torch to the body of a living pig in order to study the pathology of burns or break the back of a rat to learn how that affects the animal's capacity for penile erection. In these, as in an almost infinite number of other experiments—many of them useless by any reasonable standard—the researcher's right to know, and possibly to profit from the knowledge acquired, collides with the individual animal's right not to be mistreated in this way.

Similarly, in the creation of transgenic animals, pain is a factor that should not be left out of whatever equations one constructs: pain for the fleshy pigs whose skeleton is inadequate to bear added weight, for cows whose distended udders scrape the ground and make it difficult for them to walk. The only sensitive comment on this that I have so far encountered in a scientific journal was a letter from a Canadian veterinarian published in

Nature, I believe, in which he protested the neglect of this consideration in the literature he had read about transgenic animals. (He was referring specifically to the physical discomfort implicit in the introduction of genetic characteristics into an organism unprepared for them by its previous evolutionary development.)

Also among the innocent victims of this sort of experimentation are the millions of transgenic mice who are sacrificed (the word of choice among researchers), in the ratio of thousands used to produce one mouse in whom a gene is successfully implanted—that is in such a way that the genetic characteristic actually expresses itself in the animal.

It is well known that AIDS, in the form that afflicts human beings, is a condition—"a syndrome"—that has not naturally manifested itself in other species. Yet, a medical technology that has refused to liberate itself from the obsolete procedure of seeking cures for human ailments and injuries by making healthy non-human animals sick or injuring them is still engaged in attempts to create artificially a transgenic animal that will carry the virus, despite the misgivings of many researchers who believe that clinical studies offer the best hopes of success.

We have, I believe, a moral obligation to consider what effect is produced on an animal—any sentient creature—by introducing a genetic characteristic that is not part of its own species history, a change imposed invasively only to make use of the animal for some purpose alien to its own being.

The Moral Problems with Transgenic Industries

That purpose can, in fact, be very self-serving (publication, prestige, profit). There was, for example, not much interest in AIDS in the bio-medical industry before the money started flowing. I know of at least two of my colleagues at Stanford, who run what are known in the medical school as "mouse factories," who expanded into the AIDS business with loud cries about their service to humanity and have just started up their own profit-making companies. We may justly question the ethics of scientists who seek to enrich themselves not only through the suffering of countless animal victims, but also from research initially funded by grants of the taxpayers' money.

We should also not forget that the bio-medical use of animals has mushroomed into a multibillion-dollar industry, including, amid the breeding for sale of many species, a veritable explosion of marketable strains of transgenic mice. The manufacture of food, cages, stereotaxic devices and a multitude of high-priced gadgets, is an immense business. For a glimpse at some of its not always visible dimensions, study the trade magazine *Lab Animal*. In August 1990, Stanford's Department of Comparative Medicine hosted what it called a "rodent seminar," complete with refreshments (wine and cheese!), sponsored by the Charles River Breeding Laboratories, the world's largest lab animal factory—one example among many of the ties between today's universities and the corporate world. (See Martin Kenney's book, *Biotechnology: The University-Industrial Complex*, Yale Univ. Press, 1986, for a wealth of documentation on this.)

The Application of Two Moral Concepts

I might here invoke two of those major moral concepts that we presumably honor in our conduct toward other human beings (although often more in the breach than in the observance), but which we dismiss out of hand when it comes to our treatment of nonhuman animals:

Might does not make right. There is no question that we could not do what we do to animals if they were not powerless to resist us. What we do is "right" only for those who embrace an ethical philosophy that legitimizes power.

The end does not justify the means used to attain it. (See Simone de Beauvoir's *Pour une morale de l'ambiguïté* for a perceptive analysis of this often grossly simplified issue.) Assuming that the ends sought by the creation and use of transgenic animals are desirable (an assumption that deserves to be freshly questioned in each instance), does this end justify the means? How legitimate is it to "use" sentient creatures as means to an end? Moral philosophers have long argued against treating human beings as means to an end, rather than as ends in themselves. Kant's is doubtless the most familiar formulation of the concept: "So act as to treat humanity, whether in thine own person or in that of any other, in every case as an end withal, never as means only." On the threshold of the twenty-first century, we ought to be morally advanced enough not only to actualize at long last that precept for human beings, but to consider its extension to nonhuman animals.

Or are we to cling to our self-appointed role of master species, as some of us refuse to relinquish the myth that they are a master race or a master gender? Are nonhuman animals so alien, so inferior to us, as Jews and gypsies were to the Nazis and people of color to white supremacists, that we are morally at liberty to discard ethical principles when it comes to what we do with and to them?

Certainly, in practice our species has proceeded generally on that assumption, and has used nonhuman animals as economic resources to exploit and as products for consumption. To abandon these practices and the attitudes that legitimize them will doubtless represent a revolutionary ideological and behavioral change for humankind. We might recall, however, that it has been only recently in the history of our species that the legitimacy of slavery came into serious question (for example, the

157

framers of the U.S. Constitution resisted proposals to deal with the issue in that document), as well as the use of women for breeding children and for cheap labor. In fact, the treatment of women as the property of their husbands and as a morally, intellectually and physically inferior "subspecies" continues unabated in many areas of the world.

Animals as Human Property

Genetic engineering represents the concretization of the *absolute* claim that animals belong to us and exist for us. We have always used animals, of course, either for food, fashion, or sport. It is not new that we are now using animals for farming, even in especially cruel ways. *What is new is that we are now employing the technological means of absolutely subjugating the nature of animals so that they become totally and completely human property.*

Andrew Linzey, *Animal Theology*, 1995.

In theory, too, we have still not liberated ourselves (or our nonhuman animal victims) from the archaic idea that even very bright men, like the great 17th-century French philosopher and scientist René Descartes, clung to, namely, that nonhuman animals are soulless automatons, animated not by thought or feelings, but by some sort of clockwork mechanism.

Today's scientists who try to still their conscience as well as ours by denying animals of species other than our own the capacity to think and have emotions and feelings, including pleasure and pain, must confront the contradiction between that anthropocentric fallacy and the practice of exploiting animals because they are like us and may even be related to us (assuming we don't wish totally to repudiate Darwin—who wrote, incidentally, with great warmth of individual animals for whom he had come to have real affection and a strong feeling of kinship).

Is It Ethical to Improve Animals Transgenically?

The engineering of transgenic animals inevitably brings to mind all the disputes about eugenics, as applied to the "improvement" of domesticated animals and human beings—a notion that received much attention in Hitler's Germany, but which had been conceived and practiced earlier and is still with us.

There is, however, a substantial difference between the relatively slow process of selective breeding (not natural selection, but selective by human design) and what has come to be called genetic engineering, even though some of the scientists working in this field minimize the distinction, obviously because they hope that will make what they are doing seem less disturbing. (A striking example is the 1987 statement on "Introduction of Recombinant DNA-Engineered Organisms into the Environment" issued by the National Academy of Sciences.) It is true that both practices are alike in that they thwart the slow natural evolutionary process, but genetic engineering is far more radically invasive of the organism and destructive of its integrity.

But just how sacred is the "natural" evolutionary process? A group of scientists recently made modest newspaper headlines by declaring that we have always tampered with "nature" and that an absolute opposition to any interference with a "natural" environment calls into question practically all of human history. Their gambit seems to me on the order of setting up a straw man, the demolition of which proves very little. Of course, we have always "tampered with nature"; only the most benighted dogmatist would pretend otherwise. But it is equally evident that we have not always done so very wisely. Witness the massive deforestations both past and present and today's truly criminal destruction of the environment. The real question is: how far do we go? Can we best deal with this problem by concocting a rigid formula for setting bounds to our interventions or should we be unrelentingly critical and constantly reevaluating a situation that is not fixed and permanent, but in perpetual flux? Above all, when the interests—indeed, the very lives—of groups other than the "tamperers" are involved, must there not be ethically guided control?

To pursue this line rigorously means to question the moral value, as well as the feasibility and utility, of every invention or innovation that promises to alter the conditions of our existence and that of the other animals with whom we share the earth. Moreover, the questions and the decisions that follow them ought not to be left to scientists. In a democratic society, we should all claim the right to participate in decisions that affect all the inhabitants of the planet.

Rifkin's Desacralization of Nature

The question is thus not whether we are to refrain absolutely from transforming the world we live in. Rather, we, as thinking beings whose consciousness (or conscience) has come to require ethical decisions, must assume responsibility for oversight and regulation of the changes proposed by scientific activists.

This issue is related to what Jeremy Rifkin calls the "desacralization" of nature. In an argument he developed in his 1983 book *Algeny*, Rifkin describes the success of a mechanistic model of the universe, laying particular stress on the triumph of the Darwinian conception of evolution, which Rifkin sees as leading to the present-day mechanistic ideology of the genetic engineers—and, for that matter, of behaviorists like the late B.F. Skinner and the sociobiologists. For Rifkin, desacralization "allows human beings to repudiate the intimate relationship and likeness that exist between ourselves and all other things that live."

Rifkin's analysis of the profanization of nature and desacralization of animals is consonant with his critique of the reductionist definition of life as a code to be deciphered and of living entities as so many bundles of information. To be sure, that has become an important aspect of our contemporary conception of what a lifeform is, what with the development of both DNA technology and computers, and also with what I might call the *desubjectification* of life in this century, in both the capitalist and the socialist countries. It should also be evident, however, that these perceptions amount to only a small segment of our experience of the total phenomenon of life.

What place does this reductionist vision offer to the ethical considerations which are not part of the genetically transmitted "code" of life, but which are inseparable from the human race's history—not only the history that others have made in the past, but the history that we ourselves have the capacity to participate in making and which, when all is said and done we may well deem the most precious part of our identity?

The Reductionist Conception of Life

There are other kinds of reductionism relatable to that of the mechanistic biological engineer, among them that view of economic and political behavior that minimizes moral factors so as to enable those who control our society—like those who have come to dominate some areas of scientific activity—to subordinate ethical considerations to the quest for power and wealth. In what is now being called "corporate culture" (and, sad to say, university "culture" too), this can mean that the material success of the institution transcends the individuals who constitute it, although the individual is presumed to find personal fulfillment in helping the institution to realize its goals. It is that kind of thinking that has facilitated the corporatization of many of our universities—those (like the University of California, for example) that we call "public," as well as those that call themselves "private" (like Stanford).

Our choice is, therefore, not simply between secularism and retaining a belief in the "sacredness" of life. Without having a set of beliefs consistent with those of the established supernatural religions, without divinizing "Mother Nature," one may still reject or at least be skeptical of the impoverished mechanistic reductionist conception of life that we associate with both Descartes and Skinner.

Compare the present ideology of the scientific establishment (as represented by some of its avatars, like the American Medical Association, the American Association for the Advancement of Science, the National Academy of Sciences and the great established research universities), characterized by its reverence for material achievement, with Albert Schweitzer's doctrine of reverence for life, mindful that he, too, was a scientist, a practicing physician, and not a comic-strip guru. Which do we want to impart to our students?

What Do We Want?

Do we want students at our universities to be coopted into a creed of greed, that subordinates humane values to financial gain (a concept that also expresses itself in oppressive labor policies and indifference to political and social justice)? Do we want them to internalize the values of academic administrators who have supported the selling of the universities to corporate interests and the racist apartheid regime in South Africa with their investment policies and continued war research and the production of nuclear weapons as part of the university's mission?

Are these the attitudes, the goals, the values we prize? Let us not be naïve. Neither the universities' institutional behavior nor their ideology is truly impartial or neutral. Our science is not value-free, and we should have the candor to recognize that. Our science, like our other institutions, is oriented toward the maximization of profits and the minimization of human values and ethical concerns. (Indeed, we have seen something of a new discipline developing in some faculties: the study of ethics as a branch of learning dedicated to legitimizing in pseudo-ethical terms what humane ethics condemns as monstrous and inhumane.)

The Choice Between Two Ethics

What then is our bottom-line choice? I suggest that it is, broadly speaking, between two ethics, two courses of action:

A. The perpetuation of a mechanistic science dedicated to the survival of a profit- and power-oriented society. We might also recognize that the treatment of both human and nonhuman animals as objects under our control and made to serve our ends, instead of as conscious subjects—what Rifkin calls desacralization—reflects an ethic of domination, in which control of both animals and humans is associated with a general domination of nature. At least since the Renaissance, our civilization ("Western Civilization") has seen nature as our adversary, to be fought, conquered, mastered, harnessed, "raped," and, of course, exploited for economic advantage—an aggressive, invasive, selfish and totally anthropocentric and doubtless phallocentric view of the world.

B. The inculcation of an ethic of compassion and empathetic understanding that respects the subjective experience of other sentient beings, both human and nonhuman, and an intellectual attitude that questions authority, distances itself from subservience to the corporate world and to those who seek to corrupt our institutions of higher learning by making them dependent on it for trickle-down handouts.

Is what I have said tantamount to intransigent opposition to any modification of the genetic structure of animals? Not quite. I can conceive of legitimate applications of genetic research, provided that they are not exploitive of human or animal subjects (*i.e.* acknowledging their *subjectivity*) or inconsistent with their welfare. That would, I fear, rule out almost everything presently going on in our laboratories, because the welfare of the nonhuman animals experimented on there is totally disregarded. Transgenic animals are being created primarily to benefit corporate interests, researchers and the institutions they serve. Most are condemned to death and even the survivors are treated as objects without moral value.

One last word. If the subject is not to be exploited, even benevolent action intended to promote its welfare presents a moral issue. Can it be imposed without being invasive? The "informed consent" that only recently has been required for experimentation on human subjects is obviously out of the question for nonhuman animals. It is, therefore, imperative that their interests be represented, however imperfectly, by human advocates. I should like to believe that some of those advocates who will lend their voice to speak on behalf of the animals will be found among our students. Why should they not include students of biology—the science that studies and that should respect—if not revere—life?

Periodical Bibliography

The following articles have been selected to supplement the diverse views presented in this chapter. Addresses are provided for periodicals not indexed in the *Readers' Guide to Periodical Literature*, the *Alternative Press Index*, or the *Social Sciences Index*.

American Dietetic Association
"Position of the American Dietetic Association: Vegetarian Diets," *Journal of the American Dietetic Association*, November 1993. Available from 216 W. Jackson Blvd., Suite 800, Chicago, IL 60606.

Digby Anderson
"Vegemaniacs," *National Review*, November 1, 1993.

Michael Castleman
"Flesh Wounds," *Sierra*, March/April 1995.

Stanley Curtis
"Acting Responsibly," *Agricultural Engineering*, May 1993. Available from 2950 Niles Rd., St. Joseph, MI 49085.

Alan Farnham
"Skewering Perdue," *Fortune*, February 24, 1992.

Greta Gaard
"Milking Mother Nature: An Ecofeminist Critique of rBGH," *Ecologist*, November/December 1994.

Kathryn Paxton George
"Should Feminists Be Vegetarians?" *Signs*, Winter 1994.

Suzanne Hamlin
"Eating in 1994: The Year Beef Came Back," *New York Times*, December 28, 1994.

Tony Hiss
"How Now, Drugged Cow: Biotechnology Comes to Rural Vermont," *Harper's Magazine*, October 1994.

Thomas Jukes
"Today's Non-Orwellian Animal Farm," *Nature*, February 13, 1992.

Steve Kopperud
"What's Animal Agriculture Doing About Animal Rights?" *Agricultural Engineering*, May 1993.

Charles McCarthy and Gary Ellis
"Philosophic and Ethical Challenges of Animal Biotechnology," *Hastings Center Report*, January/February 1994.

Colman McCarthy
"Why 'Free Willy' and not Elsie the Cow?" *Washington Post*, September 14, 1993. Available from Reprints, 1150 15th St. NW, Washington, DC 20071.

T. B. Mepham — "Transgenesis in Farm Animals: Ethical Implications for Public Policy," *Politics and the Life Sciences*, August 1992. Available from Association for Politics and the Life Sciences, Northern Illinois University, DeKalb, IL 60115.

Lauren Mukamal — "Going Vegetarian," *Ms.*, July/August 1994.

Kevin Ropp — "New Animal Drug Increases Milk Production," *FDA Consumer*, May 1994. Available from Superintendent of Documents, Government Publications Office, Washington, DC 20402.

Henry Spira — "Your Dinner Led a Horrible Life," *Wall Street Journal*, July 1, 1993.

Paul Thompson — "Genetically Modified Animals: Ethical Issues," *Journal of Animal Science*, vol. 71, Supplement 3, 1993. Available from 309 W. Clark St., Champaign, IL 61820.

Sallie Tisdale — "Meat," *Antioch Review*, Summer 1994. Available from Box 148, Yellow Springs, OH 45387.

Wall Street Journal — "Animal Farms," June 14, 1993.

Thomas Witherell — "Notes from the Vegetarian Underground," *America*, April 23, 1994.

Does Wildlife Need to Be Protected?

ANIMAL
RIGHTS

Chapter Preface

Many animal rights activists are concerned with the issue of wildlife conservation. These advocates contend that wild animals need to be protected from the threats to their survival posed by various human activities, including the destruction of natural habitats, the capturing of live animals for entertainment purposes, the poaching of wild animals for commercial exploitation, and hunting.

Critics argue that hunting especially is a barbaric activity that serves no practical purpose and results in the needless suffering and death of countless animals. According to Matt Cartmill, the author of *A View to a Death in the Morning: Hunting and Nature Through History*, hunters are often described in derogatory terms, characterized as compulsive, blood-thirsty, beer-drinking men who are "eager to shoot anything that moves." Cartmill suggests that some men hunt out of a need for male bonding and to affirm their masculine identity and their sexual virility.

Hunters, who insist that this portrayal is an exaggeration, defend hunting with at least three arguments. First, they justify killing their prey on the grounds that they use the animals for food and other useful purposes. Second, they maintain that hunting serves an ecological function by controlling the number of prey animals (especially deer) that would otherwise starve and/or damage people's crops and gardens. Finally, hunters view hunting not as a destructive activity, but as perhaps the ultimate communion with nature. According to artist Ryland Loos:

> Many hunters also enjoy such outdoor activities as bird watching, nature photography, mountain climbing, hiking and canoeing. But in these pursuits, the human is not part of nature's system. The hunter, a predator, is part of nature.

The debate over hunting is one of the issues discussed in the following chapter on the protection of wildlife.

> *"People who hunt have most often been the ones who come to love and appreciate these animals enough to make their welfare a life's dedication."*

Hunting Animals Is Morally Acceptable

Ryland Loos

Ryland Loos works as an artist in the biological sciences at the State University of New York in Albany. In the following viewpoint, drawing upon his experience as a naturalist and hunter, Loos describes the pleasures he and others have traditionally received from hunting. While emphasizing the aesthetic pleasure derived from hunting, he acknowledges that, as human predators, "there are few hunters who do not feel some remorse at reducing a beautiful bird or mammal to a possession." Hunting, however, helps man find his place in the natural world, he insists. Indeed, according to Loos, "spending contemplative hours and days with wildlife heightens rather than diminishes the hunter's reverence for life."

As you read, consider the following questions:

1. According to Loos, why is it important to remember that famous naturalists and ecologists have themselves been hunters?
2. How, in Loos's view, might hunters see themselves as justifiably an integral part of the natural world?
3. How is hunting different from other outdoor activities, according to the author?

From Ryland Loos, "Friends of the Hunted." Reprinted with permission from the November 1993 issue of the *Conservationist* magazine.

On a morning in late November, ducks were coming out of the north, arriving in flocks of a dozen to several hundred. They circled high, out of range of my gun, before dropping into a mass of quacking comrades 150 yards away, just inside a refuge. With each wave I would crouch low and do my most convincing quacking, inviting them to join my 18 plastic decoys. A few would babble a polite "No thank you, we're going to join the thousands of real ducks that we see right over there."

Hours later while picking up the decoys it occurred to me that though I had never before seen so many ducks in New York State, I hadn't fired a shot. My human companion and my dog both agreed that it had been a memorable day.

It reminded me of a recent fall walk along the shores of Lake Champlain. I met a hunter who had been there since dawn enjoying the view of New York and of Vermont down the lake. The only ducks around had dropped in to his dozen cork-bodied decoys and he had shot one, a beautiful mallard. Feeling that he needed to defend his actions, he said in a soft, apologetic voice, "It's a decent thing to do." This man's need for understanding would once have surprised me, but it doesn't any longer. At least, not since an evening gathering I attended shortly after moving to Albany. Bill Severinghaus, New York State's pioneering whitetail deer researcher, was introduced to a well-dressed couple who immediately took offense at the mention of deer hunting. "Anyone who would kill a poor defenseless deer is a cruel and heartless person indeed, and certainly not very well educated. Hunters are nothing but a bunch of redneck beer drinkers." All attempts by Severinghaus to disagree were interrupted by increasingly loud remarks fueled by rising emotions. This man I much admire who, through his dedicated research and knowledge, has done more for the deer of New York State than anyone, had to walk away from insulting shouts of uninformed emotionalism.

Famous Naturalists Who Hunted

Let's quietly listen to the researcher's point of view and also look at some people who have enjoyed hunting to see how well they fit the "redneck" stereotype.

It would surprise many bird-watchers to know that John James Audubon, according to biographer Alexander Adams, "loved hunting for its own sake, rejoicing in the sound of the shot and the sight of the falling bird." In his formal portraits he holds his gun in hand.

Nearly every bird and wildlife painter since Audubon and his fully armed rival, Alexander Wilson, "the Father of American Ornithology," enjoyed hunting. Louis Agassiz Fuertes, Francis Lee Jacques, Richard Bishop, Lynn Boque Hunt, and DEC's own recently retired Wayne Trimm are highlights of a long list.

"Well!" the shouter says, "Everyone knows that painters are weird. A pure naturalist or scientist would never hunt." In response, I give you Charles Darwin. He returned from partridge shooting to find the letter that sent him aboard the *Beagle* to the Galapagos to begin the era of modern biology. On board ship, this killer of game was nicknamed "philosopher" because he was known to be "sensitive, beauty loving and scholarly."

Again, the list of scientist hunters would be long and would include all 25 distinguished founders of the American Ornithologist Union, C. Hart Merriam, founder of the government organization that evolved into the present U.S. Fish and Wildlife Service, Spencer Fullerton Baird and forestry pioneer John Quincy Adams. It would also include Paul Heye, my favorite professor, who made ornithology, conservation and ecology classes as interesting as the dove hunts we shared in the sand counties of Southeast Missouri.

Another noted midwestern ecologist also loved to hunt. His journals and writings are filled with details about trips such as this example for December 6, 1926: "Saw a large flock of doves but couldn't get near them. Coming back I unexpectedly flushed a big mallard drake out of the head of the buckbrush lake. I shot through some saplings at him but failed to connect." This lifetime hunter is the much revered author Aldo Leopold.

The Biotic Community

Leopold came to see how economic self-interest clashed with an ecologically informed conscience and wrote, "A thing is right when it tends to preserve the integrity, stability and beauty of the biotic community. It is wrong when it tends otherwise." He knew that the human species is a part of the biotic community and not a thing above it, and that man plays his role as a predator and as a steward of the land. He further wrote, "I believe that hunting takes rank with agriculture and nature study as one of three fundamentally valuable contacts with the soil."

During the first years of this century, Theodore Roosevelt's love of animals founded on knowledge and his abilities as a hunter teamed with George Bird Grinnell, editor of *Forest and Stream* magazine, to stop rampant market hunting and to establish the nation's first effective game law. Grinnell, whose enthusiasm for birds began while taking drawing lessons from Audubon's widow, wrote many magazine articles and books fostering conservation. He promoted a heightened sense of ethics and helped to establish hunting seasons and bag limits and to outlaw market and plume hunting. He established the first Audubon Society and along with Roosevelt and a distinguished group of hunters established the Boone and Crockett Club, parent organization to the New York

Zoological Society.

In 1900, as Governor of New York State, Roosevelt revitalized the ineffective political state Fisheries, Game and Forest Commission and placed W. Austin Wadsworth, president of the Boone and Crockett Club, at its head. In many ways, the ideals of this forerunner of DEC became a model for the nation when Roosevelt became president. Under Roosevelt, 100 million acres were added to American forest reserves. Five national parks, 17 national monuments, a professional forest service and an extensive system of wildlife refuges were established. John F. Reiger contends in his excellently researched book, *American Sportsmen and the Origins of Conservation*, that practically every leader who has risen to a position of prominence in the defense of wildlife has been a hunter. People who hunt have most often been the ones who come to love and appreciate these animals enough to make their welfare a life's dedication. Spending contemplative hours and days with wildlife heightens rather than diminishes the hunter's reverence for life.

Real Hunters

There are still real hunters in America. The number of hunters has stabilized at about 7 percent of the population since 1937 (6.9 million then, 15.5 million now). But these hunters are not seen clearly. The media increasingly resorts to cartoon stereotypes of hunters, and this hurts them. They are not mean-spirited rednecks or drunken Bubbas, and they are tired of offhanded references to Bambi.

Terry McDonell, *The New York Times*, June 3, 1995.

Hunters are not all uneducated ruffians, even though, unfortunately, those who make themselves most visible seem to fit this category. For every mudspattered pickup with guns displayed in the rear window and boisterous, camo clad, knife-carrying drivers, there is a car or two with hunting gear and coveralls stowed out of sight in the trunk, driven by someone whose greatest fall enthusiasm you would never suspect. Hunters do run the gamut of personality types; but, in most cases, even the reddest neck, through the work done by his license and other fees, befriends wildlife more than does the best intentioned shouter.

Hunting Controls Animal Populations

"I don't care who hunts! What about the animal's rights?" erupts the shouter. They do have rights. A deer has the right to live out its life in the natural process Leopold referred to as the "Round River," a river that flows into itself, a system in which rocks produce soil which grows an oak which produces an acorn that is eaten by a deer which is eaten by a man who eventually dies to return to the soil. The deer feed upon plants and we, as predators at the top of a food chain, feed upon them. Deer have a right to outwit us, as they most often do in our days afield. If we do not do our part to control their numbers, they also have the right to eat our crops, gardens and shrubs and to cross roads, smashing fenders, windshields and, on occasion, us. In the natural cycle that is their right, a deer will die, by a bullet or an arrow, or slow starvation, disease or freezing. In the scheme of things the latter are no more natural and no more humane than the former.

The Hunter as Predator

Even with this knowledge, there are few hunters who do not feel some remorse at reducing a beautiful bird or mammal to a possession. Most, as the Spanish philosopher Ortega observed, do not hunt in order to kill, but rather kill in order to have hunted. For most of us, like window-shopping without the possibility of buying or gardening without vegetables to gather at season's end, hunting requires the possibility of occasionally bringing home game.

Many hunters also enjoy outdoor activities such as birdwatching, nature photography, mountain climbing, hiking and canoeing. But in these pursuits, the human is not part of nature's system. The hunter, a predator, is part of nature. Leonard Lee Rue III has probably taken more published photographs of whitetail deer than anyone while researching and writing numerous books on their habits; but still, he hunts them in season with a bow. It's a different experience.

The Pleasure of Hunting

At three o'clock on an October afternoon, I climbed onto my 15-inch-square platform strapped 12 feet above the ground to the trunk of an ash tree. The woods' edge glowed golden from the maples all around. For minutes at a time, I faced the corner of a field of goldenrods to the north before turning ever so slowly to the wooded slope immediately to the south—glancing over a green field to the west as I turned—to which I thought deer might come before sunset. On their way, I hoped they would pass within range of my bow.

On one turn, I was surprised to find the woods full of dark feathered basketballs whose arrival had been masked by the sound of falling leaves. Having a turkey permit with me, I drew on the nearest Tom. The arrow fell inches low, a complete miss, but the blade did clip off a wing feather. Straight up into the air the gobbler sprang, before landing not far from my tree. He cocked his head as if to say "What, pray tell, was that?" before trotting back to his friends who went, clucking with questions, over the ridge. The silent arrow hardly interrupted their afternoon stroll.

At four o'clock a ruffed grouse, sitting on the top stone above a gap in the fence bordering the goldenrods, commenced drumming. My watch revealed an average wait between drums of four and one-half minutes. Drumming was preceded by three or four nods of the head. Two seconds separated the first and second wing beat, and one second separated beats two through 14 before he speeded up to a blur ending around beat 29. Perfectly spaced drumming continued for an hour and 35 minutes until six o'clock shortly after three young raccoons tumbled over the low stones in the gap below the grouse's perch on an early beginning to a night ramble. Mice moved under the leaves below my tree in an area where earlier a chipmunk had scurried back and forth. Gray squirrels performed at intervals their usual tail twitching, "what are you doing in my tree?" antics.

Just before dark, as an unseen woodcock twittered away, I picked up the arrow and the clipped wing feather that lay beside it. Shuffling through a deep carpet of dry leaves toward the road with my first turkey trophy protruding from my pocket, I ended perhaps the best afternoon of the fall. I saw no deer that day, but I had gone to the woods with that intent. I had hunted. Toward the end of that season after many such afternoons and mornings, in another woods, I put an arrow through a deer and felt my moment of remorse, as well as a reinforced feeling of oneness with the ages of men who have hunted. Something very basic to my species had again been satisfied in a socially and environmentally non-destructive way. Since then, each month's outdoor activity has been enjoyed in its turn while looking forward to another autumn and days afield in search of game—it is a decent thing to do.

"If killing animals is wrong as a spectator sport, it ought to be equally wrong as a participatory sport."

Hunting Animals Is Morally Objectionable

Matt Cartmill

Matt Cartmill is professor of biological anthropology at Duke University in Chapel Hill, North Carolina. In the following viewpoint, Cartmill examines the self-declared motives of hunters and concludes that many of them are either dishonest, openly sexist, or blatantly sadistic. He contends that hunting is morally wrong.

As you read, consider the following questions:

1. In what ways, according to Cartmill, do hunters attempt to justify their behavior?
2. How does Cartmill respond to the suggestion that people continue to kill animals to satisfy a human instinct to hunt?
3. In the author's view, why is it morally wrong to hunt?

Excerpted from *A View to a Death in the Morning: Hunting and Nature Through History* by Matt Cartmill (Cambridge, MA: Harvard Univ. Press, 1993); © 1993 by Matt Cartmill. Reprinted by permission of the publisher.

The motives of hunters are vague and visceral, and non-hunters find them hard to understand. To most of us, ceremoniously going into the woods once a year to kill deer with a rifle sounds about as attractive as marching into the dairy barn once a year to bash cows with a sledgehammer. Because hunters have trouble articulating and defending their motives, non-hunters often conclude that they are simply crazy. From the Renaissance to the present day, writers who have seen hunting as a sign of man's depravity have assumed that the hunter takes a psychopathic pleasure in inflicting pain and death. As Joseph Wood Krutch put it:

> Killing "for sport" is the perfect type of that pure evil for which metaphysicians have sometimes sought. Most wicked deeds are done because the doer proposes some good to himself . . . [but] the killer for sport has no such comprehensible motive. He prefers death to life, darkness to light. He gets nothing except the satisfaction of saying "Something which wanted to live is dead. There is that much less vitality, consciousness, and, perhaps, joy in the universe. I am the Spirit that Denies."

Lunatics and Yahoos

Many others see hunters in this same light, as inscrutable bloodthirsty lunatics. Hunters, writes Joy Williams, "are persecutors of nature who should be prosecuted":

> They're overequipped . . . insatiable, malevolent, and vain. They maim and mutilate and despoil. And for the most part, they're inept. Grossly inept. Camouflaged toilet paper is a must for the modern hunter, along with his Bronco and his beer. Too many hunters taking a dump in the woods with their roll of Charmin beside them were mistaken for white-tailed deer and shot. Hunters get excited. They'll shoot anything— the pallid ass of another sportsman or even themselves. A Long Island man died last year when his shotgun went off as he clubbed a wounded deer with the butt. Hunters get mad. They get restless and want to fire! They want to use those assault rifles and see foamy blood on the ferns.

Williams thinks sport hunting should be prohibited by law. That proposal is supported by a large number of pro-animal organizations, from hardcore animal-rights groups like PETA [People for the Ethical Treatment of Animals] and Friends of Animals all the way over to mainstream humane societies like the Massachusetts SPCA [Society for the Prevention of Cruelty to Animals]. One recent poll indicates that almost a third of all Americans agree with them. And pro-animal activists are not the only ones who see hunters as crazy killers. Even some U.S. Fish and Wildlife agents, who presumably ought to support sport hunting if anyone does, complain about "four-wheel-drive, assault-rifle, gun-and-run, shoot-anything yahoos who think they're Rambo."

This stereotype of the hunter—as a violent, psychopathic male compulsive eager to shoot anything that moves—is a staple of popular culture, recurring in innumerable films, TV shows, and comic strips. It has been set to music, in Tom Lehrer's *Hunting Song:*

> I always will remember,
> 'Twas a year ago November,
> I went out to hunt some deer
> On a morning bright and clear.
> I went and shot the maximum the game laws would allow:
> Two game wardens, seven hunters, and a cow.

Even some hunters concede that the main motive for hunting is a simple, weasel-like joy in killing things and seeing foamy blood on the ferns. "We *like* to kill animals," admits the hunting journalist Humberto Fontova. "Hunters are simply guys who get a thrill out of killing animals." Fontova thinks that evolution has implanted an instinctive love of killing in his breast. "I recognize the urge as a predatory instinct to kill. Man is a predator—has been for tens of thousands of years. It's going to take a while to breed that out of us, and thank God I won't be around by then."

Born with an Urge to Kill?

Fontova is not the only hunting writer who offers the hunting hypothesis as a rationale for hunting. A lot of them insist that their urge to kill is something they were born with, an instinctive blood lust inherited from our killer-ape ancestors. Those who do not thrill to the chase seem rootless and degenerate to them. "For some unfortunates," wrote Robert Ruark,

> prisoned by city sidewalks and sentenced to a cement jungle more horrifying than anything to be found in Tanganyika, the horn of the hunter never winds at all. But deep in the guts of most men is buried the involuntary response to the hunter's horn, a prickle of the nape hairs, an acceleration of the pulse, an atavistic memory of his fathers, who killed first with stone, and then with club, and then with spear, and then with bow, and then with gun, and finally with formulae. How meek the man is of no importance; somewhere in the pigeon chest of the clerk is still the vestigial remnant of the hunter's heart; somewhere in his nostrils the half-forgotten smell of blood.

The hunting writer Tom McIntyre thinks that a distaste for the hunt is a perversion of our instincts, like celibacy or anorexia:

> Being hunters is what made humans what they are . . . from millions of years of a hunting past that shaped everything from our bodies to our brains to our social relationships. Ten thousand years of grubbing in the dirt is hardly an adequate period for the impulse to hunt to be extinguished in our lives. And so the real aberration is not that some humans still hunt and kill, but that some do not.

But if the desire to hunt and kill is a human instinct, it is a curiously restricted one. Only about 12 percent of Americans hunt, and their numbers grow smaller every year. Though most of us still think it all right to hunt for meat, polls show that large majorities are opposed to hunting simply for trophies or for recreation. If killing animals were an intrinsically pleasurable activity like eating, drinking, and making love, then the majorities would presumably lean the other way—and, as the hunting naturalist Valerius Geist points out, a lot more of us would be eager to land a job cutting steers' throats in a slaughterhouse.

©Mike Thompson and Copley News Service. Used with permission.

In short, there is no reason to think that human beings have any innate fondness for bloodshed. No doubt some people hunt because they enjoy killing animals. But those people are kidding themselves when they claim that their love of killing is something all of us are born with—or even something they have in common with all hunters. Other hunters, in fact, argue the reverse: that "buck fever," the nervous trembling and paralysis of the trigger finger that afflicts novice hunters, stems from an ingrained *reluctance* to kill that the beginner must learn to overcome. And at the other end of their hunting careers, many experienced outdoorsmen finally hang up their weapons because they have simply grown sick of killing. In an interview with the great bowhunter Fred Bear, John Mitchell asked him why he had given up hunting. Bear thought it over before he answered:

> "Oh, I suppose it was all those years, and trips," he said. "Every damn time I went hunting, I had to *kill* something." He stopped then and turned his face toward the rain, and in a voice so soft and low I could barely hear it, said at last, "I figure you know damn well what I mean."

If hunters themselves often start out and end up with a distaste for killing, then why do they hunt? The writings of hunters and the studies that have been undertaken of their motives show that different people hunt for different reasons. Some of these reasons are easy for the nonhunter to understand. Others are not.

What About an Economic Motive?

Simple economic need furnishes the best and most easily understood reason for hunting. But it is not a real motive for most modern hunters, many of whom spend large sums of money every year in the hope of fetching home a few wildfowl or a few dozen pounds of venison. The hunters who sink $20,000 or $30,000 into building specialized all-terrain vehicles to chase deer through the swamps of southern Florida are not trying to economize on their grocery bills. In the past, many people hunted because the bodies of wild animals provided them with food and clothing and other materials that they could not so easily obtain in any other way. This still holds true for a few rural Americans today. For the vast majority of hunters in modern America, however, hunting is a net drain on assets and has no real economic value. One sign of this fact is the carrion that accumulates during hunting season alongside many rural American roads where hunters have killed deer or wildfowl, hacked off a few choice cuts of meat, and left the rest of the carcass for the crows.

Some hunters condemn this sort of careless slaughter as "unethical," and make a point of trying to eat, wear, or utilize in some other way every possible scrap of their quarry's body. "I don't waste anything," proclaims one hunter held up as a model in a 1985 National Rifle Association ad. "I process the meat, tan the buckskin, make thread and lacings from the sinew, even scrimshaw the bones." The underlying notion here, that a truly ethical hunter is one who wastes no part of the animals he kills, is a fairly new idea. There are hints of this clean-plate ethic in the nineteenth century—for example, in the pronouncements of Cooper's Deerslayer or in Oscar Wilde's famous characterization of English fox hunting as "the unspeakable in pursuit of the uneatable." But before World War II, the plebeian "pot hunter" or meat hunter was commonly looked down on as the social and moral inferior of the classier sport hunter, who killed for amusement rather than from vulgar need. The clean-plate ethic seems to be mainly a postwar phenomenon, probably connected with the general rise in ecological consciousness during the second half of this century.

Another ecology-related rationale sometimes offered for hunting is the need to keep population numbers down so that the prey animals will not die a lingering death from starvation in lean seasons. A great deal of ink has been expended in articulating and attacking this rationale, but all that needs to be said here is that population control has never been a *motive* for hunting. Hunters do not trudge reluctantly off into the woods out of a sense of humanitarian duty, to locate starving animals and put them out of their misery. In fact, hunters are usually the first to protest when wolves, coyotes, cougars, feral dogs, or other non-human predators move into an area and start taking over the job of controlling game populations. Perhaps the most interesting fact about this whole controversy is that it is always focused exclusively on those archetypal martyrs of the wildwood, the deer. No one has much to say one way or the other about the hunter's obligation to keep opossums, foxes, or ravens from starving to death in the snows of winter.

Many hunters hunt for social reasons that have nothing to do with hunting as such. Whenever hunting has been a marker of the ruling class, social climbers have joined the chase in order to gain status and cozy up to the gentry. Conversely, hunting is a seasonal ritual of working-class solidarity for many rural American men. When they go hunting, they feel that they are renewing their bonds with friends and kinfolk and reaffirming their ties to the land and way of life they have inherited from their ancestors. Still other men like to go hunting precisely because it gets them away from their kinfolk and into the exclusively male company of old buddies, with whom they can relax, "drink beer, shoot at inoffensive animals, and talk about pussy," in the words of R. Blount Jr. For such men, hunting addresses a different kind of social need—a need for what is sometimes called "male bonding."

To Affirm Masculinity?

The connection of hunting with masculinity runs deep, and both hunters and their critics often comment on it. Hunting has been a stereotypically male activity throughout most of Western history. In America today, the vast majority of hunters are male; some 21 percent of men but only about 2 percent of women hunt. Women who hunt generally do so with male companions, and their participation in a hunt is often resented by male hunters. Many male hunters believe that hunting affirms their identity as men, and feel that taking a boy hunting cements his bonds to other males and helps make a man of him.

Some hunters think that their sport affirms their virility as well as their masculine identity. "The sentiment of self-importance makes the enjoyment of women all the more pleasant after hunting," wrote the sixteenth-century Indian king Rudradeva of Kumaon. Though few modern hunters would put it that candidly, some of them obviously believe that hunting makes them sexier. You can see it in the double-entendres on their bumper stickers. BOWHUNTERS HAVE LONGER SHAFTS, asserts one such sticker. I HUNT WHITE TAIL YEAR ROUND, proclaims another (which is decorated with drawings of a deer's scut and a woman's buttocks to make sure nobody misses the pun). And some women do seem to be attracted to the aura of deadly force and competence that surrounds an accomplished hunter. That aura presumably explains why some clothing manufacturers peddle hunting togs to nonhunters as intriguingly sexy getups.

Since hunters often think of hunting as a marker of manhood, each side in the debate over hunting tends to suspect that there is something shaky about the other side's sexual identity. Opponents of hunting are not above intimating that hunters go out and kill things because they are neurotically anxious to prove their virility. For their part, hunters have been known to suggest that their critics are either limp-wristed sissies with too little testosterone or bull-necked viragos with too much. Antihunting activists, scoffs one hunting writer,

> are mostly aging hippies still asking what's called their women if 1968 was their best year. . . . What's called men in that group wear turtlenecks and Earth Shoes, and have granny glasses hanging around their skinny necks. The men would rather be eating a bowl of granola than chasing pipefitters from Pittsburgh but their larger women and matriarchal mores won't let them.

Going back and forth over this muddied ground is not likely to yield any clear answers. No doubt some men are attracted to hunting because it makes them feel manly. But there are many devoted hunters who show no evident need to prove themselves in this way, and who hunt for reasons that apparently have nothing to do with their gender identification.

To Be a Part of Nature?

Many articulate hunters, the ones who are most apt to write books on the joys of the hunt, say that they hunt in order to feel that they are part of nature. Hunting is for them mostly a pretext for being outdoors, an "excuse to get out into the hills, away from the crowds, to live, if only for a few days, beyond the wall," in the words of E. Abbey. Such hunters relish the pursuit of the quarry because it disciplines and focuses what might otherwise become a careless stroll through the woods. John Mitchell recalls that he and his other boyhood friends who took up hunting were set apart from their fellows by their "land sense," their love of and sensitivity to the natural order: "a way of looking at the land, and noting where the acorns fell, and which side of a tree the moss grew on, and how the prickly buckeye fruits split open October, and why the stirred-up leaves and wisp of rabbit fur probably meant there was an owl nearby, dozing on a full stomach." Hunting, writes the sports columnist Craig Holt, is a way of "keeping a promise with the land," which prevents him from becoming "isolated from the natural world." Valerius Geist, struggling to define his reasons for hunting, describes it as an "intercourse with nature":

> It's a welcome weight on one's shoulders when one hikes home with game in the bag and a set of antlers or horns protruding from the pack. During a rest break, the hand touches the gleaming points (or the horn tips), caresses the antler beams (or the burr), and plays with the soft hair on the head. Hunting is a passion better men than I have tried to describe . . . and attempted to explain. Some have called it sport. I disagree. Some have called it cruel and unjust—an uncultured act, done for the sake of killing. I disagree. It is no more "sport" than is gardening; it is no more done for the sake of killing than gardening is done for the sake of killing vegetables. If it is sporting, with whom is one competing? The animals? I should blush at such a comparison, given the weapons we possess and the skills in hunting we are capable of. . . . Were someone to call it an intercourse with nature, I should shake my head at the choice of words, but I shall know what that person gets out of hunting. When stalking, one's guts must tell one that one is doing something right, that one is reliving the very drama that caused man's ancestors to rise from the apes to become men.

There Is Really No Good Reason to Hunt

. . . We need to ask whether hunting is wrong. There may be no clear-cut answer to this question. But we can at least decide whether the answer we give is in principle compatible with other things we believe.

There is a consensus today, at any rate in the industrialized West, that the suffering of sentient animals is something that is intrinsically undesirable: that, other things being equal, the deliberate infliction of such suffering is something that must be *justified*, by showing that it serves a higher or more urgent goal. If we accept any sort of laws against cruelty to animals, we

180

must accept this proposition. And if we do, it is hard to see how we can justify sportive hunting, since it inflicts grave suffering for the sake of mere amusement. If killing animals is wrong as a spectator sport, it ought to be equally wrong as a participatory sport.

Hunters generally dismiss this issue as irrelevant. After all, everything dies sooner or later. Something must kill these animals eventually, they say, and it might as well be us. The trouble with this argument is that it provides an equally good (or bad) rationale for sportive homicide. Hunting writer V. Bourjaily argues that the suffering of the quarry is not the sort of thing that grownups can afford to worry about: "We must, by the time we finish growing, have learned that you can never stop and think or it will break your heart." But this is exactly backwards. Children, not grownups, are the people who are unconcerned about the results of their behavior. Growing up involves learning to recognize the consequences of our actions and taking responsibility for them; and one consequence of hunting is the infliction of pain and death for no very urgent reason.

"*Although today's zoos are not the ultimate centres for captive breeding, in the immediate future their role is vital.*"

Zoos Help Preserve Endangered Species

Colin Tudge

In the following viewpoint, Colin Tudge, author of *Last Animals at the Zoo*, argues that zoos maintaining captive breeding programs can help solve both the short- and long-term problem of species extinction. Responding to a British report stating that zoos are no longer useful institutions for preserving endangered species, Tudge contends that even the establishment of numerous national wildlife parks is an inadequate solution to the problem of diminishing biodiversity. Tudge contends that zoos provide a vital backup to habitat protection for numerous animals now listed on the endangered species list.

As you read, consider the following questions:

1. How, according to Tudge, has *The Zoo Inquiry* understated its own case?
2. Why are national wildlife parks less than satisfactory as a means of preserving endangered species, in Tudge's opinion?
3. What arguments does the author use to support his contention that zoos may help preserve a large number of endangered species?

Colin Tudge, "Captive Audiences for Future Conservation," *New Scientist*, January 28, 1995. Reprinted with permission.

captive breeding has most to offer the land vertebrates. Among these, an estimated 20 000 species are now threatened. Of this 20 000, about 2000 are thought to need special protection from captive breeding.

In short, present-day zoos could, in theory, protect all the land vertebrates that require captive breeding. This 2000 includes all the rhinos, several big cats and bears, and so on.

Still, the numbers to be saved seem small, compared with those endangered. But what does "biodiversity" really mean? We could reasonably argue that the two remaining species of elephant encompass as much true "diversity" as 50 000 variations on a theme of rogue beetle. Neither is it true as some have argued that the small creatures are the true shapers of landscapes, simply because their total biomass is greater. The big animals largely determine what plants can grow, and they in turn determine which of the tiny ones can survive.

Financial Considerations

Finally, comes the matter of cost. *The Zoo Inquiry* tells us that it costs $16 800 a year to maintain a black rhino in captivity, and only $1000 per rhino in the wild. Actually it seems impossible to calculate the price of true protection in the wild, since no one has done it. The Zimbabweans have tried very hard, but the poachers are still winning. They are spending all they can afford but much more is needed. The Indian rhinos at Chitwan in Nepal are protected by more soldiers than there are rhinos. Nepalese labour is among the cheapest in the world outside Africa, which keeps the cost down wonderfully—yet this is hardly desirable.

More to the point, at the 1992 world conference on rhino conservation in San Diego, Tom Foose of the World Conservation Union showed that no wild population of rhinos could be considered "safe" unless it contained at least 2500 individuals. But a well-kept captive population could be maintained indefinitely with only 150 individuals. The captive ones are safer, and better bred. In some rhino species (like the black) a few dominant males do most of the breeding, which reduces overall genetic diversity; while in captive groups, every male should pass on its genes. Thus in crude arithmetical terms, each captive rhino is equivalent to 16 6 in the wild. Suddenly the price discrepancy disappears.

Captive breeding is not an alternative to habitat protection. Increasingly, however, it is a vital backup. If those zoos that devote themselves are impoverished, then animals will suffer. An order of magnitude increase in public expenditure is far more pertinent than closure.

"*Animal welfare organisations such as Zoo Check argue that conservation should really take place in the animals' natural home, thereby effectively conserving the whole habitat as well as the species.*"

Zoos Do Not Help Preserve Endangered Species

Eileen Murphy

Writing for the *Vegetarian*, the official journal of the Vegetarian Society in England, Eileen Murphy argues in the following viewpoint that zoos are in crisis. Often advertising themselves as educational institutions whose purpose is to inform the public about endangered animals, she contends zoos are often little more than "sordid amusement parks" with animal entertainment. She concludes that because the zoos' captive breeding programs are not useful, the public and endangered animals are better served through the preservation of natural habitats.

As you read, consider the following questions:

1. What arguments do zoos use to justify their existence, according to Murphy?
2. What alternatives to captive breeding programs does Zoo Check propose to more effectively preserve endangered animals, according to the author?

Excerpted from "Zoos and Endangered Species: A Special Report," *Vegetarian*, February 1993. Reprinted with permission.

Who doesn't have fond childhood memories of a trip to the zoo? But what we probably failed to realise as children was that a fun day out for us meant a life sentence behind bars for the animals we saw.

Zoos are a relatively new phenomenon, the first modern examples being set up in Vienna, Madrid and Paris in the 18th century. London Zoo opened to the public in the 19th century when its curators realised that the collection of animals brought from around Britain's empire was becoming a financial burden they could not carry.

The Zoological Society of London, which governs the work of the zoo, stated its mission in 1825 as offering the public an exhibition of "animals brought from every part of the globe to be applied either to some useful purpose, or as objects of scientific research—not of vulgar admiration!"

While this may have sounded great on paper, in reality many of Britain's zoos have since become little more than sordid amusement parks with 'live' entertainment. Animals are housed in often outdated, totally unsuitable conditions that cause both physical and mental anguish. Who can forget the distressing scenes of great cats or polar bears incessantly pacing out their torment in the cramped confines of their cages?

Considering that you now have to do no more than switch on a television set to learn all about wild animals and their natural environment through documentaries whose intimate contact with their subjects takes your breath away, is there any need for zoos in the 20th century? Zoos of course argue that there are plenty of reasons for their continued existence. They point to the need for education about other species and have quickly cottoned on to the conservation argument. London Zoo claims that its commitment to preserving endangered species and eventually returning them to the wild is clearly indicated by its inter-zoo captive breeding programmes. Allowing people to see endangered animals in the flesh is also one of the best ways of educating them about conservation matters, claims the zoo. "One case in point is the Arabian oryx—people wouldn't be able to see this animal in the wild if it wasn't for our captive breeding programme. The public often don't appreciate how much conservation work we do," explained education officer Rod Humby.

Zoo Check's Point of View

On the other side of the fence, animal welfare organisations such as Zoo Check argue that conservation should really take place in the animals' natural home, thereby effectively conserving the whole habitat as well as the species.

Founded in 1989 by Virginia McKenna and Will Travers, Zoo Check has been campaigning to ensure a reappraisal of the way animals are kept in zoos. The group runs a number of individual conservation projects itself, maintaining that the best place to conserve wildlife is in its own habitat, not in a cage in an urban city. Zoo Check is involved in projects in Africa to try to save the black rhino population, and in Spain to set up sanctuaries for the endangered Iberian wolf whose population has decreased to a few hundred.

No Need for Zoos

The problems of zoo animals and the crisis of wildlife's threatened annihilation are primarily man-made and need a political, not technocratic, solution. If the right policies toward nature were pursued, we should need no zoos at all.

Michael W. Fox, *The Animals' Agenda*, June 1986.

According to Will Travers of Zoo Check, as many black rhinos in zoo-based captive breeding programmes die as are bred. Compare that with Zoo Check's own project in Kenya's Tsavo National Park. Will Travers explains:

The black rhino population in Africa is still falling, but in Kenya where we are working with around nine controlled areas the population is increasing. We have over 200 acres of natural habitat allowed for each rhino, protected by solar powered fencing and guarded by rangers. The population will be released from the sanctuaries once the trade in rhino horn has stopped. This provides a real glimmer of hope for the species. I'm far more willing to accept captive breeding in the natural habitat as an answer to extinction than keeping small pockets of endangered animals in zoos all over the world.

Such captivity in-situ has been a necessary concession within the Iberian wolf project, where Zoo Check has had to set up a rescue and rehabilitation centre. The difference between this and captive breeding in zoos, as Zoo Check points out, is that it takes place in the animals' natural habitat, is a single species centre, and its main aim is to rehabilitate this endangered species so that it can continue living in the wild.

This is not to say that there are no problems with in-situ projects, the main one being that endangered animals' natural habitat is in danger just as much as the animals themselves. "With some of the problems in the wild, people have just been throwing money at them, but they haven't gone away. What we're saying is that you shouldn't throw the opportunity of zoos away," says Rod Humby. "It's alright to say we should close zoos and give the money to other types of conservation but what if they don't succeed? You haven't got any back-up. People don't seem to understand that there is nothing we'd like more than to see animals conserved in the wild, which is exactly why we are developing the science of reintroduction.". . .

Do Zoos Really Educate Us About Animals?

With technological advances since zoos were first set up, everyone can now see the real wilderness while sitting at home in front of their television, and there would seem little reason to bring back examples of animals from around the world when we can see them in the dramatic productions of people such as David Attenborough and Julian Pettifer. Yet the presence of live exhibits at zoos is exactly what Rod Humby believes is their unique selling point:

> Any other experience just can't compete with meeting a live animal. Through the collection we address the aspect of educating people about respect for animals—as individuals and as species. We also educate people about conservation through our schools programme, our adult education classes in animal ecology and conservation and with our new membership scheme called Lifewatch.

This last scheme allows members special reductions on admission to the zoo and regular updates on the work of the Zoological Society. "When people visit they usually have strong preconceptions about zoos but once they receive the information we present, some of them change their minds," explains Rod. "That flow of information is very important in breaking down barriers that are often based on what the zoo was doing 20 or 30 years ago."

While many zoos have little justification in claiming that they run more than a token education programme, some have good departments that use slide shows, lectures, models and resource packs to teach people about endangered species and the natural world. The question that begs to be asked, of course, is why such departments can't function in their own right without the need for a live collection of animals. Enter Will Travers and his plans for an innovative new concept called the Worldlife Centre. Still in the initial planning stages, the centre will be based around world habitats and include thematic exhibits incorporating virtual reality special effects. Will believes that such a centre will signal an end to the live animal-based zoos that have been the only option since Victorian days. "With Worldlife people will be able to decide whether they believe the incarceration of wild animals is a 'unique feature'. We will be producing an exciting and innovative, non-animal experience for people. The general public has an enormous thirst for knowledge about the environment and wildlife—that is the challenge that Worldlife is set to meet," he enthuses.

Periodical Bibliography

The following articles have been selected to supplement the diverse views presented in this chapter. Addresses are provided for periodicals not indexed in the *Readers' Guide to Periodical Literature*, the *Alternative Press Index*, or the *Social Sciences Index*.

Gary Anderson and Luke Dommer	"Does Hunting Contribute to Sound Wildlife Management Policies?" *CQ Researcher*, January 24, 1993. Available from 1414 22nd St. NW, Washington, DC 20037.
Betsy Carpenter	"Upsetting the Ark: Zoos Are Under Increasing Pressure Today to Justify Their Existence," *U.S. News & World Report*, August 24, 1992.
Matt Cartmill	"The Bambi Syndrome," *Natural History*, June 1993.
Jeffrey Cohn	"Decisions at the Zoo," *BioScience*, October 1992.
Jared Diamond	"Playing God at the Zoo," *Discover*, March 1995.
Sarah Ferguson	"Strike a Pose," *New York*, November 7, 1994.
Toni Hopman	"Liberate the Zoos," *Los Angeles Times*, April 9, 1992. Available from Reprints, Times Mirror Square, Los Angeles, CA 90053.
Walter Kuentzel	"Skybusting and the Slob Hunter Myth," *Wildlife Society Bulletin*, Summer 1994. Available from 5410 Grosvener Ln., Bethesda, MD 20814.
Colman McCarthy	"A Small Town Tradition of Massacre," *Washington Post*, August 25, 1992.
Suzy Menkes	"Is There a Future for Fur?" *Vogue*, August 1994.
Richard Miniter	"Saving the Species," *National Review*, July 6, 1992.
New Yorker	"Making the Fur Fight Fly," February 28, 1994.
Kathryn Olson and G. Thomas Goodnight	"Entanglements of Consumption, Cruelty, Privacy, and Fashion: The Social Controversy over Fur," *Quarterly Journal of Speech*, August 1994. Available from 5105 Backlick Rd., Bldg. E, Annandale, VA 22003.

George Rabb	"The Changing Roles of Zoological Parks in Conserving Biological Diversity," *American Zoologist*, February 1994. Available from 401 N. Michigan Ave., Chicago, IL 60611.
Nathaniel Wheelright	"Enduring Reasons to Preserve Threatened Species," *Chronicle of Higher Education*, June 1, 1994. Available from 1255 23rd St. NW, Suite 700, Washington, DC 20037.
Ted Williams	"Canned Hunts," *Audubon*, January/February 1992.
Robert Worcester	"Scenting Dissent," *New Statesman & Society*, April 21, 1995. Available from Foundation House, 38 Kingsland Rd., London E2 8DQ, U.K.
Richard Wornshop	"Hunting Controversy," *CQ Researcher*, January 24, 1992.

CHAPTER 5

What Issues Need to Be Resolved Within the Animal Rights Movement?

Chapter Preface

The animal rights movement is the subject of a great deal of criticism. For example, because they are opposed to the use of animals in medical research that could ultimately prove beneficial to humans, animal rights activists are often accused of placing the welfare of animals above that of humans. They are also often charged with being overly zealous in both their actions and rhetoric as they attempt to "liberate" animals from what they view as exploitation by humans. Targets of their intense criticism include the agricultural industry, hunters, zoos, and circuses.

However, debate about animal rights issues is not confined to arguments between animal rights activists and those who disagree with them. Within the animal rights community itself, various leaders, coalitions, and organizations carry on considerable discussion—at times quarrelsome, contentious, and decidedly polemical—as to how the animal rights movement should pursue its goal of improving the lives of animals. For example, some activists promote the complete liberation of all animals from all human uses. Others contend that while complete liberation would be ideal, it is not practical as an immediate goal. Because animals will undoubtedly continue to be used for food and other purposes, these activists maintain, efforts should be directed at ensuring that such animals are treated in as humane a manner as possible.

Differing views also exist on how the animal rights movement can attract followers. Some believe that in order to draw a larger constituency, the movement should shed its image as a radical fringe group and adopt a more moderate tone. Others promote the teaching of animal rights issues in elementary and middle schools as a means of encouraging young people to join the cause.

The following four viewpoints point out differences in understanding and strategy current within the animal rights movement.

"There are fundamental and profound differences between the philosophy of animal welfare and that of animal rights."

The Animal Rights Movement Must Reject Animal Welfarism

Tom Regan and Gary Francione

Tom Regan, professor of philosophy at North Carolina State University and author of *The Case for Animal Rights*, is president of the Culture and Animals Foundation. Gary Francione is professor of law at Rutgers University School of Law and director of the Rutgers Animal Rights Law Clinic in Newark, New Jersey. In the following viewpoint, Regan and Francione, comparing the philosophy of animal rights with that of animal welfarism, conclude that animal welfarism ultimately works against the best interest of animals. The promotion of a strong animal rights philosophy, on the other hand, serves both the short- and long-term interests of animals, they conclude, and therefore it alone should guide the animal rights movement.

As you read, consider the following questions:

1. According to Regan and Francione, what are the fundamental differences between the philosophy of animal rights and that of animal welfarism?
2. Why does animal welfarism actually work against the promotion of animal rights, according to the authors?
3. What "abolitionist steps" do Regan and Francione advocate?

Tom Regan and Gary Francione, "A Movement's Means Creates Its Ends," *Animals' Agenda*, January/February 1992. Reprinted with permission.

Many animal advocates hold that there really is no difference between animal welfare and animal rights. Others claim that while there is a difference, advancing animal welfare is a necessary prerequisite to advancing animal rights. Given either assumption, many conscientious activists conclude that we must support welfarist means in our march toward animal rights ends.

We believe these views are mistaken. Not only are the philosophies of animal rights and animal welfare separated by irreconcilable differences, and not only are the practical reforms grounded in animal welfare morally at odds with those sanctioned by the philosophy of animal rights, but also the enactment of animal welfare measures actually impedes the achievement of animal rights.

We emphasize at the outset that we do not intend to be critical of past activities of the movement or of the admirable efforts of individuals to end animal suffering. Rather, we are discussing the *future* direction of the movement as a matter of movement policy, and the campaigns chosen by the movement pursuant to that policy.

Fundamental Differences

There are fundamental and profound differences between the philosophy of animal welfare and that of animal rights. Animal rights philosophy rests on the recognition of the moral inviolability of the individual, both human and nonhuman. Just as people of color do not exist as resources for whites, or women for men, so other animals do not exist as resources for human beings. The goal of the animal rights movement is nothing less than the *total* liberation of nonhuman animals from human tyranny.

No one who accepts the philosophy of animal rights would be satisfied with a continuation of our society's rapacious consumption of farm animals, for example, even if these animals were raised in an ecologically sustainable fashion, and were transported and slaughtered "humanely." Animal welfarists, by contrast, are committed to the pursuit of "gentle usage." They believe it morally permissible to use nonhumans for human benefit, but think humans should try to "minimize" suffering. Thus, whereas welfarists seek to *reform* current practices of animal exploitation, while retaining such exploitation in principle, rights advocates oppose all such exploitation in principle and seek to *abolish* all such exploitation in practice.

Recognition of the moral inviolability of individual animals not only helps shape the ends that the animal rights movement seeks, it should also help articulate the morally acceptable means that may be used. And this is important. Many animal rights people who disavow the philosophy of animal welfare believe they can consistently support reformist means to abolition

195

ends. This view is mistaken, we believe, for moral, practical, and conceptual reasons.

Moral Concerns

The view that animal welfare means can be used to achieve animal rights ends rests on unsupported, implausible speculation about the future. For example, why should we believe that making "animal model" research more "humane" will persuade people in the future to stop using nonhuman animals in research? Why not draw the *opposite* conclusion—namely, that the "humane" exploitation of nonhuman animals will lead to the *indefinite perpetuation* of such exploitation? By analogy, why think that permitting "gentler" rape or "more humane" slavery would lead to the absolute prohibition against rape and the total abolition of slavery? Clearly, when so much depends upon beliefs about the future, a minimal respect for rationality demands more than a minimal amount of empirical support. The thesis that reformist means will lead to abolitionist ends is entirely lacking in just such support.

More than troubling, a reformist response to animal oppression is morally inconsistent with the philosophy of animal rights. Advocates of this philosophy must reject the idea that the end justifies the means; thus, they must refuse to support the institutionalized exploitation of *some* nonhuman animals *today*, no matter how "humane," in the hope that *other* animals will benefit in the *future*. Since reformist measures *necessarily* authorize such exploitation (this is true by definition), consistent animal rights advocates cannot support them.

Practical Concerns

The belief that making animal exploitation more "humane" through legislation now will help end it in the future is mistaken for a second reason: the real world doesn't work that way. For an example we need look no further than the federal Animal Welfare Act. Many of the supporters of the 1985 amendments to the AWA argued that they were simply one step in the struggle to end vivisection.

It is clear in hindsight that these expectations have remained miserably unfulfilled. Rather than hastening the demise of vivisection, the amendments fortified it through explicit Congressional recognition of its legitimacy, and gave vivisectors an ostensibly strong law to point to when questioned about abuse of animals in laboratories. For example, in a recent *New England Journal of Medicine* article, vivisectors, pointing to the AWA and its amendments, state that the public need not be concerned about the treatment of animals because "[t]here are stringent regulations, [which] carry the force of federal law, governing the care and use of animals in medical research." What the authors do not point out—and what the American public does not know—is that the AWA prohibits "unnecessary" animal suffering, but *leaves to the exclusive discretion of vivisectors* the determination of what constitutes "necessity."

Moreover, as a result of the amendments, which require that each research facility have an Institutional Animal Care and Use Committee, vivisectors now argue that the committees provide animals protection equivalent to that provided by human experimentation review committees. What the vivisectors do not mention, however, is that human experimentation requires the *informed consent* of the human subject—a crucial concept that cannot be applied in the context of animal experimentation—and that these committees are composed almost exclusively of other vivisectors who for the most part "rubber stamp" what the vivisector wants.

The Wizard of Id. Reprinted by permission of Johnny Hart and Creators Syndicate.

Small wonder, then, that many activists who worked for the 1985 amendments to the AWA now realize that the AWA serves as a most convenient tool in the biomedical industry's bag of public relations tricks.

We should add that animal rights advocates who support animal welfare means are playing into the hands of the biomedical establishment's current strategy of portraying this "temporary" acceptance of animal welfare as proof of the "dishonesty" of the animal rights movement. Patrick Concannon of Cornell Veterinary School argues that animal rights advocates often support welfarist reforms, but "are not bound by any moral requirement to be truthful about their ultimate goals and intentions." The animal rights movement must be careful to ensure that these untruths do not succeed in creating an impression of the movement as dishonest in any sense.

The belief that animal welfare reforms advance the cause of animal rights is also mistaken conceptually. As long as humans have rights and nonhumans do not, as is the case in the welfarist framework, then nonhumans will virtually always lose when their interests conflict with human interests. Thus welfare reforms, by their very nature, can only serve to retard the pace at which animal rights goals are achieved.

In order to understand this point, we need to remind ourselves of the nature of rights. In the ordinary course, rights are not subject to violation simply because others will benefit from that violation. For example, under the U.S. Constitution, people enjoy a right to liberty that may not be violated without due process. This right, among others, prevents people from being used in biomedical experiments against their will—even when such use would produce substantial benefits for many other people. The whole purpose of a right is to act as a *barrier* of sorts between the rightholder and everyone else.

In our society at the present time, and indefinitely into the future under the welfarist framework, only people have rights enforceable by law. Animals are regarded as the *property* of humans, and rather than having rights, animals are almost always regarded as the *object* of the exercise of rights on the part of humans. When we confront a situation in which human and nonhuman interests conflict, we should attempt to balance those interests, but, under the animal welfare framework, we balance two very dissimilar interests: the interest of the nonhuman animal, who is regarded as property and the object of the exercise of human rights (usually property rights), against the interest of the human rightholder. And the animal is almost always bound to lose because by weighing the human right so heavily, a presumption in favor of exploitation is created.

Thus the moral framework established by the animal welfare philosophy guarantees that nonhuman animals will almost always lose when their interests are balanced against the claims of human rights. This moral framework can only serve to impede animal rights.

Animal Rights Activism

Many animal advocates will agree with us up to this point, but will then make the familiar charge: "We cannot end animal exploitation overnight. We must take things one step at a time, and we must be content with the reform of the system. The abolitionist philosophy would have us do nothing, and we need to do something."

This charge rests on a misunderstanding. It is perfectly consistent with the philosophy of animal rights to take a gradual approach to end animal exploitation. It is just that the steps that need to be taken must themselves be abolitionist in nature.

What would such abolitionist steps be like? Here are only a

few examples: an end to the Draize, LD50, and all other toxicity and irritancy tests; an end to the use of animals in product testing; an end to the use of animals in maternal deprivation, military, and drug addiction experiments; an end to commercial whaling; an end to the killing of elephants, rhinos, and other "big game"; and an end to the commerce in fur.

As far as the billions of animals used for food are concerned, the abolitionist means is found in education. Those who advocate animal rights must seize the vegan initiative that contemporary society, for a variety of reasons, presents to them. Americans are, in unprecedented numbers, prepared to stop eating nonhuman animals and animal byproducts, and the advocates of animal rights should direct their time and effort to getting those ranks to swell through education and rational persuasion. A "No veal at any meal" campaign, not "Eat happy veal raised in larger social units," is the realistic abolitionist place to begin.

Abolitionist Philosophy Divisive?

Some activists might object that the demand for abolitionist "purity" will "divide" the animal rights movement and thereby slow its progress. Some have even gone so far as to denigrate the philosophy, which we along with many thousands of grassroots activists espouse, as the "new fundamentalism." This is, in our view, an unfair, harmful perjoration of a serious, well-developed philosophy, and represents the type of rhetorical excess activists have learned to expect from image-makers in the employ of the American Medical Association or the American Farm Bureau, but not from persons committed to working to advance the struggle for animal rights. These issues to one side, we believe that a clearer understanding of the two philosophies—animal rights and animal welfare—coupled with the determination to work for abolitionist means to abolitionist ends, does not divide people otherwise united by their commitment to animal rights; rather, it serves to clarify whether any unity exists in the first place.

The acceptance of our position does not mean that animal advocates—whether adherents of animal rights or animal welfare, or others—must be at constant war with one another, or that those who advocate animal rights should strike a "holier than thou" pose. There is plenty of room for justified humility by everyone, plenty of opportunities for displaying tolerance and patience toward people who are just beginning to think about the issues, and plenty of occasions calling for cooperation among the partisans of conflicting philosophies, from educating the public about how badly other animals are treated, to joining forces on specific actions, such as the Hegins pigeon shoot, opposition to particularly egregious research, students' rights in the classroom, and anti-fur campaigns. But it is our view that animal *rights* organizations should pursue animal *rights* campaigns, and not spend their human and economic resources on projects that seek to promote the welfare but do not vindicate the rights of nonhumans.

The purpose of our remarks is not intended in any way to disparage the efforts of people who perform acts of kindness toward animals. People can clearly help animals even though they do not share the rights perspective. We are talking here about the future direction of the animal rights movement, and although we value those individual acts of kindness that result in the amelioration of animal suffering, the movement simply cannot afford to formulate its philosophies, policies, strategies, and campaign so that everyone who has any concern for animals will be able to agree on the principles informing and directing the movement. To do so would be to adopt views that are so broad as to be meaningless, and that would frustrate, rather than forward, the achievement of animal rights goals.

There will always be organizations espousing a moderate welfarist message, whose primary aim will be attracting those people who have a genuine concern for animals but who, for whatever reason, do not accept the rights position. Those organizations serve a valuable role in providing a niche for such people, who often evolve to accept a rights approach. Those groups, however, are not animal *rights* organizations, and indeed they often quite explicitly disavow the rights position. Over the past several years, some groups that once advocated animal rights appear to have backed away from that position, claiming that they must have a position that will be comfortable for everyone who wants to help animals. But no organization can be all things to all people; indeed, advocating an approach that everyone can live with is substantially certain to result in a position that will appeal to the lowest common denominator, and that will ensure that animal rights will remain an unattainable ideal.

The Larger Social Context

The philosophy of animal rights views the systematic exploitation of animals as a symptom of a society that tolerates the systematic exploitation of "the other," including those human "others" who lack the economic and other means to resist oppression. Thus, the philosophy of animal rights necessarily calls for human, not only animal, liberation; by contrast, the philosophy of animal welfare neither addresses nor advocates why and how justice for humans is to be achieved.

The philosophy of animal rights is an inclusive philosophy. Rights for nonhumans only make sense if we accept the total inclusion of our human sisters and brothers as full and equal members of the extended human family, without regard to race, sex, economic status, religious persuasion, disability, or sexual preference. Thus the philosophy of animal rights entails far-reaching social change. Animal liberation is human liberation. The philosophy of animal rights illuminates why this is. But it is no less true that human liberation is animal liberation. To believe in and work for our oppressed and exploited brothers and sisters in fur and feather and fin commits animal rights activists to believing in and working for our oppressed brothers and sisters in human flesh. Perhaps our movement has not yet arrived at this degree of inclusion, but in our view, such inclusion is the goal to which our movement must aspire.

"Sometimes philosophy can get in the way of helping animals suffer less during the many years before they achieve the rights we wish for them."

The Animal Rights Movement Must Embrace Animal Welfarism

Ingrid Newkirk

Ingrid Newkirk is cofounder and national director of People for the Ethical Treatment of Animals (PETA). Speaking on behalf of and in appreciation for those who promote animal welfarism, Newkirk argues that the animal rights movement must avoid ostracizing anyone who promotes animal well-being. She contends that animal welfarists have done much to lessen the suffering of animals, and their devotion to animals, however deficient from the viewpoint of animal rightists, must be appreciated as intrinsically valuable and ultimately helpful in improving the quality of animal life.

As you read, consider the following questions:

1. In Newkirk's view, why should animal rights activists respect people who wish to help animals but who may not be fully committed to the philosophy of animal rights?
2. According to the author, what practical concerns will always prevent the animal rights movement from purifying itself of those who disagree with its philosophy?
3. In what ways, as Newkirk describes them, are both animal welfarists and animal rights activists walking the same road?

Ingrid Newkirk, "Total Victory, Like Checkmate, Cannot Be Achieved in One Move," *Animals' Agenda*, January/February 1992. Reprinted with permission.

Like Tom Regan and Gary Francione, I hold dear the vision of a world in which other-than-human beings are respected to the fullest.

This is a most unrealistic view, of course, because no one has yet been able to reason, bully, or cajole human beings out of warmongering against one another, or even stealing from, cheating, and undercutting their own friends and relatives. (Take, for example, the pettiness of group rivalries, and the energy wasted arguing over which way is *the* best way, by every group of human beings, from model airplane enthusiasts to civil rights advocates.) However, while utopia may be unattainable, most forms of animal slavery will be abolished, I'm sure, if we push for them without embarrassment or hesitation and force ourselves to accept that total victory, like checkmate, cannot be achieved in one move.

Constructive Criticism

Although I expect [Tom Regan and Gary Francione's viewpoint] to be a well-reasoned call for us to go beyond the admittedly ridiculous—albeit, in my opinion, sometimes necessary—task of trying to regulate atrocities, I have a concern: Recently, I hear audiences being told that "animal rightists" must take an all or nothing approach. Further, that we must cast out "animal welfarists" and others who happen not to endorse that speaker's own views on issues involving not only other-than-human beings but our own species. It was a very destructive call.

My appeal here, therefore, is for us always to try, at least, to be constructive in our criticisms; welcoming to all new arrivals; and tolerant of people who are trying, in their own diverse ways, to help animals, even if we don't agree with them.

I will go to bat for "animal welfarists" (many of whom I respect enormously and consider my dearest professional friends); argue very briefly that there are pitfalls in attempting to reduce the membership of the animal rights movement to "purists," whatever each of us imagines that to mean; and give an example of why I believe that each step in the right general direction can only bring us closer to our ultimate goal.

Steps in the Right Direction

To take the last point first, here's the example: Some years ago, the government was about to succumb to pressure from the cattle industry to withdraw a requirement that cows and steers awaiting slaughter—sometimes for up to three miserable days—be given water while they wait. Water, they reasoned, is expensive, and the cattle are going to die anyway.

Animal protectionists began circulating petitions trying to counter the influence of the cattle lobby. I sent some of these petitions to a vegetarian community, asking for signatures, but the petitions were returned unsigned. A note that came back with them read, "We are ethically opposed to the slaughter of animals for food, therefore we cannot get involved."

Luckily, the water requirement remained in place, but I cannot imagine how those vegetarians with clean hands, who declined to help, could explain their politics to the poor cows, sitting in the dust with parched throats. The issue was not to slaughter or not, it was to water or not. Sometimes philosophy can get in the way of helping animals suffer less during the many years before they achieve the rights we wish for them.

Movement "Purity"

Secondly, in regard to "purifying" our movement: only dead people are true purists, feeding the earth and living beings rather than taking from them. Most vegans drive cars, buy consumer goods, and live in buildings that have displaced hundreds to thousands of other-than-human beings. We know it is impossible to breathe without hurting or exploiting; we can simply try to keep improving and eliminating old habits we don't need.

Cooperation Should Be Universal

Animal advocates are a diverse group of people with wide-ranging ideas and convictions about ethics, strategies, tactics, and even animals themselves. Consequently the animal rights movement has become an eclectic confederation of local groups, national societies, and unaffiliated individuals. Cooperation among these elements is not as universal as it should be. Until it is, we risk losing the momentum provided by growing public support for animals and, even worse, we allow the powerful vested interests opposing animal rights to define us as a movement driven by anti-human, anti-scientific zealotry.

The Animals' Agenda, vol. 14, no. 3, 1994.

At the Alliance conference [in 1991], I listened to two people who have each contributed enormously to people's understanding of animal rights. They addressed the audience within minutes of each other. One argued that, "to be consistent," people who are fighting for animal rights must be "pro-choice." The other argued that, "to be consistent," we must fight for all life, even that of unborn babies. Each was sincere, vehement, and wholly committed to his/her position on abortion.

The animals, judging by what is going on in slaughterhouses and on mink farms, among other places, need the good works of both speakers and everyone in the audience. To ostracize one speaker (and perhaps half the audience who supports that speaker) because his or her opinion on abortion does not conform to mine would diminish our collective work in areas where we do agree.

All Walking the Same Road

Finally, [concerning] the "welfarists." Imagine that there were no anticruelty statutes in America and that we were starting from scratch in trying to persuade people that animals are not ours to eat, wear, experiment on, use in entertainment, and so on.

It is only within the last hundred years that the "animal welfarists" have worked to compel society to accept that cruelty to animals (beating lame horses who no longer had the strength to pull heavy carts, drowning crates of stray dogs in the rivers—that sort of thing) is more than wrong, it is illegal. (Incidentally, the public's perceived self-interest prohibited it from accepting the anti-vivisectionist movement, even though it emerged at the same time as the humane movement; thus the circa 1890 anti-vivisection societies became dormant for some decades.)

The Springboard to Animal Rights

It is certainly thanks to the "welfarists"—many of whom have embraced animal rights, but some who still have bull roasts, breed purebred dogs, and do other things I wish they wouldn't—that we are now able to springboard into animal rights. It is also thanks to them that spaying and neutering, euthanasia (as opposed to drowning, bludgeoning, electrocution with jumper cables, death by inhalation of hot, filthy carbon monoxide) and humane education are no longer considered radical ideas. Frontline "welfarist" workers' jobs are lousy, thankless, and stressful enough as it is without animal rights purists jumping all over them. (Yes, euthanasia is a miserable solution, but if any euthanasia critic out there knows where they can put the 14,000 unwanted animals who will come through just one of my area shelters this year, please drop me a line. Those who offer living deaths and slow deaths—furriers, butchers, experimenters, guard dog companies, and people who think an acceptable home need only mean food, water, and air—need not apply.)

It is almost impossible for even one of us to find another of us who agrees on *everything* we hold true. Some people hunt but believe the Hegins pigeon shoot is cruel. Some are vegan but still believe that *some* animal experiments are justified. Differences are the norm. What's important is where we agree.

Wherever we decide to put our own energies, time, and money is our decision. We can disagree heartily as to what will bring about animal liberation the soonest, but all of us are guessing, so let's not try to undermine each other and be accusatory of each other's motives. We are, after all, walking along the same road, changing our behaviors as we go, stalling periodically, but trying to find the strength to do what we believe is right.

May Tom and Gary's article be the (positive) voice of the "loud-howling wolves [who] arouse the jades that drag the tragic melancholy night."

"*It is . . . important for both extremes to resist falling into an 'us' versus 'them' mentality wherein the issue gets reduced to opposing the enemy instead of advancing a cause.*"

The Animal Rights Movement Must Learn to Compromise

Peter Wilson

Peter Wilson, a researcher in the Department of Astronomy at Cornell University, studies the origin, production, and distribution of organic matter in the solar system. In the following viewpoint, posted on the World-Wide Web in 1995, he argues that real progress in the animal rights debate is made by way of compromise. To support his argument, Wilson reviews examples of compromise described in Deborah Blum's *The Monkey Wars* that have been instrumental in improving animals' lives. Deriving encouragement from such examples, Wilson urges both animal rights activists and those traditionally opposed to their movement to forge new alliances in order to benefit animals.

As you read, consider the following questions:

1. According to Wilson, why is the Animal Welfare Act a good example of how opposing parties may come to agree on issues involving the welfare of animals?
2. In what way is Deborah Blum's *The Monkey Wars* biased, according to Wilson?

Peter Wilson, "In Defense of Compromise," *Animal Life*, Fall 1994. Reprinted with permission.

In a democratic and pluralistic society, extremism on controversial issues is unavoidable. And when the issue centers on the intentional taking of life, especially a life incapable of defending itself, strong animosity is inevitable between the two extremes. But one need only consider murders by anti-abortionists to recognize the danger that this animosity can represent. It is thus important for both extremes to resist falling into an "us" versus "them" mentality wherein the issue gets reduced to opposing the enemy instead of advancing a cause. Otherwise, a workable compromise will never be achieved.

The Animal Welfare Act: An Example of Compromise

It wasn't too long ago that only one side of the animal rights debate had any clout in the United States, and that was the pro-research side. Scientists once had total freedom to perform any experiment they desired and to treat the animals in whatever manner was most convenient. As it has become increasingly clear that animals are not Descartes's automata, but are instead truly capable of suffering, the animal rights movement has gained strength and legitimacy. The two extremes are currently represented by scientists defending the old status quo of unrestricted research and animal rights activists opposing all uses of animals. Over the years a compromise has been forged by the people caught between these extremes. That compromise is in the form of the Animal Welfare Act.

The Animal Welfare Act endorses the use of animals in research, but at the same time it mandates the humane treatment of those animals whenever not prohibited by the needs of the experiment. The law no longer views animals as just tools, but neither does it view animals as individuals possessing rights. As such, neither extreme can claim total victory, although this is clearly a step away from the absolute power scientists once held.

Deborah Blum's *The Monkey Wars*

In *The Monkey Wars*, Deborah Blum chronicles many of the battles fought between animal rightists and animal researchers over the use of primates in experiments. Because we are ourselves primates, the arguments both for and against the use of nonhuman primates are strongest and, therefore, the emotions on both sides run the highest. Because the biologies are nearly identical, there is a high probability that experiments done on nonhuman primates will advance the understanding of human diseases. But for exactly the same reason, there is a high probability that nonhuman primates have a capacity to think and feel similar to humans, so it is very easy to empathize with them and to believe them deserving of rights similar to humans.'
Also, because they are our closest relatives, chimpanzees serve

as the test case for both sides. Since only humans currently have recognized rights, whether or not rights are ever extended beyond our species and to chimpanzees will have important implications for every other animal rights battle.

Deborah Blum has attempted to write a balanced presentation of the many sides of this issue by profiling people from across the philosophical spectrum. Most of the book is spent with the animal experimenters, though, with the animal rightists profiled only to the extent that they are the adversaries of the experimenters.

S. Gross. Reprinted with permission.

The first four chapters explore the range of primate research from the noninvasive sign-language studies of Roger Fouts to the brain damage experiments of Stuart Zola-Morgan. The reactions that these researchers have had to the rise of animal rights have a similarly large range. Whereas Fouts frequently sides with animal rightists in fighting for increased emphasis on the welfare of the primates, Zola-Morgan retains the old-school attitude that any effort to restrict the activities of scientists is inherently anti-science and should be fought against.

The next four chapters detail a large number of confrontations between the extremes. These range from the legal battle over custody of the Silver Spring monkeys to a letter writing campaign over an episode of *Quantum Leap*. Blum then examines in the following three chapters many of the complications involved in the use of primates. One chapter focuses on the uncertain but sometimes useful animal model of disease; another deals with trans-species organ transplants and the possibility of thereby exposing humans to new viruses; and finally a chapter follows the effort of Robert Gormus to obtain mangabeys from Africa.

In the twelfth and final chapter Blum criticizes both sides for their unwillingness to compromise and urges each extreme to move towards the middle. The main conflict, however, between the two extremes is not whether animal experiments should occur, although this difference of opinion motivates both sides, but rather ensuring the welfare of the animals as mandated by the Animal Welfare Act. This act clearly supports the use of animals in research, yet animal rightists almost unanimously endorse this law, so in this regard one side has already accepted compromise. And in defending this compromise the animal rightists have allied with the people which the book holds up as holding the rational middle ground.

LEMSIP: One Example of a New Alliance

One glowing example of this alliance is the relationship animal rightists have with Jan Moor-Jankowski, the director of the Laboratory for Experimental Medicine and Surgery in Primates (LEMSIP). Moor-Jankowski intentionally employs animal lovers to care for the primates at the facility. His chief veterinarian, Jim Mahoney, even admits, "I don't feel so right about what I do that I could turn to an animal rights advocate, and say, you are wrong. In the end, I think I'm wrong." And at one point when Moor-Jankowski wanted to kill some birds nesting in the facilities, an employee reported him to state wildlife officials, much to Moor-Jankowski's amusement. LEMSIP is also very open about the research performed there; nothing is hidden in a shroud of secrecy. When Alex Pacheco, president of People for the Ethical Treatment of Animals (PETA), was at Cornell he pointed out that he could visit LEMSIP at any time unannounced and would be allowed to inspect the facility and make sure the conditions were satisfactory. And on several occasions, Moor-Jankowski has sided with animal rightists in their confrontations with researchers. By keeping an open facility and showing genuine concern for the animals, Moor-Jankowski is allowed to do his animal experiments in relative peace.

Because of this truce and the common interest—the welfare of the animals—of two of the three sides presented, [*The Monkey*

Wars] is too one-sided against the fanatical experimenters who fight against the current compromise.

Some Researchers Oppose Compromise

Peter Gerone, the director of the Tulane Regional Primate Research Center, is the primary antagonist in the book opposing compromise. Gerone objects to having the standards for animal welfare exceed those for the worst outcasts of human society—criminals in prison. When the Centers for Disease Control (CDC) cited and revoked the import license of his animal supplier for unsanitary conditions, Gerone was more concerned about the fact that Shirley McGreal of the International Primate Protection League had sent him a copy of the CDC report with a note that essentially said "thought you'd like to know." Just one of the 46 problems found by the CDC was that the monkey cages were stacked such that monkeys were being urinated on by those above them. What prison treats its prisoners like this?

And when USDA inspectors issued some complaints about Tulane's facilities, Gerone blasted them for not keeping the complaints just between them and Tulane since official records are available to animal rightists through the Freedom of Information Act. Gerone sees any criticism of experimenters and their treatment of animals as persecution intended to end all research. Despite, or possibly because of, the fact that the complaints were relatively minor and of little use to those opposed to animal experimentation, his letter ended with the paranoid statement, "You will only satisfy them if you decided to ban animal research."

Yet another example comes following an inspection of Gerone's treatment of the Silver Spring monkeys. Roy Henrickson, a veterinarian from the University of California, Berkeley, suggested Gerone treat the monkeys better. But according to Henrickson, "[Gerone] was so set by that point, he couldn't even hear me. He wouldn't have done anything that he thought might have made PETA happy. "

This one-minded crusade against animal rightists, even at the expense of the animals, seems only to be fed by Gerone's own refusal to interact with the monkeys. "I don't let monkeys hug me. It's not good to let them get too close." "I don't relate to monkeys and I don't want to. It would bias my ability to direct a center that does research on them." He wants to assure "the ability to pursue interesting questions unfettered." Concern for the animals' welfare, therefore, is an impediment to research and is to be opposed at every turn. But by distancing himself from the monkeys, he denies himself the possibility of understanding why animal rightists are so opposed to the use of monkeys in research.

Whereas Gerone comes across as a pit bull looking to exact a pound of flesh from his enemies, Stuart Zola-Morgan, a neuro-surgeon at the University of California, San Diego, appears to simply be a man with an outdated mindset lacking the ability to comprehend the changes occurring around him. Zola-Morgan is curious about how the brain works, so he inflicts brain damage on monkeys in order to study where and how memories are stored. His justification for his experiments is that he is curious. He does not stand behind the claim that he does it to save human lives. In his own words, "the major reason I'm doing this is that I want to know." Because animal rightists don't consider that sufficient justification, he labels them "anti-knowledge and anti-progress." He accuses animal rightists of having lost their curiosity about the world around them. All knowledge, according to him, has a price but he fails to recognize that sometimes the price can be too high.

Some Animal Rightists Also Oppose Compromise

Despite all the faults with the fanatical animal researchers, the fanatical animal rightists aren't perfect angels, either. First of all, although not interviewed for the book, the people who make personal threats, especially death threats, against researchers or illegally harass them are to be condemned by all, researchers and animal rightists alike. And for the most part, they are. Such behavior violates one of the principles upon which animal rights are founded: sympathy for others. But, sometimes people of good conscience are driven to illegal actions. Just as the actions of the Underground Railroad and the civil rights groups of the 1950s and 1960s violated laws at the time but are now admired as heroic, some of the actions of the Animal Liberation Front (ALF) are justified responses to situations where the mistreatment of animals is hidden behind locked doors. And as the book points out, the ALF has never caused physical harm to any person, and they probably never will. But feeling justified does not excuse the crime. If caught, members of the ALF should still be punished. Anyone who breaks the law, even for a good cause, should be willing to accept the consequences.

From the interviews with mainstream animal rightists, only PETA's insistence that no experiments be performed on the Silver Spring monkeys at the time they are euthanized appears excessively dogmatic. Although Pacheco's intentions are easy to understand given the lies and double crosses he encountered with the National Institutes of Health, including a promise that the monkeys would not be used for research while they were still alive, he should have compromised. If they were going to be euthanized, it should have been irrelevant if a coma was induced first and the brain exposed. Although Pacheco appears to believe that such actions would not be tolerated if done on a human, experimentation on animals or humans should be allowable when euthanasia becomes necessary, so long as consciousness is lost first and never regained. Except for Pacheco's belief that the health of the monkeys would improve if only Gerone would give them proper treatment, there was no justification for Pacheco to refuse his own veterinarian's request to euthanize Billy, one of the Silver Spring monkeys. PETA had little chance of changing Billy's situation, so his current poor health took precedence over what his health would have been under better conditions. Gerone, though, fed Pacheco's fear of deception by refusing to allow Pacheco to even visit the primate facility.

Concluding Observations

Overall, the book is a fascinating discussion, detailing the ugly politics underlying animal rights battles. But the noted absence of truly fanatical animal rightists like the members of the ALF or animal rightists opposed to the Animal Welfare Act makes it unbalanced against fanatical experimenters. The book would also benefit from a chapter discussing the philosophies each side utilizes to justify their beliefs. The animal rights side, however, is readily available from another wonderful book called *The Great Ape Project* by Paola Cavalieri and Peter Singer. The absence of a philosophical discussion is probably to the experimenters' advantage, though, since even Peter Gerone admits, "once someone raises the philosophical question . . . what is it that makes me feel I have a right to use animals, I'm at a loss for an answer."

"Significant progress lies in establishing animal rights as a mainstream political issue."

The Animal Rights Movement Must Be Politically Pragmatic

Kim Stallwood

Kim Stallwood is the editor in chief of *The Animals' Agenda*, a bimonthly journal published by the Animal Rights Network. In the following viewpoint, Stallwood argues that animal liberationists—and especially leaders of various animal rights organizations—must put aside their ideological divisions and unite themselves for the "pragmatic politics of animal advocacy." Encouraging her audience to develop a well-defined platform, she urges "actions, not positions" as the best way to balance "the utopian vision of animal liberation" with the "reality of the world in which we live."

As you read, consider the following questions:

1. What, in Stallwood's view, are the problems that the animal rights movement now faces?
2. According to Stallwood, why does Britain's General Election Coordination Committee for Animal Protection provide a model for American animal rights activists?
3. What note of caution does the author express to those who articulate an animal rights ideology?

Excerpted from "Utopian Visions and Pragmatic Politics" by Kim Stallwood, a paper presented to the National Alliance for Animals, June 25, 1995. Reprinted with permission.

There are two fundamentally important challenges which we face individually as animal advocates and collectively as the animal rights movement. Our ability to respond to these challenges will inevitably determine whether we are successful in confronting the cultural, political, and scientific assumptions of speciesism on which animal exploitation is predicated.

Our Challenges, Our Vision

The first challenge is learning how to balance the utopian vision of animal liberation with the pragmatic politics of animal advocacy.

When I say the utopian vision of animal liberation I refer to our cherished ideals of a world where human and nonhuman animals can peacefully coexist together.

When I say the pragmatic politics of animal advocacy I refer to the reality of the world in which we live and the day-to-day experiences we encounter which shape our opinions on what it is possible to achieve for animals.

The second fundamental challenge that we face is learning how to construct a united and professional animal rights movement that balances the utopian vision of animal liberation with the pragmatic politics of animal advocacy.

[This] presentation will be in three parts. First, I will summarize the progress of the British animal rights movement toward establishing animal rights as a mainstream issue. Then I will outline the steps that are currently under way in this country toward a similar objective. Finally, I will describe how you can make animal rights a mainstream political issue in your state.

The Present Situation

We are a diverse group of people with wide-ranging ideas and convictions about ethics, strategies, tactics, and even animals themselves. Consequently we have created a movement that has become an eclectic confederation of local groups, national societies, and unaffiliated individuals. Cooperation among these elements is not as universal as it should be. Until it is, we are at constant risk of losing the momentum provided by growing public support for animals and, even worse, of allowing the powerful vested interests opposing animal rights to define the movement as one driven by anti-human, anti-scientific zealotry.

To be sure, we are currently experiencing a crisis in leadership at both the local and the national levels of our movement. This leadership crisis manifests itself in our inability to articulate a long-term plan to accomplish specific objectives. And even if we could articulate a long-term strategy, I suspect that our leadership crisis disqualifies us from being able to discuss it, for virtually every discussion about our movement's future degenerates into a battle over egos and organized turf.

England's General Election Coordinating Committee for Animal Protection

One way that I thought we could learn more about how to confront successfully these challenges is by meeting with animal advocates in the U.K. In 1995 I organized with Environmental Travel the first "Animal Rights View of England" tour. Fourteen wonderful animal advocates from ten states accompanied me on an intensive six-day program. This program included a visit to Britain's leading animal rights organizations, a meeting with sympathetic Members of Parliament, participation in an anti-vivisection protest comprised of 1,000–2,000 people, and attending a national exhibition, "The Animal World Show."

We had many opportunities to discuss with individual activists—ranging from grassroots organizers to nationally recognized advocates—the actions of the animal rights movement in the United Kingdom. These discussions enabled us to appreciate the successes of our British colleagues, including:

- Widespread public support for animal rights, vegetarianism, and cruelty-free living;
- Sympathetic media coverage in national newspapers, radio, and television;
- Parliamentary all-party support for increased legal protection.

Participation in the tour confirmed my belief that the foundation for this significant progress lies in establishing animal rights as a mainstream political issue. This was accomplished through a series of movement-wide coalitions over the last 20 years.

The original campaign, which was called "Putting Animals into Politics," was launched in 1977 by the General Election Coordinating Committee for Animal Protection. Better known as GECCAP, this committee consisted of individual animal rights experts and representatives from national animal protection groups.

The campaign comprised a general mission statement, the identification of four areas of concern (companion animals, farm animals, laboratory animals, and wildlife), and a list of goals (abolishing the battery cage, banning the use of dogs for hunting, halting the live export of food animals, and so forth).

GECCAP was based on two simple premises:

- Political candidates and elected representatives care about votes and campaign contributions.
- Political candidates and elected representatives will care about animal rights when they are linked to votes and campaign contributions.

Proceeding from these assumptions, the animal rights movement in the U.K. succeeded in demonstrating a significant fact to the three major political parties: A sufficient number of voters would be influenced by a party's or a candidate's position on animal rights—and by a party's or a candidate's track record on animal rights issues.

The Future of the Movement

The animal rights movement is now old, but still has momentum, which could be used, together with friction raised by the newly empowered wise use movement, to win the reduction of meat to condiment status, if it is eaten at all; the abandonment of sport hunting; the end of the fur trade; more popular and effective means of protecting wildlife habitat; and perhaps much else. We are at the outset of a new growth phase for pro-animal activism, *if* leadership can leave the rhetorical shell of past growth phases, making use of new understanding.

Animal People, April 1995.

GECCAP's approach combined national and local action focused on the same program. This program was nonpartisan, and although its ultimate goals were abolitionist, no positive action for animals was derided—or worse yet, rejected—because it was considered unworthy of some philosophically or politically correct theory. The campaign concerned itself with the real world, for that is the world in which animals suffer. As a result, the major political parties accepted animal protection as a legitimate political issue, one that was included in their manifestos for the first time. This acceptance came about after politicians had been convinced that their positions regarding animals could gain or could lose them votes.

Consequently, veal crates are now banned in England, the single-sow stall will become illegal in 1999, many county and town councils have banned not only hunting with dogs but also circuses with performing animal acts from their land. The British county is the equivalent of a state in this country. All of these issues were included in GECCAP's original platform.

Actions, Not Positions

We noticed during our recent visit two animal protection issues that were continually in the public eye and the media spotlight: the hunting on horseback and on foot with packs of dogs of foxes and other wild animals and the live export of two million lambs and sheep and half a million young calves annually from Britain to Europe. Currently there is widespread public support for laws to prohibit both of these issues. At the next general election significant numbers of voters will determine which political party they will vote for based on the current government's scorecard on these and other animal protection issues and the manifesto pledges of the other two major political parties. All the talk and the theorizing notwithstanding, there is one inescapable conclusion about leadership: It ultimately consists of actions, not positions.

The mission of *The Animals' Agenda* is to "inform people about animal rights and cruelty-free living for the purpose of inspiring action for animals." Among the most important groups we need to inform about animal rights and cruelty-free living are the groups that comprise this nation's elected officials at the federal, state, and local levels. Toward that end, I have urged the formation of a professional association of animal advocacy groups that would represent the animal rights movement by presenting a united voice for animals. The group, modeled after GECCAP, would articulate a clearly defined animal rights mission. It would also incorporate a legislative and public education program that would amplify the voice of the animal rights movement to the public, the media, and local, state, and federal lawmakers.

In 1994 I convened a small and informal group of animal advocates to discuss how we could establish animal rights as a mainstream political issue in the U.S. This group, which consisted of Peter Gerard, Holly Hazard, Wayne Pacelle, and Ken Shapiro, compared the progress in the U.K. with current developments in this country. We also explored the different approaches that could be taken. Is it better, for example, to form first a professional association of animal advocacy organizations before embarking on a movement-wide campaign or would our chances of success be greater if we organized first a movement-wide campaign and allowed the formation of an association to develop out of it? We also looked at the environmental movement and met with the League of Conservation Voters to learn of their progress. Finally, we began to develop our own written plan of action.

Our discussions identified the National Alliance for Animals and *The Animals' Agenda* as two organizations that uniquely serve the entire animal advocacy movement. The National Alliance for Animals organizes annually movement-wide conferences that bring together a cross-section of grassroots activists and national representatives. *The Animals' Agenda*, which publishes information, commentary, and analysis on animal exploitation, is the *Time* or *Newsweek* of our movement.

A Platform for Action

When we combined our deliberations on making animal rights a mainstream political issue with the role of the National Alliance and *The Animals' Agenda* we agreed that our next course of action will be to develop a platform. . . .

This platform, which will be published in *The Animals' Agenda* . . . , will consist of three components:

- A mission statement that enshrines the spirit and purpose of what we believe, what we seek to accomplish, and who we represent. It will also include some additional goals, including making animal cruelty a federal offense in every state of the union, awarding animal advocacy organizations legal standing to sue on behalf of animals, and endorsement of the Great Ape Project;
- The platform will identify five priority areas of concern: companion animals, free-roaming or wild animals, animals in entertainment, animals in agriculture, and animals in science and education;
- Each of these five priority areas of concern will detail specific goals that we will seek to accomplish; for example, a ban on the battery cage, the abolition of factory farming, and an end to all toxicity testing.

I welcome anyone who is interested in participating in the drafting of this platform to contact me. Also, I welcome your feedback on the platform once it is published in *The Animals' Agenda*. It is healthy to have an exchange of views, but debates must be carried out in a respectful and meaningful way. We must not permit disagreement to divide us. Nor must we mislabel a respect for civility in discourse as censorship. . . .

It is our sincere hope that many local and national animal advocacy organizations will endorse [this platform] and circulate it widely to their members and supporters. The circulation and endorsement of a movement-wide platform will help focus our message to the people, the media, industry, and the government.

It may be easy to dismiss this initiative as naive and unrealistic. But what is the alternative? How many times have you asked why are there so many organizations and why can't they get along? Unless these goals are achieved, the animal rights movement will slip from the forefront of this country's movements for equality and will become, instead, a sad, desolate footnote in the history of our times.

Local Action

Now is the time to organize similar initiatives within your state. Get together with animal advocates in your state and plan a state-wide long-term strategy. Write your own mission statement. You may have different issues and needs than other states. Develop your own priority areas of concern and determine what specific goals you would like to accomplish. Follow the plan but never allow your plan to become an excuse not to do something to help animals because it is not included. Keep seizing every opportunity to speak up for the animals. Revise the plan. Update it. Perhaps one day you will be able to check off accomplishments. Get involved with city hall or your local county government. Join a political party. Stand for election. Remember to make the point that there is a unity of oppression between the workers exploited by the poultry industry and the chicken slaughtered for human consumption, between the workers exploited on the backstretch of every racetrack and the systematic disregard of the welfare of racehorses, between the suffering of animals in the research laboratory and the suffering of people who take drugs that were not as safe as animal tests had certified them to be. . . .

Finally, I want to express a note of caution about ideologies. There is occasionally within the debate about animal liberation spirited discussion about the different philosophical traditions that are used to justify a new relationship with nonhuman animals. These philosophical traditions include utilitarianism, natural rights, painism, ecofeminism, and others. Philosophical theories are to be used like tools but beware when they become dogmatic ideologies. . . . Some animal rights proponents use particular philosophical theories as yardsticks to measure how real an animal rights activist you really are. Reject these artificially constructed devices at every opportunity. Under this rubric animal welfarists become the enemy. If, by their reasoning, animal welfarists are the enemy what does that make the public? If we view the public as far more heinous than the "enemy," how can we ever reasonably believe that we will ever have a winning strategy to empower them to understand and accept the arguments for animal liberation? Let's be clear: this is a divisive and—may I say—elitist strategy that only succeeds in making enemies of our friends. The animals need all the friends that they can get.

Periodical Bibliography

The following articles have been selected to supplement the diverse views presented in this chapter. Addresses are provided for periodicals not indexed in the *Readers' Guide to Periodical Literature*, the *Alternative Press Index*, or the *Social Sciences Index*.

Animal People	"Remembering the Aim," April 1995. Available from PO Box 205, Shushan, NY 12873.
Anna Charlton et al.	"The American Left Should Support Animal Rights: A Manifesto," *Animals' Agenda*, January/February 1993.
Josephine Donovan	"Animal Rights and Feminist Theory," *Signs*, vol. 15, 1990.
Philip Jamieson	"Animal Welfare Law: Foundations for Reform," *Between the Species*, Winter 1992. Available from PO Box 8496, Landscape Station, Berkeley, CA 94707.
Louis Jacobson	"Animal-Rights Battle Spills into Schools as Both Sides Target Next Generation," *Wall Street Journal*, September 2, 1992.
Roberta Kalechofsky	"Jewish Law and Tradition on Animal Rights: A Usable Parable for Christians and Jews in the Movement," *Between the Species*, Fall 1991.
Harriet Ritvo	"Toward a More Peaceable Kingdom," *Technology Review*, April 1992.
Howard Rosenberg	"Fighting Tooth and Claw," *Los Angeles Times*, March 22, 1992. Available from Reprints, Times Mirror Square, Los Angeles, CA 90053.
Ken Shapiro	"Toward Kinship: Ethics of Advocacy," *Animals' Agenda*, vol. 14, no. 6 (1994).
Kim Stallwood	"An Animal Rights View of England," *Animals' Agenda*, vol. 15, no. 5 (1995).
Jerrold Tannenbaum	"Veterinary Medical Ethics: A Focus of Conflicting Interests," *Journal of Social Issues*, Spring 1993.
Gary E. Varner	"The Prospects of Consensus and Convergence in the Animal Rights Debate," *Hastings Center Report*, January/February 1994.
Joe Weil	"Education: A Fundamental Strategy for Animals," *Animals' Agenda*, vol. 15, no. 3 (1995).

For Further Discussion

Chapter 1

1. Peter Singer bases his philosophy of animal rights on the belief that human and nonhuman animals experience suffering and pleasure in similar ways. R.G. Frey, on the other hand, emphasizes that human life appears to be intellectually and culturally richer than nonhuman life. In tracing the development of their arguments, where do Singer and Frey appear to agree with each other and at what point do they disagree?

2. Peter Singer and Tom Regan both seek to liberate and dramatically improve the lives of animals. They do not, however, agree with each other when arguing for a philosophical basis for animal liberation. Comparing their arguments, which seems to be easiest for the general public to understand and accept—and why?

3. The 1988 Annecy Report to the World Council of Churches tells Christians that their teachings and beliefs take seriously the need for compassion toward animals. James Parker, however, is not convinced. Which argument is more persuasive? Why?

Chapter 2

1. At one time, Michael Allen Fox contended that the American Medical Association's arguments for using animals in biomedical experimentation were convincing. Does the fact that Fox later changed his mind and now argues against such experimentation make his present position more or less compelling? Explain your answer.

2. Although Elizabeth Baldwin and Bernard E. Rollin are both respected scientists and researchers, they come to different conclusions about the merits of using animals in psychological research. Comparing their viewpoints, determine the audience to which each is speaking and evaluate how effectively their arguments target those specific audiences.

3. Susan Offner and F. Barbara Orlans present opposing arguments about the usefulness of classroom dissection in biology classes. Offner argues that students gain experiences in understanding biology that only dissection provides; Orlans disagrees. Based on your experience as a student who may have been required to study biology and practice dissection, who do you believe makes the better argument? Why?

Chapter 3

1. In making her argument that modern farming practices are inhumane, Laura Ten Eyck provides graphic descriptions of alleged cruelty to animals. Steve Kopperud, who defends the agricultural industry against such charges, contends that it would be against farmers' economic self-interest to treat their animals in an inhumane manner. Which argument is more persuasive? Why?

2. Daryn Eller's viewpoint was originally published in a mainstream women's magazine. The viewpoint by the People for the Ethical Treatment of Animals originally appeared as a pamphlet distributed by that animal rights organization. How do the rhetorical styles of the viewpoints reflect these different contexts?

3. Tabitha Powledge and Raymond Giraud argue from quite different backgrounds: Powledge from within the scientific community; Giraud as a professor of literature. To what extent are the arguments of each made more or less persuasive by the knowledge of her or his background? What possible merit is there in such trans-discipline argumentation and discussion?

Chapter 4

1. When Ryland Loos and Matt Cartmill analyze the reasons people hunt, they come to conflicting conclusions. For Loos, hunting provides an experience within which hunters discover themselves profoundly linked to the animal world; for Cartmill, such an analysis, if not an outright lie, is at best a sophisticated self-deception. Which author do you find more persuasive? Why?

2. Both Eileen Murphy and Colin Tudge are concerned with the welfare and future of animals, especially those belonging to endangered species. They disagree, however, as to how such animals are best preserved and humanely served. Murphy argues that many zoos are in crisis. Tudge, however, is less severe in his judgment. If Murphy and Tudge were to work toward a synthesis of their positions, might they come to some common understanding? If so, what might they agree on?

Chapter 5

1. While working to reduce animal suffering, people within the animal rights movement argue among themselves about the best ways to accomplish their goals. Tom Regan and Gary

Francione argue for the more radical position while Ingrid Newkirk promotes a more moderate view. How divisive do these arguments appear to be? From a strictly pragmatic point of view, which set of arguments seems best?

2. Peter Wilson and Kim Stallwood, each in his and her own way, also make suggestions as to how best to work for animal welfare and rights.

   Wilson believes that Deborah Blum's *The Monkey Wars* illustrates what can be done when people with opposing viewpoints listen to and learn from one another. Is Wilson right? Does compromise help? Why or why not?

   Stallwood's plea is for more action and less talk. What kind of action does she promote? How, if at all, do her recommendations differ from traditionally more dramatic boycotts and demonstrations? Stallwood suggests that the strategies of British animal rights activists have proven to be effective. Would such strategies work in the United States and other countries? Why or why not?

General Questions

1. Do you believe animals have rights equal to those of humans? Cite arguments found in at least two viewpoints to defend your answer.

2. Do you support the animal rights movement adamantly, a little, or not at all? Why?

3. Do you believe the animal rights movement is a radical or a moderate movement? Cite at least two authors to support your view.

Organizations to Contact

The editors have compiled the following list of organizations concerned with the issues debated in this book. The descriptions are derived from materials provided by the organizations. All have publications or information available for interested readers. The list was compiled on the date of publication of the present volume; names, addresses, phone numbers, fax numbers, and e-mail addresses may change. Be aware that many organizations take several weeks or longer to respond to inquiries, so allow as much time as possible.

The American Anti-Vivisection Society (AAVS)
Noble Plaza, Suite 204
801 Old York Rd.
Jenkintown, PA 19046-1685
(215) 887-0816
fax: (215) 887-2088

AAVS advocates the abolition of vivisection, opposes all types of experiments on living animals, and sponsors research on alternatives to these methods. The society produces videos and publishes numerous brochures, including *Vivisection and Dissection and the Classroom: A Guide to Conscientious Objection*. AAVS also publishes the bimonthly *AV Magazine*.

American Association for Laboratory Animal Science (AALAS)
70 Timber Creek Dr., Suite 5
Cordova, TN 38018
(901) 754-8620

AALAS collects and exchanges information on all phases of management, care, and procurement of laboratory animals. Its publications include *Contemporary Topics in Laboratory Animal Science* and *Laboratory Animal Science*.

The American Society for the Prevention of Cruelty to Animals (ASPCA)
424 E. 92nd St.
New York, NY 10128
(212) 876-7700
fax: (212) 348-3031

The ASPCA promotes appreciation for and humane treatment of animals, encourages enforcement of anticruelty laws, and works for the passage of legislation that strengthens existing laws to further protect animals. In addition to making available books, brochures, and videos on animal issues, the ASPCA publishes *Animal Watch*, a quarterly magazine.

The American Vegan Society
501 Old Harding Highway
Malaga, NJ 08328
(609) 694-2887

The society is dedicated to advocating a purely vegetarian diet. It publishes brochures, booklets, the quarterly *Ahimsa*, and books on nonviolent living and ethical eating.

Animal League Defense Fund (ALDF)
1363 Lincoln Ave., #7
San Rafael, CA 94901
(415) 459-0885

ALDF is an organization of attorneys and law students who promote animal rights and protect the lives and interests of animals through the use of their legal skills. It publishes the *Animals' Advocate* quarterly.

Farm Animal Reform Movement (FARM)
PO Box 30654
Bethesda, MD 20824
(301) 530-1737
fax: (301) 530-5747

FARM seeks to moderate and eliminate animal suffering and other adverse impacts of commercial animal production. It promotes the annual observance of March 20th as "The Great American Meatout," a day of meatless meals, and provides a variety of brochures and fact sheets for consumers and activists.

Food Animal Concerns Trust (FACT)
PO Box 14599
Chicago, IL 60614
(312) 525-4952
fax: (312) 525-5226

FACT promotes better care of farm animals and improved farming methods to produce safer foods and focuses on the food safety problems that arise from intensive animal production. Believing that factory-farming methods should be abolished, FACT helps farmers fund operations that raise animals humanely. Its trademarks are Nest Eggs and Rambling Rose Brand free-range veal. It publishes a quarterly newsletter, *FACT Acts*, as well as fact sheets and numerous brochures and pamphlets.

Foundation for Biomedical Research (FBR)
818 Connecticut Ave. NW, Suite 303
Washington, DC 20006
(202) 457-0654

FBR provides information and educational programs about what it sees as the necessary and important role of laboratory animals in biomedical research and testing. Its videos include *Caring for Laboratory*

Animals, The New Research Environment, and *Caring for Life*. It also publishes a bimonthly newsletter, *Foundation for Biomedical Research*.

The Humane Society of the United States (HSUS)
2100 L St. NW
Washington, DC 20037
(202) 452-1100
fax: (202) 778-6132

HSUS works to foster respect, understanding, and compassion for all creatures. Among its many diverse efforts, it maintains programs supporting responsible pet ownership, elimination of cruelty in hunting and trapping, exposing painful uses of animals in research and testing, and abusive treatment of animals in movies, circuses, pulling contests, and racing. It campaigns for and against legislation affecting animal protection and monitors enforcement of existing animal protection statutes. HSUS publishes the quarterlies *Animal Activist Alert*, *HSUS Close-up Reports*, and *HSUS News*.

Institute of Laboratory Animal Resources (ILAR)
2101 Constitution Ave. NW
Washington, DC 20418
(202) 334-2590

Organized under the auspices of the National Academy of Sciences, ILAR advises, upon request, the federal government and other agencies concerning the use of animals in biomedical research. It prepares guidelines and policy papers on biotechnology, the use of animals in precollege education, and other topics in laboratory animal science. Its publications include *Guide for the Care and Use of Laboratory Animals* and the quarterly *ILAR News*.

The Jane Goodall Institute for Wildlife Research, Education, and Conservation (JGI)
PO Box 599
Ridgefield, CT 06877
(203) 431-2099
fax: (203) 431-4387

JGI's goals include the support and expansion of field research on wild chimpanzees, assisting studies of chimps in captive environments, conducting comparative studies of captive and free-living chimpanzees, and enriching captive chimpanzees' lives. JGI also participates in conservation programs in Africa. It publishes the *Jane Goodall Institute—USA World Report*.

John Hopkins Center for Alternatives to Animal Testing (CAAT)
111 Market Pl., Suite 840
Baltimore, MD 21202-6709
(410) 223-1693
fax: (410) 223-1603

CAAT fosters the development of scientifically acceptable alternatives to animal testing for use in the development and safety evaluation of commercial and therapeutic products. The center conducts symposia for researchers and corporations. Its publications include *Alternative Methods in Toxicology, Animals and Alternatives in Testing*, and a periodic newsletter.

National Cattlemen's Association (NCA)
PO Box 3469
Englewood, CO 80155
(303) 694-0305

The NCA functions as the central agency for national public information and legislative and industry liaison for farmers, ranchers, breeders, and feeders of beef cattle. It publishes the monthly *National Cattlemen* and the weekly *Beef Business Bulletin*.

National Livestock and Meat Board (NLSMB)
444 N. Michigan Ave.
Chicago, IL 60611
(312) 467-5520

Representing numerous organizations of marketers, growers, packers, retailers, and food service firms, NLSMB serves the livestock and meat industry. It conducts promotional programs and provides information about beef, veal, pork, lamb, and associated meat products. A producer of films, manuals, catalogs, and brochures, NLSMB also publishes the semimonthly *Beef Promotion Bullhorn*.

People for the Ethical Treatment of Animals (PETA)
PO Box 42516
Washington, DC 20015
(301)770-PETA
fax: (301) 770-8969

An international animal rights organization, PETA is dedicated to establishing and protecting the rights of all animals. It focuses on four areas: factory farms, research laboratories, the fur trade, and the entertainment industry. PETA promotes public education, cruelty investigations, animal rescue, celebrity involvement, and legislative and direct action. It produces numerous videos and publishes *Animal Times, Grrr!* (a magazine for children), various fact sheets, brochures, and flyers.

Psychologists for the Ethical Treatment of Animals (PSYETA)
PO Box 1297
Washington Grove, MD 20880-1297
(301) 963-4751
fax: (301) 963-4751
e-mail: kshapiro@capaccess.org

PSYETA seeks to ensure proper treatment of animals used in psychological research and education and urges revision of curricula to include ethical issues in the treatment of animals. It works to establish procedures reducing the number of animals used in experiments and has developed a tool to measure the invasiveness or severity of animal experiments. Its publications include the *PSYETA Newsletter*, *Humane Innovations and Alternatives*, and the journals *Society and Animals* and the *Journal of Applied Animal Welfare*.

Putting People First
4401 Connecticut Ave., Suite 210
Washington, DC 20008-2302
(202) 364-7277
fax: (202) 354-7219

Composed of members using animal products, Putting People First works to inform the public of the wrongs of animal rights and disseminates information that opposes animal rights philosophy and actions. It publishes the biweekly *From the Trenches* and the periodic *The People's Agenda*.

Student Action Corps for Animals (SACA)
PO Box 15588
Washington, DC 20003-0588
(202) 543-8983

SACA, composed primarily of high school and college students, encourages youth participation in the animal rights movement, serves as a national clearinghouse and counseling center on the issue of student rights and empowerment, disseminates overviews of issues for students and teachers, and coordinates a Stop Dissection Campaign throughout the United States. It publishes two handbooks, *Action Alerts* and *Non-Animal Biology Lab Methods*, in addition to *SACA News*.

Vegetarian Resource Group (VRG)
PO Box 1463
Baltimore, MD 21203
(410) 366-VEGE
fax: (410) 366-8804

VRG membership is primarily made up of health professionals, activists, and educators working with businesses and individuals to bring about healthy nutritional changes in schools, workplaces, and communities. It educates the public about vegetarianism and veganism and examines vegetarian issues as they relate to good health, animal rights, ethics, world hunger, and ecology. VRG publishes books on vegetarianism, a computer software game, and the bimonthly newsletter *Vegetarian Journal*.

Bibliography of Books

Carol Adams	*Neither Man nor Beast: Feminism and the Defense of Animals.* New York: Continuum, 1994.
Carol Adams	*The Sexual Politics of Meat: A Feminist-Vegetarian Critical Theory.* New York: Continuum, 1991.
Animal Welfare Institute	*Animals and Their Legal Rights: A Survey of American Laws from 1641 to 1990.* Washington, DC: Animal Welfare Institute, 1990.
Ted Benton	*Natural Relations? Animal Rights, Human Rights, and the Environment.* New York: Routledge, 1992.
Deborah Blum	*The Monkey Wars.* New York: Oxford University Press, 1994.
Stephen Bostock	*Zoos and Animal Rights: The Ethics of Keeping Animals.* New York: Routledge, 1993.
Peter Carruthers	*The Animals Issue: Moral Theory in Practice.* New York: Cambridge University Press, 1992.
Matt Cartmill	*A View to a Death in the Morning: Hunting and Nature Through History.* Cambridge, MA: Harvard University Press, 1993.
Paola Cavalieri and Peter Singer, eds.	*The Great Ape Project: Equality Beyond Humanity.* New York: St. Martin's Press, 1994.
Paul Clark and Andrew Linzey, eds.	*Political Theory and Animal Rights.* Winchester, MA: Pluto Press, 1990.
Vernon Coleman	*Why Animal Experiments Must Stop.* Lynmouth, Devon, UK: European Medical Journal, 1994.
Jan Dizard	*Going Wild: Hunting, Animal Rights, and the Contested Meaning of Nature.* Amherst: University of Massachusetts Press, 1994.
Nick Fiddes	*Meat: A Natural Symbol.* New York: Routledge, 1991.
Lawrence Finsen and Susan Finsen	*The Animal Rights Movement in America: From Compassion to Respect.* New York: Twayne Publishers, 1994.
Michael Allen Fox	*Animals Have Rights, Too.* New York: Crossroad, 1991.
Michael Allen Fox	*Superpigs and Wondercorn.* New York: St. Martin's Press, 1992.
Gary Francione	*Animals, Property, and the Law.* Philadelphia: Temple University Press, 1995.

Laura Fraiser et al.	*The Animal Rights Handbook.* New York: Berkley, 1993.
Robert Garner	*Animals, Politics, and Morality.* New York: Manchester University Press, 1993.
Jane Goodall	*The Chimpanzee: The Living Link Between "Man" and "Beast."* New York: Columbia University Press, 1992.
Kathy Guillermo	*Monkey Business: The Disturbing Case That Launched the American Animal Rights Movement.* Bethesda, MD: National Press Books, 1993.
E. C. Hargrove, ed.	*The Animal Rights/Environmental Ethics Debate.* Albany: State University of New York Press, 1993.
Lisa Hepner	*Animals in Education: The Facts, Issues, and Implications.* Albuquerque, NM: Richmond Publishers, 1994.
Mike Hutchins, ed.	*Ethics on the Ark: Zoos, Animal Welfare, and Wildlife Conservation.* Washington, DC: Smithsonian, 1995.
James Jasper and Dorothy Nelkin	*The Animal Rights Crusade: The Growth of a Moral Protest.* New York: Free Press, 1992.
Andrew Johnson	*Factory Farming.* Cambridge, MA: Blackwell, 1991.
Roberta Kalechofsky	*Autobiography of a Revolutionary: Essays on Animal and Human Rights.* Marblehead, MA: Micah Publications, 1991.
Roberta Kalechofsky, ed.	*Judaism and Animal Rights: Classical and Contemporary Responses.* Northvale, NJ: Aronson, 1994.
Ted Kerasote	*Bloodties: Nature, Culture, and the Hunt.* New York: Random House, 1993.
Gill Langley, ed.	*Animal Experimentation: The Consensus Changes.* New York: Chapman and Hall, 1989.
Michael Leahy	*Against Liberation: Putting Animals in Perspective.* New York: Routledge, 1991.
Andrew Linzey	*Animal Theology.* Urbana: University of Illinois Press, 1995.
Finn Lynge	*Arctic Wars: Animal Rights, Endangered Peoples.* Hanover, NH: University Press of New England, 1992.
Charles R. Magel	*Keyguide to Information Sources in Animal Rights.* New York: Mansell Press, 1989.

Bettina Manzo	*The Animal Rights Movement in the U.S., 1975–1990: An Annotated Bibliography.* Metuchen, NJ: Scarecrow, 1994.
Kathleen Marquardt	*Animalscam: The Beastly Abuse of Human Rights.* Washington, DC: Regnery, 1993.
Anthony Marshall	*The Zoo: Profiles of 102 Zoos, Aquariums, and Wildlife Parks in the U.S.* New York: Random House, 1994.
Jim Mason and Peter Singer	*Animal Factories.* New York: Harmony Books, 1990.
Jay McDaniel	*Of God and Pelicans: A Theology of Reverence for Life.* Louisville, KY: Westminster/John Knox Press, 1989.
R.E. McDowell	*A Partnership for Humans and Animals.* Raleigh, NC: Kinnic Publishers, 1991.
Mary Midgley	*Animals and Why They Matter: A Journey Around the Species Barrier.* Athens: University of Georgia Press, 1984.
Lisa Mighetto	*Wild Animals and American Environmental Ethics.* Tucson: University of Arizona Press, 1991.
Ingrid Newkirk	*Free the Animals! The Inside Story of the Animal Liberation Front and Its Founder, "Valerie."* Chicago: Noble Press, 1992.
Ingrid Newkirk	*Save the Animals! 101 Easy Things You Can Do.* New York: Warner Books, 1990.
Dale Peterson and Jane Goodall	*Visions of Caliban: On Chimpanzees and People.* Boston: Houghton Mifflin, 1993.
Charles Pinches and Jay McDaniel, eds.	*Good News for Animals: Christian Approaches to Animal Well-Being.* Maryknoll, NY: Orbis Books, 1993.
Evelyn Pluhar	*Beyond Prejudice: The Moral Significance of Human and Nonhuman Animals.* Durham, NC: Duke University Press, 1995.
Jim Posewitz	*Beyond the Fair Chase: The Ethic and Tradition of Hunting.* Helena, MT: Falcon Press-Orion, 1994.
Rod Preece and Lorna Chamberlain	*Animal Welfare and Human Values.* Waterloo, ON: Wilfrid Laurier University Press, 1993.
James Rachels	*Created from Animals: The Moral Implications of Darwinism.* New York: Oxford University Press, 1991.
Tom Regan	*All That Dwell Therein: Animal Rights and Environmental Ethics.* Berkeley: University of California Press, 1982.

Tom Regan — *The Case for Animal Rights.* Berkeley: University of California Press, 1983.

Tom Regan — *The Thee Generation: Reflections on the Coming Revolution.* Philadelphia: Temple University Press, 1991.

Tom Regan and Peter Singer, eds. — *Animal Rights and Human Obligations.* Englewood Cliffs, NJ: Prentice-Hall, 1991.

Jeremy Rifkin — *Beyond Beef: The Rise and Fall of the Cattle Culture.* New York: Dutton, 1992.

Rosemary Rodd — *Biology, Ethics, and Animals.* New York: Oxford University Press, 1990.

Bernard Rollin — *Animal Rights and Human Morality.* Buffalo: Prometheus Books, 1992.

Bernard Rollin — *The Frankenstein Syndrome: Ethical and Social Issues in the Genetic Engineering of Animals.* New York: Cambridge University Press, 1995.

Clifford J. Sherry — *Animal Rights: A Reference Book.* Santa Barbara, CA: ABC-CLIO, 1994.

Robert Silverman — *Defending Animals' Rights Is the Right Thing to Do.* New York: S.P.I. Books, 1994.

Peter Singer — *Animal Liberation.* New York: New York Review of Books, 1990.

Peter Singer, ed. — *In Defense of Animals.* New York: Blackwell, 1985.

Richard Sorabji — *Animal Minds and Human Morals: The Origins of the Western Debate.* Ithaca, NY: Cornell University Press, 1993.

Marjorie Spiegel — *The Dreaded Comparison: Human and Animal Slavery.* New York: Mirror Books, 1988.

James Sterba, ed. — *Earth Ethics: Introductory Reading on Environmental Ethics and Animal Rights.* Old Tappan, NJ: Macmillan, 1995.

Keith Tester — *Animals and Society: The Humanity of Animal Rights.* New York: Routledge, 1991.

Colin Tudge — *Last Animals at the Zoo: How Mass Extinction Can Be Stopped.* Washington, DC: Island Press, 1992.

Michael Zimmerman et al., eds. — *Environmental Philosophy: From Animal Rights to Radical Ecology.* Englewood Cliffs, NJ: Prentice Hall, 1993.

Index